MW01093443

Praise for *Mother, Creature, Kin*

"This is a heartachingly beautiful, deeply life-altering book, one I will be placing into the hands of many mothers, creatures, and kin. Tenderly we are reminded of all the ways in which we have become lost; all the ways we find to become found once more. On community, interconnectedness, and ecologies of care, this book has widened my heart beyond compare. There is grace here, and hope, and the light we need to guide us onward. A book for these times."

—**Kerri ní Dochartaigh**, author of *Thin Places*
and *Cacophony of Bone*

"This is a beautiful book—the prose, the stories, the sentiments and values. It belongs in the company of works by Ursula K. Le Guin, Rachel Carson, Terry Tempest Williams, and Robin Kimmerer, all of whom are inspiring presences in these pages. While Chelsea Steinauer-Scudder writes vividly about bearing and nurturing a child, she also invites us to understand mothering in a larger sense, as caring for all creatures—for birds and whales, trees and grasses, the entire web of life."

—**Scott Russell Sanders**, author of
The Way of Imagination

"*Mother, Creature, Kin* is both an education and an affirmation of our most essential and connected ways of being. Nuanced and layered, its language is a force of love."

—**Jamie Figueroa**, author of *Brother, Sister,
Mother, Explorer* and *Mother Island*

Mother, Creature, Kin

Mother, Creature, Kin

WHAT WE LEARN FROM NATURE'S MOTHERS IN A TIME OF UNRAVELING

Chelsea Steinauer-Scudder

BROADLEAF BOOKS
MINNEAPOLIS

MOTHER, CREATURE, KIN
What We Learn from Nature's Mothers in a Time of Unraveling

29 28 27 26 25 24   1 2 3 4 5 6 7 8 9

Library of Congress Cataloging-in-Publication Data

Names: Steinauer-Scudder, Chelsea, author.
Title: Mother, creature, kin : what we learn from nature's mothers in a
  time of unraveling / Chelsea Steinauer-Scudder.
Description: Minneapolis : Broadleaf Books, [2025] | Includes
  bibliographical references.
Identifiers: LCCN 2024020460 | ISBN 9781506495477 (hardcover) |
  ISBN 9781506495484 (ebook)
Subjects: LCSH: Motherhood. | Nature--Social aspects. | Animal behavior. |
  Parental behavior in animals.
Classification: LCC HQ759 .S6835 2025 | DDC 306.874/3--dc23/eng/20240716
LC record available at https://lccn.loc.gov/2024020460

Cover illustration by Kimberly Glyder
Cover design by Kimberly Glyder

Print ISBN: 978-1-5064-9547-7
eBook ISBN: 978-1-5064-9548-4

Printed in China.

For Aspen

CONTENTS

Prologue   xi

Introduction   xiii

Part I. Centering: Orienting to Sacred Place

  1 Heartbeat   2

  2 Axis Mundi   6

  3 Coming into Being   11

  4 The Good Mother   15

  5 A Mothering Language   18

Part II. Belonging: Taking Flight with Birds

  6 Ascendance   28

  7 Setting Bearings   33

  8 Hoopoe, i   38

  9 Sensory Orientation   40

 10 Hoopoe, ii   50

 11 Disrupted Navigation   51

 12 Hoopoe, iii   57

13 Quickening   59

14 Unraveling   61

15 Hoopoe, iv   67

Part III. Entangled: Tracking Whales

16 Bodies in Orbit   72

17 Bloodlines, Milklines   78

18 Scrimshaw   84

19 Flukeprint   88

20 Dream   89

21 Urban Whale   90

22 Devour   99

23 Whale Chase   104

24 Whalefall   109

25 Chimera   112

26 Knife's Edge   114

27 Farewell   119

Part IV. Community: Imagining Trees

28 Mythical Forests   122

29 Cultivating Roots   126

30 Cutting Down the World   135

31 Restrained Growth   145

32 Creation Story   152

33 Tree Seed   156

Part V. Edge Work: Traversing Salt Marshes

34   Vulnerable Nest   162

35   Porous Boundaries   170

36   Between the Tides   173

37   Edge Erosion   182

38   Passageways   189

39   Reclaim   195

40   Wild Transgression   202

41   Flood   209

42   Hurricane   218

43   Tide-Work   223

Part VI. Homemaking: Tending the Seasons

44   Inhabiting   228

45   Wonder (Summer)   232

46   Music (Fall)   235

47   A Particular Love (Winter)   250

48   Rebirth (Spring)   261

49   Ritual (Summer)   266

50   Creating Possible Futures   270

Acknowledgments   277

Notes   281

PROLOGUE

Down in the dark, below the rising waters of the incoming tide and the *Spartina* grasses that can withstand the repeated sweep of salt, a single-celled organism is giving birth.

It is, in this way, a mother, though it is neither male nor female; nor does it have a mate. It is, rather, dividing itself asexually, and its offspring are departing in microscopic, floating globes of genetic material.

This is foraminifera: an ancient order of protist, of which there are thousands of species. These organisms have inhabited marine ecosystems for more than 540 million years, surviving numerous mass extinction events.

The floating globe–children will soon extend their arms: hundreds of shining tendrils of cytoplasm. With these arms spread in an array around themselves, these one-celled creatures, though they are among the smallest forms of life, will take on the appearance of a cosmic starburst. Then the children will begin to build. Collecting bits of sediment and debris and cementing them together, they will each construct a complex spiral shell around themselves, featuring several chambered whorls with passages between them. Here they will live for the duration of their lives.

This generation of children may reproduce asexually for several generations and, several generations later, sexually. It is not fully known how foraminifera make their reproductive choices. But all these generations will live in the specific marine environment to which this particular species of foraminifera, *Trochammina inflata*, has adapted: in the margin between high and low tides, at the edge of land and sea.

And when each of these children ceases to be, their shells will remain. Carrying the unique chemical signature of this ocean at this point in time, the shells, many no larger than a strawberry seed, will turn to fossils that keep this story, preserving it for eons.

These dwellings will become microscopic snapshots of the deep time planetary forces at work on the sea. As the generations arise and fall away, each child will tell a piece of the story of the shifting border between land and water, a moment in the rising and falling of the oceans. Each is a witness to its particular moment of change.

The shells are a hint of what was, and of what is to come. They are pieces in the ever-evolving story of how to mother, how to endure, at the edge.

INTRODUCTION

I set out to write this book because my daughter was born into a world that is unraveling. And because there are fewer than 350 North Atlantic right whales left. And because there are single-celled organisms dwelling in the peat of salt marshes that are utterly mysterious. And because that peat is, in many places, eroding away and washing out to sea.

I wrote this book because I am afraid. And because I am grieving an ongoing loss that feels too big to name.

But, mostly, I set out to write this book because of how much I love my daughter and how much love I feel for the places I have lived—and the way the purple clover grows in a riot, and the way the first snow falls.

We are living in a time of ecological collapse. There is no way around it. But there is, I think, a way *through*. Perhaps the best we can do is to keep renewing the world and our love for it. This book is, in many ways, a real-time log, from pregnancy to my daughter's third birthday, of wrestling with how to do this.

This is not a book about saving ourselves or about fixing the future. In the end, it's a book about the fullness and flourishing of love.

"Mothering" is the closest word I have found for examining the work that love calls us to do.

* * *

This is not so much a book about Mother Earth as it is a book about mothering with and to and through the Earth. Neither is this a book about an idealized feminine trope of the all-caring, all-nurturing, all-self-sacrificing, always-holding-it-all-together human mother of human children. Thankfully, that stereotype is presently being unraveled by, among other things, neuroscience. In her book *Mother Brain*, Chelsea Conaboy writes that researchers have clarified that "'maternal behavior' is, in fact, a basic human characteristic, not uniquely maternal after all. Studies of fathers, including nonbiological fathers in same-sex couples, have found that the brains of men who are regularly engaged in caring for their children change in ways that are strikingly similar to gestational mothers."

The English language can be a limited and binding one, especially when it comes to writing about and speaking of our relationship to the living world. Words like *mother* can become rigid and constricting. When speaking about motherhood to several women in my writing community who have a range of diverse perspectives and experiences, we encountered some discord around the word *mother* in its usual definition.

One said that as a queer woman who is not planning to have biological children, she feels deeply unseen when the essentialness of womanhood is equated to motherhood.

Another said that she always assumed that somewhere along the way she would have had a child, and now, in her early forties, she is unsure if it will happen. She wonders where, then, to put her internal, persistent need for deep care, and her desire to contribute something to the future. But there are many other ways to do this, she said.

The third said, in her view, we are all mothers. We hold space for each other and help create the environment for one another in thought, word, and deed. At our best, we nourish each other, protect one another, and help each other grow.

What I took from this conversation was that the limitation of language does not preclude working with words to reveal layers of meaning, to press and pull them, to see where else they might reach—and where we might then reach, in turn. In this way, I tug at the word *mother* throughout this book. I do not intend to take away its central meaning, nor to discount the agency and power of women who are mothers of children and call themselves such. Nor do I intend to disperse or dilute the feminine. To the contrary, I hope to center the feminine all the more by claiming that it calls to all of us, as Earth creatures and as birthed creatures, in a composting and decomposing kind of way. Naming myself as the mother of my daughter is at the heart of who I am. But it is still only a part of who I am. For I am tethered, too, to my wider human community, to maple trees and earthworms.

"I live my life in widening circles," wrote Rilke, and I think that some of our words and ideas have such circles around them, too. Meanings beyond (or within) the meaning, the potential to inhabit a multiplicity of definitions, at once wide and narrow. I suggest that we imagine what happens if the act of "mothering" is permitted to *also* become non-gendered and expansive.

Allowing for such an expansive definition of *mother* helps to pull it outside of patriarchy. For not only biological females can be mothers—caregiving creatures who tend, nurture, and nourish. And we don't need to look only to single-celled organisms for proof of this, for every human being, regardless of gender or sex, is capable of being a creature who gives care. And if the Earth becomes one of the primary recipients of that care, then we are subverting patriarchy by refusing to genderize the work of caregiving, and working outside of capitalism by making our collective aim the care of the living world rather than the individual's accumulation of wealth and power. In her book *Matrescence*, which explores the physiological, psychological, and sociological processes and metamorphoses of motherhood, Lucy Jones writes that "matrescence troubles the idea that we are self-contained individuals, separated from the rest of the living world." A worthy troubling indeed.

There is, nonetheless, a lot of conditioning and socialization around the word *mother*. I have my own layers to peel back and my own work to do, especially as a white woman in a heterosexual marriage. This will therefore be an imperfect effort, one of trying again and again to break the bounds, mainly my own, in order to see what might be possible. I hope others will pick up where I inevitably fall short and add their own layers, their own definitions, their own ways of being expansive mothers.

I wish to invite you into a kind of mothering that is wild and porous. The kind that draws blood, that loves and fears, rejoices and doubts, that exposes where we are most deeply vulnerable and from there stretches us into what is beyond us. I mean the kind of mothering that works within uncertainty and mystery. The kind that leaves soil beneath our fingernails and seeds in our hair.

Donna J. Haraway writes: "It is high time that feminists exercise leadership in imagination, theory, and action to unravel the ties of both genealogy and kin, and kin and species." She continues, "making kin and making kind (as category, care, relatives without ties by birth, lateral relatives, lots of other echoes) stretch the imagination and can change the story."

The questions at the heart of this effort are as follows: What if we all have the potential to be mothers to the places where we live and the beings with whom we share those places? And what if we are also mothered by them? What healing might then be possible? What does it mean to act ethically within these webs of relationship? And what does it mean to *mother* ethically?

Mothers have particular roles within communities. In *Essential Labor*, Angela Garbes writes about the importance of expanding what she calls the *terrain of mothering*: "While 'mother' is an important identity for many women who still provide the majority of care to children in America, no one cares for children entirely on their own. My perspective has grown to consider the work of raising children as *mothering*, an action that includes people of all genders and nonparents alike."

The terrain of mothering, she says, is one of supporting and nurturing life, a definition that situates the duties and responsibilities of motherhood—of caring for children—firmly in the community. To mother is to participate in active and shared practices of care.

Garbes is focused on the ways that the foundational work of mothering in the United States, especially in terms of the caretaking roles of women of color, is woefully overlooked and undervalued. Practices of mothering, here, enter the realm of social justice as labors that demand equality and recognition.

Ecology, too, is a terrain of both motherhood and justice. The Earth is a nurturing, life-supporting being who is woefully undervalued and overlooked within a Western, capitalist system hell-bent on her exploitation. But if we expand practices of motherhood to an *ecological* terrain, we enter, quite naturally, into practices of reciprocity. "Remember the earth whose skin you are," writes Joy Harjo. And indeed we are born of our mothers, from and into bodies made up of Earth. The Earth nourishes us with our most fundamental needs—oxygen, water, food, shelter—and is also able to meet our psychological and spiritual needs.

What, then, does it look like to mother the Earth in turn?

Simply put, taking care of that same air, water, and soil means that the Earth takes care of our physical health. "It is human perception that makes the world a gift," writes Robin Wall Kimmerer. "When we view the world this way, strawberries and humans alike are transformed. The relationship of gratitude and reciprocity thus developed can increase the evolutionary fitness of both plant and animal." To nurture the body of the Earth is to receive the nurturing of our bodies. Because—it bears restating—*each of us is Earth's body*. And this embodiment requires that we nurture the beings whose existence and ways of being keep our ecosystems, and therefore our bodies, healthy.

Mothering human children, too, is inherently an Earth-embodied practice. Whether the children within our spheres of care are "ours" or not, our practices of nurturing them are grounded in a specific place, within a particular ecological community. Whether in cities or forests or deserts or mountains, we are in perpetual relationship to the places where we place our feet, where we breathe our air, where we drink our water.

Thus, ecological mothering, like social mothering, must extend beyond biological kinship, gender, identity, and—critically—species. We have to consider not only how to nurture human relationships but ecological ones as well. The terrain of an ecological motherhood is, therefore, a communal terrain. I define ecological motherhood as: *a shared, place-based responsibility to nurture and support human and more-than-human life.*

When we think of mothers caring for their children, we often imagine that care flowing in only one direction, from parent to child. But within ecological mothering practices, the relationship goes both ways. It is reciprocal. When other beings flourish, we flourish. And isn't that true of our children as well? We care for their physical, mental, emotional, and spiritual needs. They provide us with love, challenge us, teach us, bring wonder and delight. We mother, and we are mothered in turn. There is no beginning or end to that cycle of care.

Where to step into this cycle, into this reciprocity? Perhaps in imagining all of those ties of obligation, duty, service, and gift giving and receiving. What does such a map of your community look like? I've been experimenting with different versions of this, which, depending on the day, feature different beings and different pathways of connection. Here's how it looks right now.

At the center, always, are my daughter, Aspen, and my husband, Andrew. This week, we had my mom and brother over for dinner ("Bubba" and "Nay-Nay," Aspen calls them). I am part of a circle of women who write, and we offer each other support and encouragement several times a month. Recently, the man in the recycling truck gave Aspen her own yellow vest, which she elatedly wore around the house for several weeks. The local librarian found Aspen every book about bunnies for her second birthday. We are supported by the salt marshes that mediate the boundary between land and sea several miles from our home; by the white pine in our backyard that gives us cool shade all summer; by the vegetables that will soon be growing from our raised beds; by the organisms in the soil that help grow the food in our region that brings hundreds to the weekly farmer's market; by the North Atlantic right whales who cycle nutrients through the Gulf of Maine; by the migratory shorebirds who help bring those nutrients from sea to land and back again, and who run along the waves, harvesting insects where the ocean finds the shore.

What is it to mother and to be mothered within this network of living beings? Just as we might look to various iterations of human societies and social networks to learn how to nurture connections of care, we can also look to ecological communities, especially in light of the fact that one of our essential practices in the terrain of ecological mothering is extending the bounds of community to include our nonhuman neighbors. Our children must be, first and foremost, citizens of Earth: fellow creatures of the oceans and forests and grasslands and rivers.

* * *

I hope that you, reader, whether you are a mother to children of your own or not, whether you identify as a woman or not, will join me in considering that *one* of the definitions of motherhood is the capacity for expansive love and care that human beings are capable of extending to others, within and beyond the bounds of species. I hope that you will consider the greater-than-human world as being in need of this care, in a daily, obligatory, sacred, practical, nonnegotiable sort of way. In this moment of widespread, compounding, overwhelming, uncertain ecological crises, I hope you will remember that you have so much love to give.

I began writing this book when my daughter was still in my womb. Mothering her has opened a door into what mothering could look like as a wider ecological and spiritual orientation. I know I walk a careful line: definitions of motherhood will blur and overlap in these pages when perhaps they ought to stay separate, and they will be reductive and siloed when perhaps they ought to blur. But that's part of what we need: messy ways of reminding ourselves that we are not one thing, we are not one identity. We are blurred, overlapping creatures. However we are related to each other, and however we define those relations, we are interconnected beings. In every moment is the opportunity to be reborn to that interconnection.

In the Buddhist cosmos, there is the great cycle of samsara—rebirth—that all sentient beings undertake. This is also translated as "wandering," not from place to place, but from life to life. We live and die and are reborn again and again, as human beings, as insects, as gods, through all the realms of existence. The Buddhist belief in compassion is rooted, in part, in this infinite wandering. The Buddha taught that we have all been through these cycles so many times that, in one life or another, we have all been related to one another. Specifically, we have been the mothers of—and have been mothered by—every being we encounter. Every human, ladybug, amoeba, elephant. These are all beings who have given birth to us and are fundamentally part of the same existence we are. Whatever your system of belief—for I myself am not a Buddhist—I hope you will agree that this latter part is true: we are all woven into the fabric of the same cosmos.

The part of samsara that I find myself returning to is one particular understanding of the karmic cycle in which the life *before* one becomes a buddha is spent in the heaven of the contented, as a god. And it seems as though that would be the end of it, doesn't it? A contented heaven could understandably be one's ultimate aim, and indeed it is in other religious traditions. But this heaven-sent being—so few of whom ever make it this far—must enter a mother's womb, be reborn once more to a human form on the Earth. Buddhahood, the highest state of existence, is not possible from heaven, but is brought about here among the soil and forests and oceans, in service to others, where one can be present to help and to heal.

Such theologies hold within them a fundamental faith in not only humanity but in all beings. Such radical compassion that is both expansive and Earth-bound strikes me as one path through the unknown and the uncertain, because it insists upon mutual flourishing as a nonnegotiable condition of life, or at least a non-negotiable way of being on the path to healing.

And so, if we are beings moving through unending cycles of birth and death and rebirth—and I will admit to not knowing whether or not we are—then how fortunate am I to get to be my daughter's mother? To have a chance at a deeper understanding of what is needed of my present human form, as one among so many relatives? I have no expectation of reaching enlightenment in this lifetime, but motherhood is teaching me about a daily practice of mutual flourishing, ways of reaching beyond myself.

Conducive to such routine practice, the karmic cycle of rebirth, termed "dependent arising," is also said to exist on a daily, perfunctory scale. Macro and micro. In every instant, our consciousness is born, experiences sensations and feelings, forms attachments, suffers, learns, dies, and is reborn again, perhaps with an ever-so-slight reorientation toward a deeper truth. What a generous theology indeed: that change is ever possible, that there is rebirth in every moment of our existence. There is, always, opportunity for renewal.

The voices I hope to uplift in the pages to follow are those of our more-than-human kin—"companion species," in the phrasing of Donna J. Haraway. I write of mothering my daughter, but I also write of how companion kin have made that motherhood root and branch. In the coming chapters, we will hear stories of the silent flight and superpower hearing of barn owls, of nursing and endangered right whales, of real and imagined forests, of eroding salt marshes, of edge-dwelling single-celled organisms, and of newly planted gardens. The creatures within these stories have been teaching me about different aspects of mothering: language, belonging, entanglement, community, edge work, homemaking, and how to think about the future.

These pages contain but a handful of more-than-human voices. There are so many more beings to listen to. They all have things to teach us. They are speaking. They are in need of our restraint, our humility. And we are deeply in need of them. We are *Homo sapiens*, one species among many. We are interconnected in ways we know and in ways we cannot know.

Collapse is a time when many of our familiar walls will come down, whether we want them to or not, and whether or not we are ready. May we learn to listen to what is beyond them: all of the beings and ways of being that are worthy of our care and attention. For we cannot endure, much less flourish, alone.

PART I

CENTERING
Orienting to Sacred Place

O be still, while
You are still alive,
And all things live around you

— from "In Silence," by Thomas Merton

HEARTBEAT

In early March, approaching the end of my first trimester, I noticed that buds had appeared on the weeping cherry tree in our backyard. The dogwood, the apple tree, and the lilac followed suit. Given the weather, they were all right on time: mid to high forties at night and high fifties during the day. The sun shone down, and, like a siren song, it beckoned the sap to run through the veins of these trees, bringing signs of life to the tips of their branches.

As I made my rounds in the mornings after, pausing at each tree to examine the buds—fuzzy on the apple tree, elegant and scaled on the cherry, sharply pointed on the dogwood—I rejoiced. And then I began to worry.

It was too soon. One night, temperatures plummeted well below freezing. The next morning, there were snow flurries in the air. When I checked the trees, they appeared unchanged to my untrained eye, but I wondered if they'd already been damaged. I closed a hand over a few of them, as if the temporary transfer of my own warmth would make some sort of difference. It had dipped down into the twenties the previous night, to eighteen degrees the night before. I tried not to fret. However many tree buds I briefly cupped in my palms, I would not change their fate.

It's possible that I was so fixated on the budding trees that spring because of the baby growing in my belly, this new life that seemed so tender and miraculous that it made me catch my breath. As the trees were budding, it was still too early to feel any kicking or wriggling, but if I sat still, I could feel that light. In such moments, rejoicing seemed the only response I was capable of.

But when I brought my attention back to the world, there was an unmistakable sheen of fear. One night, we attended an event at Andrew's school. I was just beginning to show, and so Aspen was announcing her own presence to people we hadn't gotten around to telling yet. "Chelsea's pregnant!" one of Andrew's coworkers whispered to him—a statement, not a question.

Then the world changed. COVID-19 arrived on the East Coast. Just five days after that school event, Andrew was teaching from home. My brother was indefinitely out of a job at the restaurant where he worked. We canceled our trip to visit my dad, stepmom, and ninety-four-year-old grandmother in Nebraska. With predictions of hospitals running out of space, we breathed a sigh of relief that a close family friend who recently had a heart attack would be able to keep his scheduled date for coronary bypass surgery.

None of these things had been questions in February when we were passing our phones around to anyone who would ask to see a picture of my first ultrasound.

Then, I tried not to touch my phone—much less my face—if I was in public.

Then, I tried not to be in public.

Two early studies indicated that the virus was not passed from mother to child just before or during birth. But those studies involved just nine and four mothers, respectively. We began to hear stories of women whose partners could not be in the room during childbirth. Mothers who tested positive for the virus and were not permitted to hold or nurse their children immediately after birth.

And so many people were dying. The world was losing its elders. Black and brown and Indigenous communities were faring far worse than white communities. The virus, like so much else, cruelly highlighted the existing lines around wealth, privilege, and race.

In the best of conditions, pregnancy is a vulnerable time. This being our first child, we were doing our best to keep up with a growing stack of books and articles, learning as we went along about the stages of development of a fetus, keeping up with the numerous appointments on our calendars, deciding which optional tests to have done, seeking advice about birth plans. My body was changing—my weight, my energy level, my ability to focus, my appetite, my mood—often with little discernible pattern or consistency.

Up until March, in the midst of all of that change, there had been information readily available. Our questions generally had answers, in part because many aspects of pregnancy are well-charted territory, and in part because I was fortunate to have an uncomplicated pregnancy and privileged access to care, where the standard answers and expectations tended to apply.

There were few answers, expectations, or comforting words when it came to those long, early months of a global pandemic.

And so, the line between joy and worry, vulnerability and safety, became confused. One followed the other, which followed the other. The trees were budding and beautiful, and it was snowing outside; my child was growing in my belly, and the world was screeching to a halt. I had trouble locating the difference between common sense and paranoia.

We saw my obstetrician a week or two after the consecutive nights of frost. I hoped she would tell Andrew and me with confident expertise that our social distancing measures were likely to work, that by taking extra precautions we had a good chance of riding out the storm and staying healthy. She didn't. Instead she told us that social distancing was just to keep the hospitals from getting overwhelmed.

Andrew and I sat there somewhat stunned. We, like so many, still believed then that things were going to go back to normal after just a few weeks. We could not yet fathom that this disease was here to stay. We would not have believed that in the United States alone, the numbers of the dead would climb far above one million.

I remember so clearly that moment in the doctor's office. How I hadn't truly considered the possibility that we could do everything right—for the sake of our new child, for ourselves, for the most vulnerable members of our community—and that this disease would still make a home among us.

And then she asked: "Do you want to hear the heartbeat?"

And there, lying on the table, I remember, too, how the worry dissipated completely for a long moment. All I could hear, at 156 beats per minute, was *joy, joy, joy.*

AXIS MUNDI

My first fragment of memory is of my mother. We are standing together in golden, waving grass. There is the sense that the sun is setting behind us because what I see in the memory is not our physical bodies but our shadows, cast before us, wavering as the grass bends and circles in the wind. My mother and I are holding hands, and in our silhouettes there is no distinction between where she ends and I begin. And the grass of the rolling plains grows and reaches through our conjoined image.

When I was one and two years old, we lived on a Nature Conservancy preserve that spanned more than fifty thousand acres along the Niobrara River in north central Nebraska—a landscape of Sandhills prairie, bur oaks, and bison. Later we would move to Omaha, and shortly after to Oklahoma. For a long time, I wasn't sure that this grass-memory with my mother was of a real moment. Perhaps it was an impression, a vague recall of a distant place and time that my mind gave shape to, filling in the blanks. But my mom confirmed that this did happen: she remembers it, too.

This memory has been with me for a very long time. It has had different things to say to me at different points in my life. We all have these, I think: encounters with the living world that not only stay with us but take on more meaning and power over time. Perhaps it's an early memory that stays firmly planted, or an unexpected swell of awe, or a fleeting but deeply felt connection.

These experiences can become fixed points, poles around which parts of us will always turn, orbiting again and again around the truth that lies at their center.

One of my favorite questions to ask people is whether they experience the sacred in the living world. Everyone I have ever put this question to has, near-immediately, answered "yes," even if they would not call themselves spiritual or ever employ the word *sacred*. The affirmative answer to that question is also always paired with a specific place or experience. I've heard countless stories of what I've come to think of as *axis mundi* experiences: encounters that have pulled someone into a deep experience of felt belonging upon the tiny bit of Earth that they find themselves upon. It's often very simple: a passing deer or a bathing bird that somehow opens a window into their sensory being, and, from there, the relationship flows freely, not between *I* and *it*, but *I* and *thou*.

Within the study of religion, an *axis mundi* is a sacred pole, literal or figurative, which is fixed in a particular place, connecting Earth to the realms of heaven, underworld, and divine. These holiest places are often mountains, as in the case of Mauna Kea on Hawai'i's Big Island, known by the Indigenous Kanaka Maoli to be the umbilical cord—the place from which the world emerged. Mount Meru in Hindu mythology is the home of the gods and the center of the universe. An axis mundi may also be a cosmic tree, as in Norse mythology, or a temple or a shrine. In Islam, the Ka'aba in Mecca, which pilgrims circumambulate seven times, contains within it the stone given to Adam upon his expulsion from paradise, that his sins might be forgiven. The cosmic world turns around these poles, providing a mythic context for understanding one's place in the universe.

When comparative religions scholar Mircea Eliade presented axis mundi as a concept within Western religious discourse, he introduced it as a generalized universal mythology, and subsequently received the valid criticism that he failed to account for historical context and the complex ways in which diverse people orient to the sacred and understand that orientation.

Limited and flawed as his theories were, Eliade contributed something important to Western thinking: he put forth what became an accepted language for a place-based understanding of the sacred. Many cultures and religions have sustained and lived out this understanding, without the need to name it as such. But many of the world's Judeo-Christian traditions—certainly many of those here in the United States—have deviated widely from an understanding of sacred-as-Earth. My religious roots—Judaism on my mother's side and Catholicism on my father's—are faith traditions in which God is often disembodied, transcendent-and-therefore-removed, not to be found to be running as sap in the trees or squirming microscopically in the soil or washing ashore in the tide.

I don't mean to imply that the sacred cannot be found in a book or in the shared faith of a human community. Certainly it can, and it demonstrably is. Rather, my point is that the idea of the axis mundi gives language to something important: that human beings *also* encounter the sacred in place. It is this, I think, that is the universal attribute of the axis mundi: not a catch-all for how the world's religious traditions understand the sacred but an *inherent capacity for place-based awe* that is encoded into all human beings.

I've come, therefore, to think of axis mundi in two ways (though this, too, runs the risk of oversimplifying): There are *capital-A, capital-M* Axes Mundi: those most sacred of places for cultures or religious communities—those world-beginning places whose mythological histories weave the people into the past, present, and future of particular landscapes. And then there are *small-a, small-m* axes mundi: those small, daily irruptions of majesty, those any-place-based encounters with the sacred.

I define "sacred" as that which pulls us beyond the bounds of our individual selves, envelops us within mystery, and gives us a glimpse into the vast, entwined, eternal network of living beings that we are in relationship with. A simpler way of saying it: *the moments when we are most fully human via our awareness that we are fully entangled*, down to our nuclei and electrons, in the Earth and the cosmos. Such an orientation does not require a belief in God or gods. The living world can illuminate this understanding in the forms of awe and wonder, as well as in the forms of grief and loss. And such illuminations can arise spontaneously into our consciousnesses, precisely because this sacred truth is always present everywhere upon the Earth, whether or not we are aware of it. Those small-a axes mundi, then, arrive as discrete moments in particular places. They are the moments when that sacred reality comes into focus, inviting us to orient ourselves, even if briefly, to the particular, small bit of the cosmos where we have placed our feet. Perhaps this has happened for you upon reaching the summit of a mountain, or while sitting beneath the boughs of an old growth tree, or simply while hearing the voice of a bird you recognize from your childhood home.

Which is to say: whatever we believe (or don't) about God and gods, about holy texts and pilgrimages, all of us hold within ourselves the potential to be pinned in place by a sacred pole. And in this time when there is so much disconnect from the living world, so much separation, in this time of razed forests, deserted pockets of warmed oceans, and the echoes of extinct species, orienting ourselves around these fixed points becomes more crucial than ever.

We are a species in need of centers. Place-based centers. *Particular* place-based centers, around which we can build our orientation to the world. Places that ask for our attention and care as sensory beings. Small-a axes mundi that guide us in moving through this uncertain time.

I am learning what it means to orient myself to such centers. My own history as a white, middle-class woman from pioneering ancestry is a long, multigenerational process of wandering. It's time to come home. I believe this is possible. The search itself is a practice, a ritual of perpetual return.

"There are no privileged locations," writes Scott Russell Sanders. "If you stay put, your place may become a holy center, not because it gives you special access to the divine, but because in your stillness you hear what might be heard anywhere. All there is to see can be seen from anywhere in the universe, if you know how to look; and the influence of the entire universe converges on every spot."

I have come, then, to see this memory of my mother and me in the prairie grass as one such convergence, an enduring manifestation of the sacred. A pole that has, for reasons I still don't fully understand, pinned part of me forever in that prairie grass. It is one way of organizing my relationship to sacred place.

Since my own daughter's arrival into the world, this memory has returned again to ask me a question.

What is it to be a mother in a time of ecological collapse?

COMING INTO BEING

It's an early morning at the beginning of April, the day still dark—darker still with a steady rain falling. I turn on the lamp and open the window in my office. It's in the midforties, but I love the sound of rain on the plexiglass roof that covers our porch, slanting between my office window and the backyard, where the green is returning to the grass. I welcome the rush of cold, damp air and the gentle, pattering hush of water that smells of spring. In the other room, my husband, Andrew, and six-month-old, Aspen, are listening to John Denver's *Rocky Mountain High*, a record that we recently recovered from my father-in-law's attic. We've listened to it over and over. In his "Season Suite," on side two, Denver sings these lines that I haven't been able to get out of my head for weeks: *And oh, I love the life within me, I feel a part of everything I see.*

Maybe it seems a bit frivolous, given everything that is going on in the world, to have been so fixated on this piece of Americana from a 1972 country album. But in this time of spreading pandemic, with a new baby, and our loved ones kept at a painful distance, I think I've needed Denver's unapologetic and joyful affirmation of our connection with something greater than ourselves. Or perhaps these lyrics are pointing me toward this *inner-outer* aspect of motherhood that I'm struggling to understand: How the boundaries of my individual body have blurred. How Aspen's gestation began a mysterious process of osmosis that I can't fully comprehend. How her arrival expanded my understanding of ritual as something ancient, bodily, and animal, as together we underwent the initiation of birth.

At six months old, Aspen is the only one in our small family who truly understands Denver's lyrics. This child intuits that she is in relationship to what is around her, something I only experience glimpses of before I *think* about it, my critical mind taking things into the realm of abstract thought. I always have to stop and remind—or re-body—myself. My senses have to chase this intuition through a fog of conditioning and concepts. Aspen *is* this intuition. Every morning she wakes to greet a world that greets her back. She takes it all in with generous attention and curiosity. She is startled, she is awed, she is frightened, she is patient. There is a fluidity to the boundaries of her being. She is a willing pupil of a world that, in every moment, rises anew to meet her.

In my midthirties, I have come up in a Western culture that has taught me to look back on my life with the reverse perspective: the world does not continually rise anew; it is already there, almost a foregone conclusion, with the inevitable, linear drive of human history behind it. "Nature," Western culture tells me again and again, is separate from "me" and operates apart from my enlightened, rational, human reality. I am the doer; the Earth is acted upon.

The A:shiwi (Zuni) elder and farmer Jim Enote tells the story of how his great-grandparents awoke every morning before dawn to say a prayer to help the sun rise. He expresses regret that the science-based mindset of our time makes it extraordinarily difficult to be a twenty-first-century person and still hold such beliefs. It's not that Jim is anti-science. It's that he mourns the loss of this intuitive reciprocity.

The widespread loss of the belief that the world needs our prayers and attention—and might not rise to greet us without them—is a tolling bell for the species and ecosystems that have vanished or been pushed to the brink. I'm remembering Jim's story as I hear Aspen babbling away in the other room. I mourn how violently Western culture has stomped out this intuition, driving us to orbit instead around ourselves as individuals, around the sacred center of the ego. But then I am struck: Aspen's world *is* coming into being. *My god*, I realize: *she has not yet been taught to forget that inherent, reciprocal relationship with the world.*

I attend a workshop in which cultural ecologist David Abram speaks about animism as the "spontaneous experience of how the world reveals itself to us." He says: "If you allow that everything has vitality and agency, then you notice that everything is expressive." Everything, he says, has meaningful speech.

The sound of this morning's rain enters Aspen's consciousness. What does she hear? What is the sound of rain without the word for rain? I don't know. I hear this sound, and while I want to stay present, I find myself led from the word "rain" to fretting about a winter that was too warm and a spring that came too early. As Charles Foster writes: "When I think I've described a wood, I'm really describing the creaking architecture of my own mind."

In a Western capitalist culture that feels so irreversibly conditioned to its own internal logic, its own seemingly unstoppable momentum, its own monied tongue—all of which have wrapped their threads around me, too—I can hardly believe that thirty feet away from me in the other room, beneath the rain that runs down the roof, is a human being who is currently free of this conditioning. I wonder how, as a mother, I can nurture this freedom.

We read books to Aspen and sing to her. I speak to her in my halting, intermediate French, hoping she might have some sense of another (human) language, even if my pronunciation is rusty. But listening to the rain this morning, I feel a little tug of resistance in giving her these human words at all.

Aspen has started making what seem to be her first intentional attempts at language. All day she says, "na-na-na-na . . . ba-ba-ba," which Andrew and I, of course, interpret as "ma-ma" and "da-da." But mostly she makes these sounds without any particular attention to either one of us. She spontaneously expresses herself as she explores, discovers. The sounds she makes are mostly in conversation with something other than us. She, like all infants, is a little animist in an animate world.

On mornings like this, I remind myself to be silent. I remind myself to give her ample space to listen to a much wider, deeper, more complex language than that which extends from my tongue. It is within this wide space of silence that I can witness the way Aspen meets Rain. It is in stillness that I can ask, What realities are possible at this meeting place of the world and our perception of it?

And I suppose that what is possible is this: that the meeting place itself might blur, and then disappear.

In a moment, I'll close my computer and turn off the light, and I'll bring her out to the porch. I'll try to pull myself out of my mind. We'll stand under the plexiglass roof and listen to the birth of spring—as dynamic as the drops that are falling in ever-new patterns from the gray sky like little prayers. Together, we'll witness a world coming into being.

THE GOOD MOTHER

So many of the stories we hear today are about a world falling *out* of being. Falling away. Falling from grace. The US Fish and Wildlife Service proposes declaring twenty-three species extinct. Weather and climate disasters—including floods, hurricanes, tornadoes, severe cold, drought, wildfires, and heat waves—cause nearly five hundred deaths and incurred a cost of $92.9 billion in a single year. The Earth could be out of topsoil in as few as sixty years. The number of people displaced by climate-related disasters is predicted to reach 1.2 billion by 2050.

These are stories of the mass-scale unraveling that is taking place as we pull more and more threads out of the Earth's ancient pattern to weave something that is entirely of our own making. Biodiversity and balance are sacrificed in the upkeep of a global, capitalist-driven civilization. Forests are felled to heat our homes and grow our food. The Earth is carved open to manufacture our phones, our weapons. Aquifers are drained, disrupting the migration patterns of sandhill cranes, as warming oceans change the migratory seasons of humpback whales. In doing all of this, humanity is building a world that is, increasingly, a reflection only of ourselves: our needs, desires, and wants. We continue this hungry work even as the stunted design we are creating spells our own demise.

In Linda Hogan's book *Dwellings: A Spiritual History of the Living World*, she travels to the Boundary Waters, where a group of wildlife biologists is studying a vulnerable population of timber wolves. Hogan is there with several other visitors who have come to tour the region, with the hope of glimpsing a wolf in its native habitat. But the first up-close glimpse of a wolf that they get is in the form of a carcass, pulled out of the back of a pickup truck. Many of these visitors are neither ecologists nor what one might classify as conservationists. Some hunt and trap wolves, others are curious, and others are what might be called ecotourists. But Hogan is struck by the fact that none of them can resist the urge to reach out and stroke the pelt of this animal, or to pose with it for photographs, in order to "touch a lost piece of the wild earth." To connect with something that we have severed from ourselves.

One night, the group is walking outside in the cold, wanting to hear the howl of a wolf. At last, a long howl breaks through the moonlight. A hush falls over them. Then there is another howl. But the second howl, they realize, is coming from one of the men in their party, who is calling back to the wolves "in a language he only pretends to know," and the group of people surrounding him—as well as the woods, and the wolves, and the world beyond—answer with silence. Linda writes: "We wait. We are waiting for the wolves to answer. We want a healing, I think, a cure for anguish, a remedy that will heal the wound between us and the world that contains our broken histories."

Is it possible, I wonder, to build a bridge between these broken histories and an uncertain, deeply troubled future?

Here are the paradoxes that I hold as a new mother: I believe that the world can simultaneously fall out of being and come into being. I believe that the cracks and chasms of our fragmenting civilization will widen and deepen in my lifetime, and certainly in our daughter's. I believe that bringing new life into a world in collapse is still a morally sound choice—and that the decision *not* to bring new life into the world is morally sound as well. I believe that even our limited languages might lead us—if we continue to listen and reach for knowing—to a truer expression. I don't believe there is any cure for our anguish that will stop our present downfall; but I do believe there is a cure.

The cure, the healing, is that which will bring us back into a deep, loving, entwined relationship with the living world. And this, I believe, is the work of mothering.

Again, by "mother" I do not mean only the noun that refers to a female with a uterus and children. I mean a way of being that is open to any gender, any age, perhaps even any species. As Robin Wall Kimmerer writes in *Braiding Sweetgrass*, "A good mother . . . [knows] that her work doesn't end until she creates a home where all of life's beings can flourish." I mean "mother" as a verb, and "mothering" as the good work of being in service to "all of life's beings."

I don't pretend to know what the future will look like. But I believe that, more than anything, it will need mothers.

A MOTHERING LANGUAGE

What is a mothering orientation in a time of great uncertainty? There is no one answer of course. There are spaces of stillness and silence. There is the annual flood of nutrients that washes over the riverbank and into thirsty wetlands. There is ritual and ceremony. There is the wolf spider who carries her young on her back. There is listening. There are the Mother Trees that Suzanne Simard studies, those who recognize and care not only for their kin but for "strangers too, and other species, promoting the diversity of the community." Notably, the Mother Tree, "facing an uncertain future, [passes] her life force straight to her offspring, helping them to prepare for changes ahead."

As a writer, I gravitate toward practices of words and stories. This is often where my mind goes when I think of mothering my daughter. But often, what comes instead of clear words or coherent stories are anger and fear. My words thicken and become paralyzed. There's a primordial howl frozen somewhere down in my chest. I don't know how to let it out.

Sometimes, when that memory of my mother and me standing in the grass returns to me, I can't stop thinking about shadows.

An article in the *New Yorker*, "Green Dream," yanks a knot in my stomach that has been tightening for some time. "Is limitless clean energy finally approaching?" reads the subtitle. It's a story about nuclear fusion energy offering the potential for, among other things, "a carbon-free way to power a household for a year on the fuel of a single glass of water"—if only scientists could at last figure out how to safely unleash this unending source of energy.

I won't pretend to understand nuclear fusion. Perhaps it could, in fact, be a "solution at the scale of the problem," as one aerospace engineer is quoted as saying. Yet I suspect not. This is a telling misunderstanding: that the climate crisis is a problem for science with an as-yet undiscovered scientific solution. But it is our separation from the Earth herself that lies at the heart of our crisis. But these are the gospels of our scientific age: "Clean" alternatives mean we can keep living like we're currently living. We can keep consuming. We can keep ignoring that collective lack of center.

But no, what is troubling me is not so much nuclear fusion as it is that word: *limitless*. What is troubling me is a misplaced understanding of the infinite. The desire to forget that living within limits, with restraint, is the way back to balance. These are the shadows that can disorient me: shadows that impose, shadows that desire to cast our own image onto the land. As a writer, I see the way that those sorts of shadows often take the form of words. I notice the way that I, too, employ them.

"The English language can wield our collective shadow like a weapon," I write. And that feels like a very satisfying thought. The critical part of my mind likes to sink my teeth into words like *limitless* and shake them around, asserting that such hubris will only result in our self-destruction. I use language to write about how we have forgotten that we are beings of, among, and dependent upon a living Earth, as we have oriented ourselves instead around human supremacy (leading to, among other things, white supremacy and patriarchy). I use language to write about how language perpetuates such consciousnesses.

But isn't this only another violence? Isn't this my own shadow at work? Who, for example, is "we"? What is "ours"? Rooted in my own pride, my own self-assurance, my anger, I find myself framing the problem within a linguistic structure that is built by the same forgetting and separation that plagues our shared planet.

Many have thought and written about this, and there is no need to go into great detail here. The questions I'm concerned with are: How and where within this fraught structure do we locate a language of mothering? Can mothering practices utilize Western languages toward another end? Are there different ways to think about shadows? Different dimensions?

And this is when the image of my mother and I in the grass returns to me, yet again. With a profound lightness, with a shushing wind, it asks me to look closer. *Look again at your shadows there in the grass*, it says. So I look.

And here is what I see.

That when my mind is critical, it is prone to forgetting—even resisting—love. Because loving a world that is collapsing can be too painful. But there in my memory I see that our shadows have lain down ahead of us, not to shade out the grass, not to make our mark, but to be *with* the grass, and the grass is dancing through us. There is no pain. There is no imposition. Instead, there is an easy and full love between my mother and me. And I can't see where my mother ends and I begin, and where I end and my daughter begins; and I think this melding must be true, too, for where our shadows end and the grass begins.

And when the word *limitless* comes to me this time, it alights softly and waits.

❄ ❄ ❄

Aspen, too, continues to teach me about ways of using language that open us to that which is beyond language. She turned one in early September. Her first human word is *Hi!*, which she says, every time, with that exclamation point. (Her other first word was a dog word: *woh woh!* in response to dogs barking.) "Hi!" she says to the willow tree as she pets its bark and shakes its leaves. "Hi!" she says to the neighbor's sheep, bleating in their pasture. "Hi!" to ants, crows, stuffed animals, fruit flies, and Jon Lester, our Portland Seadogs novelty bobblehead. "Hi!" she says, occasionally, even to people. Everyone thinks this is very cute—which, of course, it is. As her mother, I can confidently say that just about everything she does is cute. But other people often think it's cute because, in her endearingly naive way, she doesn't yet know that in our culture we don't say "hi" to anything that's not human.

But Andrew and I think that her greetings are, in fact, radical. This wasn't something we taught her. And it's something we've seen plenty of other children do. Their innate intuition ascribes personhood to every being they encounter. Aspen does not discriminate. She delights in the *inherent being* of all creatures. What a simple act that carries so much awareness and recognition! For me, the fact that this inclination is still present in the open minds and imaginations of children, even twenty-first-century Western ones, holds so much more promise and potential for our salvation as a species than the theories of nuclear scientists who are working on fusion.

"Hi!" is now a family practice. Together we greet crab apples, blackberries, the osprey that dives into the churning sea, the quiet shell on the beach, each other, the dewy morning, and the brisk evening.

❈ ❈ ❈

There is a lot of talk today about the ways in which our modern Western stories are not working. Certainly not the stories of capitalism and progress. Not even many of the stories of environmentalism. I agree. But I stumble a bit when there is talk of the *new* stories we need. I mostly agree with this, too, but I wonder how to tell stories—new or old—from a rooted, grounded place.

Where *are* these stories when you come from a culture whose sense of place is widely malnourished? There is much to learn from Indigenous teachers, whose voices ought to be centered. But even with the best intentions, we who are not Indigenous also ought to be very cautious of plucking Native stories from their own cultural ecosystems. There is a difference between learning and transplanting. I don't think one can simply pull stories from others' rooted traditions and fold them into one's own.

We might turn to our own wisdom and religious traditions. I spent the better part of a decade studying comparative religion, and it was clear to me that our diverse faith traditions carry stories, symbols, and rituals that, as Joseph Campbell says, speak to us "of matters fundamental to ourselves, enduring essential principles about which it would be good for us to know; about which, in fact, it will be necessary for us to know if our conscious minds are to be kept in touch with our own most secret, motivating depths." This includes the makings of myth. Of course, the expression of that wisdom—and the way in which myth works on our conscious and subconscious minds—is influenced by the present-day culture in which it is situated. But part of the power of ancient traditions is that they speak to something archetypal and evergreen within the human experience and can be drawn upon again and again, in new ways, for new contexts. I have encountered many recent examples of people doing the work of healing our separation from the Earth, grounded in the myth, symbols, and rituals of their religious traditions: Buddhist monks ordaining trees in Cambodia to protect them from logging; my dear friend and mentor Steve Blackmer's Church of the Woods, where the Eucharist is offered to people, ferns, and black bears alike; the Kanaka Maoli in Hawai'i protecting Mauna Kea. Examples abound.

But again, these symbols and rituals are not for us to fully access if we are not members of these traditions. And what of the growing numbers of people who identify with no religious or faith tradition? This is, I think, when we can turn to place itself: the places that have shaped and molded us. The places that we are in deep relationship with. The places that are, or can become, our *axes mundi*, our sacred centers.

A mothering language is one that strives to bring a sacred world into being through story. It reaches for a space in our collective imagination where all of life's beings find their home. This means that in addition to listening for the human stories that root our traditions, and in addition to listening to the stories that come through the innate knowing of our children, we must also seek out and tell the stories of the land itself. As creatures born of this Earth, we must tell the stories of the landscapes that have shaped and held and mothered us.

As mothers, we can practice listening to the voice of the land and allow ourselves to be vessels that share that voice with others. Where does the story of the land intersect our own history, our present, our future? If we are to make a home for all of life's beings, both in our actions and in our stories, then we must listen not only for our human stories but for stories of land and place.

These place-stories will be deeply imperfect, as they are translated through human language. We will fret about whether we are anthropomorphizing, or about how such stories are prone to our projections and our biases, our egos and our limited minds. But I hope we will not allow these worries to silence us.

So let me return, once more, to the time when my family lived along the Niobrara River and to that first *axis mundi*, there in the grass. As I turn round it yet again, it invites me to turn my language, to shift my perspective, to ask: if I imagine the Niobrara River as a mother, what learning might it impart?

Here, then, is one such place-story from this mother.

Once, there was a river.

She came into being, found her present valley twelve thousand years ago, fed by the springs and groundwater of the Great Plains. She wended and braided. She carried silt and sand. She flowed west to east, carving into the land. Through this weaving of water, River came to be.

Who was River as she found her shape so many millennia ago? She was, for one, a home for many different waters. Meltwater. Rainwater. Stream water. Aquifer water. These waters came from many different places: Sky. Stream. Dune. And the deep dark of the Belowground.

But the true majesty of River was this: as she welcomed more and more water, and as that water flowed faster and faster, River became a time weaver.

Picture in your mind: River's waters were always flowing, flowing. Sometimes as steady and wide as a soft line of cloud. Sometimes tumbling, cascading, and splashing over stone on their way. As these different dances of water were moving over the land, they picked up and carried with them, bit by bit, little pieces of that land. They took sediment and sandstone, chalk and ash, shell and bone. As they did, as the water carved its valley, River etched her way through ancient layers of the past and thus reached further and further back into time: Through the sand dunes that were laid down and shaped by wind. Into sand and ash. Next into soft, off-white sandstone, where the water uncovered the bones of saber-toothed deer and giant tortoises. Then through siltstone, until the waters reached all the way down to shale and one-hundred-million-year-old fossils of uncanny beasts, like the ammonite and the thick-bodied plesiosaur. All of these layers of time were folded into the current and carried away. And thus, River wove the past into the present.

But here is something even more extraordinary: as River's waters reclaimed the past and pulled it into the current, the stage was simultaneously set for the future. The exposed siltstone became home to a bur oak savanna, able to grow because of spring seeps that emerged from the south canyon wall of River's valley.

Ponderosa pines took root on the particular shape of the bluffs that River carved. Mixed-grass prairie spread over the sandy soils.

And when the ponderosa pine had taken root, and the bluestem had gone to seed season after season, and the leaves of the bur oak unfurled their royal green in yet another spring, then, one day, a mother and her daughter came to the river.

In the evening, when the sun was setting, they stood, hand in hand, admiring River and her shining water, their shadows stretching before them, swaying and dancing in the grass.

River's waters flowed past them, on and on across the land, in their snaking, rolling rhythm, until they dispersed into the open mouth of a delta, and at last vanished into the wide mystery of the sea.

PART II

BELONGING
Taking Flight with Birds

Let me be to Thee as the circling bird

—Gerard Manley Hopkins

ASCENDANCE

One April, a portion of eastern Tennessee's population of golden-winged warblers vanished. This was a different vanishing from the one the species continues to endure in the Appalachians, where its population is 5 percent of historic levels. Different from the fact that this silver migrant songbird, who wears a prim yellow hat and sings a buzzy song, has experienced one of the steepest declines of any North American songbird over the last half century. Different, I mean, from erasure.

No, this April disappearance was an intentional vanishing act.

The day after the warblers left, a massive storm system barreled through the central and southern United States, generating eighty-four confirmed tornadoes and leading to thirty-five human deaths. After the storm passed, the warblers returned, having flown almost 1,000 miles to avoid the weather. The team of researchers tracking them concluded that the birds had heard the infrasound waves—acoustic waves inaudible to human ears—produced by the approaching storm when it was as many as 560 miles away. And even though they had completed their seasonal migration and established their breeding territories, they undertook what the scientists called an "evacuation migration" and then returned home when it was safe to do so.

In myths, the presence and behavior of birds often indicates a moment of potent transition. They come to impart knowledge, or to warn, or to help. Anna Badkhen writes of how the ancient Greeks discerned prophecy from birds: "Taking the auspices—discerning divine will from the flight of birds—makes sense because birds fly closer to the empyrean, where gods dwell, which makes the bird's-eye view closer to God's."

This is a common motif across cultures and religious traditions: winged beings are taken to be closer to God. As such, birds have often been considered *thin place* creatures, able to move through the veil that separates our plane from the spirit plane: life and afterlife, or world and underworld, or Earth and heaven, or human and divine. The dove descends to Jesus at the Jordan River. In varying ways and tellings, Raven brings light to the worlds of Indigenous peoples of the eastern Arctic. In the Rig Veda: "Dark the descent: the birds are golden-colored; up to the heaven they fly robed in the waters." (These words could easily describe the Tennessee golden-winged warblers as roiling storm clouds approached.) Pigeons were associated with the Sumerian mother-goddess Ishtar. In the tomb of Tuna el-Gebel in Egypt, which was likely inaugurated in the seventh century BCE, more than four million mummified birds were discovered, a sizable percentage of which were African sacred ibis. A person of ancient Egypt, seeking perhaps a cure for illness or a longer life, could have purchased a mummified ibis and offered it in sacrifice to the god Thoth, god of magic and wisdom, a figure with a human body and the head of an ibis. In a third-century fresco in the Catacombs of Priscilla in Rome, a phoenix sits in its nest, engulfed in blood-red flames—a symbol of resurrection.

It's the wings: flight bestows upon birds the means of this boundary crossing, a dual ability to dwell in the sky and on Earth—two realms woven into one creature. I wonder if humans have been so drawn to birds in so many of our myths and stories because this is what we, too, long to be: grounded and soaring; animal and divine. And do we not have the capacity to be such beings—at once rooted and connected to something greater than ourselves?

I think what is at stake in this capacity—in reaching this rooted and interconnected potential—is an ecological and spiritual sense of belonging, in which we are at once emplaced and in deep relationship to that place. Perhaps better phrased: an *eco-spiritual* belonging, for the two are not separate.

"The world is not a problem to be solved; it is a living being to which we belong," writes Llewellyn Vaughan-Lee in *Spiritual Ecology*. "The world is part of our own self and we are a part of its suffering wholeness. Until we go to the root of our image of separateness, there can be no healing. And the deepest part of our separateness from creation lies in our forgetfulness of its sacred nature, which is also our own sacred nature."

I do not, then, mean the sort of belonging in which this computer I'm typing on belongs to me. Or this house, or this land. That sort of belonging is limited, one-sided, hierarchical, and turned easily toward destructive and diminishing ends. The question *What belongs to me?* is a dead end. But the inverse one—*To what do I belong?*—brings us both to the core of our humanity and into the relationships that sustain and nurture that humanity.

As a mother, I am circling this question of belonging, for I have brought a child into a precarious world. The storm clouds are on the horizon, and I must, nonetheless, teach her how to hold that thread of connection, to the sacred and to the Earth, even if storms roil her home. This means doing that work myself, for I cannot yet say that I truly, deeply belong anywhere. I am apprenticing to the birds. I'm tracking an intuition in wide arcs across the sky: that mothering our children, as well as extending nurture and care to the Earth, requires finding our footing, first, within an eco-spiritual center.

Such eco-spiritual belonging implies recognition *of* and *by*: that we exist within a familiar, recognized environment, and that, in turn, we are recognized and familiar *to* that environment. As Martin Shaw writes: "To be *of* means to listen. To commit to *being around*. It's participation, not as a conqueror, not in the spirit of devouring, but in the spirit of relatedness." Which is to say: such belonging is intimately connected to the belonging of human and nonhuman others. If we were to zoom out from where we stand in each of our home places, we would not simply see ourselves at the center of a circle, with spokes of relationship extending out. We would be one among an infinite pattern of such circles, many reaching toward us, each with another being in the center, and one connected to the other, which connected to the other.

This sort of relational belonging requires both the physical spaces and places and the relationships that emerge from those places. Such relationships come to serve as points of connection, or sources of mystery, or invitations into deeper knowing. At these relational thresholds—the points at which we meet what is beyond ourselves—we might become warm-blooded, feathered bodies taking flight. Some might name that form of belonging "God." Others might name it "forest." These do not need to be the same thing, nor are they mutually exclusive.

Did not the Tennessee golden-winged warblers display such belonging as creatures hopping among the branches of their native trees while tuning into the approaching storm, which was far from visible but nonetheless viscerally sensed?

Upon observing the behavior of the warblers, the researchers began asking—and this became the central question of their subsequent paper—whether paying attention to birds could serve as an accurate advance warning of disaster. My central question was: how can I be more like a warbler?

Wrapped in my physical body and attuned to a sensory universe. A weatherer of storms. Grounded and able to take flight. Both ascendant and intimately bound to creation.

Motherhood calls on us to be birdlike creatures as we seek our belonging, so that even if the ground shifts beneath our feet and the skies rend apart, our ability to be interconnected, in-relationship beings on this Earth does not waver. Whether we are warblers robed in the waters or phoenixes engulfed in flames, we can seek that belonging as we circle back, and back, toward the center.

7

SETTING BEARINGS

The first time I saw the barn owl, it was a swoop of shadow slicing through the predawn of midwinter. I was walking alone in the mist, my thoughts contained within the slender beam of my flashlight, content to leave the world to itself—wide and soft and unknown in the dark. Those mornings, I circled the mowed perimeters around two meadows, which were bisected by a stream and connected to each other by a dirt road with a culvert beneath to keep the water flowing.

Thinking I was alone was a contained thought indeed. I was just beginning my circuit around the first meadow, passing the high, deer-proof fence around the vegetable garden, when the top of one of the fence posts unraveled and took to the air. The owl's silhouette was both silent and transient. But it carried a certainty of wild presence that sent my heart into my throat. I jerked my flashlight upward, but the pale yellow light only reflected back how much water was in the air, a veil of mist between me and beyond.

We had come to live on an island in Puget Sound hoping to establish a permanent home, something I had done many times before. The journey had begun several months after my birth as my family—and later I, myself, as an adult—made and remade homes like so many beds: Nebraska, Oklahoma, Massachusetts, New Hampshire, Vermont, Maine. Now Washington.

Andrew, Aspen, and I lived on the island, accepting a generous invitation to be caretakers on a forty-acre piece of land. It is called this—"The Land"—by many who know it, for it is a special place, infused with an almost mythic ability to thrive. Singing creeks. Trees heavy with apples. Beets that grow to the size of softballs. When the woman who owned and had lovingly tended to The Land for decades confirmed her wish to donate the property to the foundation I then worked for, Andrew, Aspen, and I were invited to come and help oversee this next chapter of The Land's long life. We came in a moment of transition: for The Land, who was beginning a new phase of care under new owners; for our family, who had welcomed our first child one year before; for the world, in the grips of a global pandemic and a worsening climate crisis. We left New England and arrived in Washington on a gray day that made the towering emerald evergreens leap out from the side of the road with such stark definition as to seem almost false, like a fairy forest in a pop-up book.

And the mist spilled onto everything. What was the word for those daily winter immersions, those slow but certain soakings? Water-air? Middle-of-cloud? Some mornings, it felt like a baptism. Others, a drowning.

The move—the departure, the arrival, the orientation to a new place—was all-consuming. It took a while for the weight of homesickness to settle in, having left our families, friends, and familiar landscapes behind. I tried to walk the missing away. Morning after morning, I walked. A quiet pilgrimage round and round a figure-eight labyrinth, as if wearing the meadows' paths deeper might imprint some shape of myself here, or, as if the damp grasses would wear their way into me. Eventually, I would mark out some discernible shape of belonging. After some fated number of steps, I would truly arrive.

I did not then intend to be walking a labyrinth. But it's clear now that that's what I was doing. Human beings have been walking in such patterns for millennia. Circling in the hope of moving toward an answer, or articulating a prayer.

Every Friday between Lent and All Saints' Day, the staff of the Chartres Cathedral in France moves aside the chairs in the nave to reveal the labyrinth that coils on the floor: a stone path in eleven concentric circles, leading to a six-lobed rosette in the center. The labyrinth dates to the early thirteenth century and continues to draw pilgrims from around the world. The circular shapes of classical labyrinths like this one are often understood as symbols of spiritual wholeness or the divine center. To walk one is to overlay bodily movement with prayer, to physically circle while inwardly embarking on a spiritual journey.

Of the several theories about the original intended meaning of the Chartres labyrinth, one of them centers around mothers. The cathedral houses what is said to be the tunic worn by the Virgin Mary when she gave birth to Christ, and the labyrinth is built of 272 stones, 272 being the average number of days of human gestation in the womb. Some believe it was once used as a "birthing instrument": a woman could come to walk as a prayer for the health of her child. It's a comforting thought: the feet of so many mothers and mothers-to-be smoothing labyrinthine stones over the course of centuries.

Those mornings in the meadow, I, too, was a mother walking in circles. My prayer—sometimes articulated, sometimes only a growing pressure around my heart—to give my daughter an enduring sense of place, a refuge. My doubt: how to do this when I was stumbling over unfamiliar ground, and when it was increasingly hard to imagine what *any* place's endurance looked like in the face of planetwide ecological transformation.

In *Belonging: A Culture of Place*, bell hooks writes: "Many folks feel no sense of place. What they know, what they have, is a sense of crisis, of impending doom." She says that we live in a time defined by a "too muchness" that "creates a wilderness of spirit, the everyday anguish that shapes the habits of being for those who are lost, wandering, searching."

I had brought another human being into this troubled world, and with her arrival, the stakes of orientation had risen. We were going to have to give this child the tools and the skills to navigate a rapidly changing world. It was time to set bearings. But I felt within myself this persistent wilderness of spirit, the disorientation wrought by a sense of impending doom. And the nagging fear that I would always be shining a flashlight into the mist.

The barn owl had melted effortlessly into that liminal hour of shadows. She fully belonged there on the cusp of daybreak, while I was revealed as a creature of contrast when the sun rushed over the trees and traced the sharp, aching boundary between my body and The Land.

I walked and walked as the world felt like at any moment it might tip into chaos. For many, it had tipped long ago. For many, it was tipping now. One report estimated that nearly three billion birds had disappeared across North America in the last fifty years. Habitat loss was listed as a primary cause. This is "a staggering loss that suggests the very fabric of North America's ecosystem is unraveling," wrote John W. Fitzpatrick and Peter P. Marra in an op-ed for the *New York Times*. Elsewhere, twenty million people were being internally displaced by climate change–related disasters every year.

Where was liberation from the habits of a too-much culture, in which abundance for some meant churning out deserts for others? How could we seek our own belonging in such a way that we made space for others to belong? How could I attend to that belonging—ethically, ecologically, and spiritually?

The barn owl had given me a clue: I want to say that she pulled me out of myself, but the experience was not one of disembodiment. It was, rather, my body spilling out of pores I hadn't known were there. She unfolded me into the world alongside her, and I rippled into the shadowed trees. I spun halfway around in the dark, tracing the arc of her flight. I moved in response to her movement and, fleetingly, became a creature again—a being with senses on alert, aware of the animal in my periphery and the animal at my core, something made up of wild instinct and the forgotten ability to soar.

HOOPOE, I

In *The Conference of the Birds*, an epic poem composed in the twelfth century, Persian poet Farid ud-Din Attar gives us an allegory of the Sufi's mystical journey to God in the form of a pilgrimage undertaken by a multitude of birds.

At the beginning of the poem, the world's feathered beings are gathered together, intending to find a king. The hoopoe—a bird native to southeast Asia, Africa, and southern Europe, and known as the messenger to the prophet Solomon in the Qur'an—comes forward and beckons them to accompany him on a long and arduous journey, across "vast seas and deserts," to meet their true king, the Simorgh, a being of "undisturbed omnipotence" and "perfect grace."

At first, the hoopoe's enthusiasm is contagious; the birds are eager to set out. But it isn't long before they hedge, beginning to understand the extent of the sacrifice the journey will require—namely, that they must leave behind all that they have become attached to and all that they think they know of the world.

So begin the birds' excuses.

> But when they pondered on the journey's length,
> They hesitated; their ambitious strength
> Dissolved: each bird, according to his kind,
> Felt flattered but reluctantly declined.

The nightingale cannot leave the presence of his beloved, the rose. The finch is a coward. The partridge is consumed by greed. The mythical homa is blinded by pride. The heron is too devoted to his own misery. The owl prefers to continue to worship his idol of gold.

I'm drawn, in part, to *The Conference of the Birds* because it can be read as an ecological parable, a story ripe for this time. Each of us fully belongs here as a creature of the Earth, but the climate crisis is evidence of the veils of separation that have been placed between us and the living world. The path back to this Earth awareness, the path back to Truth and true belonging, comes in large part through seeking belonging as sensory beings attuned to what is beyond ourselves. Working to see the folds and shapes of this crisis can point us down the path to healing and reconnection. We can begin the work of removing the veils.

If my aim is to inhabit an ecological terrain of motherhood, to extend and reinforce lines of care and connection across species, then there is real, arduous work ahead.

But I identify with Attar's birds and their reluctance. I think of the comforts and privileges I've grown accustomed to and am hard-pressed to let go of, even as they become obstacles on the path back to deeper relationship. I hear my own excuses loudest of all. All the ways in which I resist. How I politely, reluctantly decline.

SENSORY ORIENTATION

The second barn owl appeared several weeks after the first.

Barn owls are nonmigratory and, if undisturbed, are often committed to the place of their birth for the duration of their lives. It's likely that both of these adult owls lived on The Land year-round. Several years ago, a nest box had been attached, fittingly, to the barn, and the pair had accepted the invitation.

The nest box was equipped with a small interior camera so that a group of us could observe the owls via an app. Paired there in one end of the box, often pressed against each other, they were haunting creatures, their white, heart-shaped faces subverting the cliches of this shape, neither familiar nor sentimental. Their speckled backs were brushed with copper and gray-blue, cast over an underlayer of downy white feathers, like broken shadows on snow. Their heads were centered by a wildness that concentrated in their bottomless inkwell eyes.

Not caught on the camera: the courtship. The male would have performed elaborate flight displays, clapping his wings together (whether he claps intentionally or simply as a consequence of the vigor of his flight is not known). He would have flown the strenuous "moth flight," hovering in front of the female, dangling his legs. Then, he would have flown in and out of the nestbox, crying out, enticing her inside. Last, he would have caught a rodent and fed it to her. She would have let out approving snores as she ate her meal. Their close presence there on the camera announced not only the success of this annual ritual but the extent to which their physical, tawny bodies were the means of their practiced actions of making a home.

We were, meanwhile, creating our own new rituals in Washington, ways of coming into relationship with a new place. Neither Andrew nor I had committed to one place for the duration of our lives, but we hoped that this place would be it, and I had seized upon rituals of belonging with the zeal of the converted. I jogged and walked the same routes, day after day, making repeated mental lists of scenic details. We took Thursday evening walks at one beach. Saturday morning outings at another. We acquired new books on the flora and fauna of the Pacific Northwest. We didn't grumble at October's endless rain or the multiple, days-long power outages, but we welcomed it all as a sort of initiation. Determined to raise a child who was deeply oriented to her home place, I needed to orient myself as quickly as possible.

The problem: my own sensory world was reeling. Somehow I had not anticipated the bodily disorientation I would experience in a cross-country move. Through relocations as a child and as a young adult, I'd been able to take such disruptions in stride. But this time was different, and while I had expected the emotional upheaval, the possible upheaval of my senses had not crossed my mind.

The new patterns and colors to the seasons, the striking lack of deciduous trees, the different smell and feel to the air—all gave me the feeling of eavesdropping on a conversation among strangers. Even the landscape's majesty felt unreachable, like staring at a portrait of a strikingly beautiful and utterly unrecognized human face. How to build a relationship with such distant beauty?

Perhaps it was because this sensory disorientation was so unexpected that it took me a long time to realize that it was happening. Or perhaps it was my resistance to acknowledging this persistent unfamiliarity, but instead of getting better, it got worse. The daily encounters with the unknown continued to untether my senses rather than anchor them. This untethering began to add to the move's toll on my mental and emotional health. And it came to feel increasingly like a failure of parenting. I had pulled my daughter away from her extended family, her wider community, and here in this new place I felt a persistent distraction and distress at not finding my footing.

Aspen's entry into the world had sped up my metamorphosis into a rooting creature—an evolution that had been underway but not yet fully realized. I no longer wanted to embark on long journeys. I wanted to burrow. That, and I had taken our family's orientation to this new place for granted, thinking it would be there to meet us upon our arrival, forgetting that such alignment is not a function of the intellect, of individual will, but a patient process of coming into intimate relationship. And that this relationship between self and land is neither one-sided nor something that can be forced, rushed, controlled.

Without any teaching from me, Aspen set about navigating this new place slowly and attentively. She created rituals on her own time, and it was a time guided not by clocks or schedules or anxiety but almost entirely by her own curiosity and her sensory, physical, animal body. She almost never moved in a straight line, instead meandering, crawling and eventually toddling on unsteady legs, guided by what she wanted to see, touch, taste. She would wander over to the crab apple tree, where she could gladly sit indefinitely, as long as we kept handing her the hard, bitter fruits to chew on. She would crawl leaf to leaf, or pebble to pebble, through the yard and driveway, squeezing found things between her thumb and forefinger before popping them into her mouth (and then, behold: the ever-fretting parents of a teething toddler). She was at home within her sensory desires and impulses. She could meet what was there to meet her, effortlessly doing the work of setting bearings that I could not.

✳ ✳ ✳

Meanwhile, I kept watching the barn owls on the owl cam. It often looked as though they were staring directly into the camera, and sometimes I would glance away under their intense gaze, as if they could see me. I thought in those moments that if I listened very carefully, I would hear in their eyes the crackle and spark of some primal energy. Ancient Egyptians must have had a similar thought: for a time, they associated barn owls with the sun god, Ra, because of those wide, black eyes that seemed to be all-seeing. But it is not, in fact, the eyes of barn owls that crackle and spark.

It is the ears.

The body and mind of a barn owl are wired for sound. The map by which the owl navigates and survives her world is built of vibrations through air. There is careful, evolutionary design behind the heart shape of a barn owl's face, which is centered not around the eyes at all (for they have a comparably limited ability) but the ears. It is more accurate, actually, to say that this disc of white feathers, called the "facial ruff," is shaped not like a heart but like a satellite dish, for that is its function. Together these feathers form a dense, curved wall that amplifies sound. The facial ruff channels sound waves to the barn owl's ears, which are hidden on either side of her head, just behind the eyes.

This ability to hear with two ears, each independently tracking the timing of a sound's arrival and its volume, is called "binaural hearing." This is how humans, too, pinpoint the origin of a sound. Binaural hearing gives us the ability to process ITD, *interaural time difference*, and ILD, *interaural level difference*. Meaning: the difference in how long it takes for a sound to arrive in each ear, and the difference in the volume each ear discerns, respectively. If a rattlesnake shakes its tail ahead of us and to the right, our brain will process our respective ears' reception of the sound such that we immediately know both where to direct our eyes and how to move our body to avoid the snake. Impressive enough, but in a barn owl, binaural hearing is practically a superpower.

Crucially, unlike our ears, the owl's ears are oriented asymmetrically on her head. The opening to the left ear is higher than the opening to the right. This asymmetry is key: it adds a level of surgical precision to the owl's binaural hearing, providing her with stunning exactitude in her response to sound.

The two barn owls would wait out the daylight in the nest box, and by dusk, the nest was empty as they set off to claim rodents from the grass. Imagine the female owl is out scouting for prey. It is a dark night with a new moon. There is virtually no light to guide her. (Not that light would matter, for her prey—a vole the size of an unshelled walnut—is hiding somewhere in a meadow of thick, two-foot-tall grass.) The owl flies, silent and nearly invisible, a shadow. Her wings, built of feathers with comb-like edges at the front and fringes at the back, mute the friction between her body and the air. They are designed to be soundless so as not to alert her prey nor to interfere with what she is listening for.

Which is this: the vole moves.

That tiny rustle of grass reaches the owl's left ear first, then her right. Her left ear is higher on her head than her right, but the ear opening is directed at a slight downward angle, so any sound below her horizon will be louder in her left ear, while a sound from above will be louder in her right ear, whose opening is directed at a slight upward angle. Her brain notes this difference in the level (ILD) and timing (ITD) of the sound between the ears and encodes it. The sound travels along her auditory nerve, to her cochlea and then to her forebrain, as the raw data of the sound is processed into information about the sound's location. It then arrives in the auditory center of her midbrain, where it comes to a network of "place-specific" or "limited field" neurons, waiting for the stimulus of this shushing rustle of grass. These neurons arrange themselves into a two-dimensional map of the owl's world. ITD provides this map with the vole's *azimuth*, or the horizontal dimension of its position relative to the owl, and the ILD provides the elevation of the vole, the vertical dimension of its position.

Is this not baffling? The barn owl hears a sound, and her brain instantly produces an internal auditory map of the exterior space in which the position of the vole is accurately displayed.

Back to the hunt: The vole is on the move. The owl snaps her head in the direction of the sound, then orients her body, changing the direction of her flight. Her wings reach back, her talons reach forward. In total darkness, she descends into the tall grass, strikes her prey.

In one study, a researcher plugged one of the ears of a barn owl. The owl became deeply disoriented and performed poorly in subsequent flight tests, making "systematic errors." Were this animal in its natural habitat and not in a lab, it would have been far less likely to have survived with this sensory stunting, nor would it have been able to successfully feed and sustain any offspring.

Thus, to feed herself, to grow her eggs, to raise the next generation, the female barn owl relies upon her keen sense of hearing, on the ways that her ears map her world and provide her with direction. Her sense of hearing is her sustenance, her survival, her way of being at home. It is her orientation to the world—and, with a clutch of eggs soon to appear in the nest, it is her ability to make orientation possible for the coming season's brood of owlets.

It's obvious, I suppose, to say that *any* animal relies on the full and robust performance of her sensory systems to thrive within her native ecosystem and to ensure the health and well-being of her offspring. But isn't it strange that this statement is far less obvious when "human" or "mother" is substituted for "animal"? The sentence then becomes almost oxymoronic. For can anyone honestly look at the Earth and say that, as a species, we are functioning to our fullest sensory capacity? Have our senses not been numbed?

So many of the models that we encounter are those provided by consumerism and capitalism, neither of which teaches or encourages us to rely on the robust functioning of our sensory bodies.

I tell you all of this about the barn owl's ears not only because it is incredible. I tell you because I was a mother walking around with one of my proverbial ears plugged.

It was not until we moved to Washington that I realized the extent to which I had taken my senses for granted, and just how much information they had been feeding me. It was only disorientation that prompted me to consider how many cues and clues my sensory systems imparted to me on a daily basis. I came to realize just how much this information provided a foundation of recognition, essential to my understanding of home. Becoming oriented to our previous home in Maine had not arisen simply from paying attention in any place, on any given day—but was the result of a *repeated* daily encounter with sounds and seasons, the particular smells of trees and waters, the patterns and noises of human movement that I had grown accustomed to over the previous years. It was accumulated experience that made a particular place familiar. Another obvious realization. But it struck me that sensory recognition and orientation, then, are not only achieved through present-moment practices of attention. They have something to do with place-memory.

❊ ❊ ❊

Two million years ago, hunting and gathering emerged as the primary means of subsisting for our distant human ancestors. As these bipedal hominins ventured into their surroundings and surveyed the landscape, they engaged their auditory and visual systems not only to know where they were but to aid in the remembrance of things like where they had been before, and what had happened there, and which seasons offered which kinds of foods. In this way, the physical demands of hunting and gathering coincided with demands on the human brain to perform increasingly complex cognitive tasks. The ability to subsist within a place drew upon both long- and short-term memory and enabled them not only to navigate physical pathways across a landscape but to engage in decision-making and planning in relation to the landscape and the food procured from it.

As was the case for early humans two million years ago, and remains the case for *Homo sapiens* today, these cognitive processes rely, in part, on the hippocampus. The hippocampus, a critical part of the brain for spatial navigation and spatial memory, is also the crucial component of what is called "episodic memory," the ability to remember specific, personal events within the context of their occurrence—the place/space and time. As described by Eran Ben-Elia, the hippocampus also aids our brains in cognitive mapping, the processes by which our audiovisual senses "filter, abstract, integrate, and store spatial information in long-term memory in order to transfer knowledge to new situations." Cognitive mapping is a place-based function of the mind, enabling us to "successfully process and encode environmental and geographical data."

Cognitive mapping is also believed to contribute to the human capacity for narrative and story. In a paper entitled "The Human Hippocampus and Spatial and Episodic Memory," the authors write that, according to cognitive map theory, in humans, "the right hippocampus is still viewed as encoding spatial relationships, but the left has the altered function of storing relationships between linguistic entities in the form of narratives."

Once thought to be exclusive to humans, episodic memory is now believed to exist across mammalian and avian species. For mammals and birds, the function of the hippocampus is similar (though there are significant differences, and the other parts of mammalian and avian brains that enable episodic memory have different neural circuitries beyond the hippocampi). Nonetheless, the presence of the hippocampus in both Aspen's brain and the barn owl's raises the theoretical possibility of a common neural ancestry.

Thus, orientation to land, for barn owls and humans alike, is rooted largely in the senses and the brain's ways of processing sensory inputs. Our senses are the points at which we directly encounter and become familiar with the myriad voices and elements of the ecologies around us.

In this way, a place-based orientation that contributes to our sense of belonging is fundamentally not abstract. It is literal. It is of the body. It is not only our way of physically inhabiting places but, through the porous gateways of the senses, the way that places come to inhabit *us*. The land enters our bodies. Just as a sound in the barn owl's outer world creates an internal map of space in her brain, we become aligned to place through our sensory encounters. We, too, make maps. As our senses feed us information, our bodies and brains translate landscapes into memories, pathways, plans, homes.

But we have become a deeply disoriented, distracted species. One study identified a causal relationship between a driver's use of GPS to navigate and a decline in spatial memory. The greater the reliance on GPS, the greater the decline, which included a decrease in the person's ability to employ "spatial memory strategies," and to engage in cognitive mapping, "landmark encoding," and "navigational learning." "These results suggest that using GPS renders individuals less able to form an accurate mental representation of their surroundings when they are navigating without GPS," the authors write, and may ultimately "negatively impact the integrity of the hippocampus."

Critically, this distraction from our own senses is paired with humanity's becoming increasingly distracted from the sensory worlds of the more-than-human beings who comprise and share our home places. Human noise, technology, development, and pollution are presently causing countless other sensory worlds to reel. A study monitoring avian reproductive success alongside a noisy Dutch highway found that traffic noise overlapped with the lower frequency band of the male great tit's song, a song used by the bird for designating territory and attracting a mate. The traffic noise ultimately had a negative impact on the birds, with female great tits laying smaller clutches in the noisier areas and fewer chicks fledging from the nest.

This brings us to an ethics of sensory orientation. If our ability to successfully navigate our home-places relies on an accumulated sensory memory that provides a foundation for relationship, for story, and for navigation, then does it not *also* rely on the healthy functioning of our ecosystems, which provide us with those consistent sensory cues? This, in turn, requires that the sensory worlds of *the creatures who inhabit those ecosystems are functioning healthily.* Our own orientation and our children's, and the barn owl's orientation and her children's, hinge on the orientation of feathered, scaled, furred, photosynthesizing bodies and their ability to continue their practiced actions of sensory recognition and navigation. These are all essential threads in the tapestry of an interconnected sensory universe.

And so, as the barn owls continued their nightly hunts, as Aspen made landmarks of fruiting trees, I set about the painstaking process of unplugging my ears.

HOOPOE, II

One by one, the hoopoe unravels the birds' excuses, speaking to each bird first directly, and then in parable. To the homa, he tells the story of "King Mahmoud after death"; to the heron, "A hermit questions the ocean"; to the owl, "The miser who became a mouse." Each a lesson woven into narrative and myth.

Stories are the hoopoe's vehicle for undermining what the birds have mistaken for purpose, helping them to navigate a path into deeper truth. Language becomes a tool of unlearning.

DISRUPTED NAVIGATION

One hundred and fifteen kilometers east of Amman, Jordan, is the Azraq Wetland Reserve, a wetland oasis in Jordan's vast eastern desert. Azraq means "blue" in Arabic. Historically, the oasis was replenished year after year with winter rains that refilled the aquifers, raised the water table, and flooded the nearby mudflats. The reserve has long been a relied-upon, permanent source of freshwater for humans and animals, and a stopover for birds migrating between Europe and Africa, drawn down from the sky by the reflection of water in the desert. Among the reeds and date palms, they would come here to rest and refuel.

Approximately one-third of Jordan's 434 species of birds are waterbirds, including the northern shoveler, a medium-sized duck with a large shovel-shaped bill and a radiant emerald head. Shovelers have a wide range. Their breeding grounds include North America and northern Eurasia, while wintering grounds extend south and west through Europe, and into parts of Africa, southeast Asia, and India. Though Jordan is one of the most water-poor countries in the world, as many as half a million birds—thousands of shovelers among them—would alight here at Azraq, finding a temporary, abundant refuge amid long migratory journeys.

Beginning in the 1980s, over-pumping of Jordan's aquifers ultimately caused the wetland and surrounding mudflats to all but disappear. The subsequent alarm bells were loud enough that 10 percent of the Azraq reserve's water was restored, via pumping from the aquifer, and the birds started coming back. But today, even this limited restoration of water is dwindling. Jordan's groundwater supply is being drained far faster than it is able to naturally refill, a fate that reflects diminishing aquifers around the world. The drop in water at Azraq is correlated with a stark decline in the numbers of birds who choose to stop here. The water table, once easily rising above ground level to replenish ponds and marshes, now sits many meters belowground. Jordan's International Waterbird Census recorded more than ten thousand total birds at Azraq Wetland Reserve in 2001. The same census recorded just fifty-three birds in 2013. This included a marked decline in the numbers of northern shovelers.

For the fall of 2013 I lived in Amman, a beige city, ancient and rapidly modernizing. Like any major metropolis, Amman carries its own flavor of stark, coexisting contrasts: ruins of a Roman theater and cranes constructing new skyscrapers; open-air spice markets and a shiny Western mall; cheap falafel stands on corners and bougie speakeasies; the palatial homes of expats, guarded by men with guns, and neighborhoods where the trash was not collected and crumbled buildings were left to crumble further. Outside the city were both tourists on vacation to Petra and the Dead Sea and refugees in sprawling camps—cities that had sprouted in the desert, necessitated by trauma and suffering. All these features were woven together by the ringing voices of the muezzins singing the daily calls to prayer that flowed down from the minarets. *La ilaha illa Allah: There is no God but God.*

Several times that fall, a night's passing rain washed the fine dust from the leaves of the city's trees, and the sudden reveal of green in the morning was like an instantaneous spring. One morning in November, snow fell, and the pomegranates in the trees sparkled and bobbed on their branches. Teenage boys whooped and slid along the slushy streets.

A friend and I had come to volunteer with several organizations that were assisting Syrian refugees who had fled the catastrophic violence of Bashar al-Assad's civil war. Over the last
seventy-five years, Jordan has received many of the Middle East's
refugees as people in the region have become displaced by violence. When we arrived, two years after the start of the Syrian war,
hundreds of thousands of Syrians had already fled their homeland. By that fall, more than half a million Syrians, mostly women
and children, had arrived in Jordan. While tens of thousands were
directed to the Za'atari refugee camp just outside the nearby city
of Mafraq, the majority resettled in Amman and other urban areas.

A surge in population due to an influx of refugees was not
unfamiliar in Jordan. With successive waves of people fleeing
violence since 1948, Palestinians now make up a fifth of Jordan's
population. During the first Gulf War in the early 1990s, tens of
thousands of Iraqis fled to Jordan, followed by another wave in the
early 2000s, when the United States invaded Iraq.

This population growth, paired with already limited water
supplies and the impacts of climate change, which have caused
precipitous decreases in the amount and predictability of annual
rainfall, has made water an increasingly dire issue. In Jordan, longer, hotter summers have stressed crops and demanded more
pumped water from aquifers. Compounding the issue, Israel and
Syria both divert the dwindling waters of the Jordan River. Were
the dove to descend again to these banks, two millennia after the
baptism of Jesus, she would find a river that has almost run dry.

Regional conflicts, too, are exacerbated by water scarcity. It
would be a great oversimplification to say that the Syrian civil war
was instigated by climate change–related events. Yet it's difficult
to ignore that—in addition to the ruthless violence of a dictator in
response to pro-democracy protests, the mismanagement of water
resources, and the ideological and religious disputes—the instiga-
tion of conflict came shortly after the country's worst drought in

recorded history, which resulted in widespread crop failures and high rates of internal economic displacement among citizens.

Coordinating with several NGOs, my friend and I brought fruit and vegetables, winter coats, school supplies, toys, soap, shampoo, menstrual pads, and diapers to Syrian families living in Amman and the surrounding towns. These families greeted us, always, with unflinching generosity, insisting on sharing the little they had. We sat on the floors of cramped, damp apartments and talked over cups of heavily sugared tea in a mix of our elementary Arabic and their stilted English, many stories unfinished and questions unanswered for lack of shared vocabulary.

The mother of one family, Umm Muhammad, was eight months pregnant with her third child when we met her. Her dignified shoulders, held straight, and the graceful curve of her belly conveyed a certain gravitas: woman with child. Her face and her flitting hands held the anxiety. She would be giving birth in a new place as a refugee of war, a place she at once did not want to be and was grateful for, having endured the flight from violence. Her child would enter the world in a foreign land, not in the birthplace of his ancestors.

While all the Syrian adults we met—the mothers, fathers, uncles, grandparents—struggled visibly under the weight of grief and trauma, the younger children retained an eagerness to learn, to play, to dream. They giggled and teased, showed off their math workbooks, gave us nicknames.

This same tendency toward joy was present in the adults when they spoke of Syria. What they conveyed then was the common language between us that needed no fluency. We couldn't catch all the words, but we understood what it meant to love a place. They showed us photographs on flip phones: lush streets, cafes with flowers in window boxes, ornate rooms in houses, smiling families.

But while I could understand a language of home, I had no frame of reference for what these families had lost in leaving theirs. After the photos of their intact worlds inevitably came the photos of the same neighborhoods, the same houses, reduced to rubble, stained with death, execution, smoke, and fire. These photographs were the ghosts of a homeland, departed. Evidence of belonging, lost. Even if I had fluently spoken the dialect, I would have had no language for this.

I was in Jordan by choice. I had an American passport. I arrived of my own will and could leave when I pleased and return home. Jordan left me with a pressing question, one that has only grown in the decade since I was there, on into mothering my daughter: How can our children, and other human beings, and other species live within prolonged disruption? If belonging is the ability to be both rooted and ascendant, embodied and emplaced, then what is *dis*belonging?

The violence of displacement. The indifference to such violence.

✳ ✳ ✳

In the years since I left Jordan, the country's population has swelled again, from eight million to eleven million. The water has continued to dwindle. In Amman, faucets often run dry, sometimes for days at a time, particularly in poorer households.

Thousands of birds no longer come down to land at Azraq. The northern shoveler is less and less likely to come to rest. Meanwhile, hundreds of thousands of people have arrived in the desert, migrations embarked upon out of desperation. Refugees have come to rest, to refuel, without knowing when or if their journeys will continue from here, whether or not they will get to return home.

What is it to become a land that no longer draws birds down from the sky?

What is it as a human being to remain suspended in a state of flight?

Both are absences. Each human and each bird one embodiment of the thousands of ways that belonging can be disrupted.

* * *

Umm Muhammad gave birth to a healthy son several weeks after we met her. He was the first infant I'd held as an adult. He lay in the crook of my arm, radiant. A tiny messenger of uncomplicated, unquestioned peace; of the deep humanity that we bring with us into the world. A graceful being, fully at home in his mother's arms. Born in Jordan to Syrian parents, his presence held both the loss and the renewed possibility of belonging.

That day, Umm Muhammad and her family were radiant, too.

HOOPOE, III

The world's mystics hold in common the desire to know God as the ultimate reality. Via different histories, different texts and practices, and different religious traditions, they long to know the Truth of truths that infuses everything. Beginning at one's birth, this Truth begins to be clouded by conditioning. The ego, worldly desires, and attachments get in the way. The mystic who embarks on the path back to God works to remove the thousand veils that exist between her soul—her true self—and God. The seeker's mystical journey is most often led by a teacher (in Attar's allegory, the hoopoe) who not only imparts wisdom but works to undo all that the novice thinks she knows. The tools of this undoing: parable, ceaseless prayer, meditation. And eventually, even these tools are discarded. Even language will be kicked away, like a ladder that is no longer of use. The layers are peeled and peeled, until the seeker reunites with God. A candle meets the sun. A drop of water returns to the ocean.

Many paths to God, the old adage goes. Mysticism has a place within Christianity, Judaism, Islam, Daoism, Hinduism, Buddhism, and on and on. Often the mystics predated these names and forms of religious practice. This is what initially led me to study Sufism, and mysticism more broadly, as a comparative religion student in college: that all religious traditions, in their complexity and diversity, have seekers within them who are searching for the same thing. Within a particular cultural and historical context, using a particular language, and with systems of symbol and ritual, they are striving toward direct experience and knowing of God. And God, for the mystic, is ultimately indescribable, will always be beyond language. This made sense to me.

Across the world's mystical traditions are countless iterations of the practices that bring one closer to God. Some mystics whirl. Some isolate. Some remain in active service to the world. Some deny themselves basic comforts. Some believe in the soul and rebirth; others believe there is no true self. Some seek God, others gods, others not God at all but enlightenment. Some perceive even the Earth as illusion or reflection, while some hear the mystery of God whispering in the trees.

Another reason I've long been drawn to *The Conference of the Birds* as a mystical text: because Attar's seekers take the form of birds, and Sufis, the mystics of Islam, are masters of the ascendant-earthbound. To achieve true belonging within much of Sufism is to be at once immersed in God and immersed in the world. The desired end is to meet the divine in this lifetime, while one still walks the Earth. Two realms woven into one creature. What better symbol than a bird to tell of such belonging?

QUICKENING

A common motif in bird lore and symbolism is that, upon death, the soul departs the body in the form of a bird. William Butler Yeats writes, in "The Death of Cuchulain": "There floats out there / The shape that I shall take when I am dead / My soul's first shape, a soft feathery shape / And is that not a strange shape for the soul. . ."

The soul departing the body as a bird would imply that, at some point, the bird *arrived* in the body. It's strange to say, but in the early weeks of my pregnancy, I felt the arrival of my child.

Around ten weeks in, two months before I would feel the quickening—the first physical sensations of a baby's movements in the womb—I was lying in bed, trying to go to sleep, when a glowing warmth arrived in my lower abdomen. That's the word: *arrived*. It was distinct, a movement that occurred within the defined space of a moment. Like sitting down on a chair. There was nothing shining, and then there was something shining. Over the course of a few minutes, the feeling settled into a pinpoint of light. From then on, I could feel that light, and I knew I was having a daughter. I have repeatedly tried and failed to explain this, even to myself.

In *Dwellings*, Linda Hogan describes her longing for an eagle feather and then a dream in which she speaks the words "Look up." She awakens to a golden eagle flying past her bedroom window. When she runs outside to follow it, an eagle feather is waiting for her on the road. She anticipates the reader's skepticism in conveying this story. "This event," she says, "rubs the wrong way against logic."

Indeed. How do I explain that light in my womb that rubs against my own logic? How do I explain my certainty of a daughter? The knowledge from then on that she was present with me, even before I could physically feel her? Sometimes I remember this night and shake my head at myself, disbelieving. I am not, in truth, sure about what I believe about the nature, or even the existence, of the soul. Maybe there's a medical explanation for this stage of fetal development, I sometimes think. Or perhaps someone could proffer a psychological explanation. Even a religious explanation has occasionally appealed to me.

Certain theologians—among them Thomas Aquinas, who was drawing upon the conclusions of Aristotle—might have told me that this sensation was *ensoulment*, the arrival of the soul. That word rings truer than any others, though it has the unfortunate baggage of having been used by some as justification for controlling women's bodies and choices around abortion.

Ensoulment or not, I'm more interested in the mystery of it rather than any certain definition. I'm interested in Linda Hogan's words. She continues: "I can only think there is another force at work, deeper than physics and what we know of wind, something that comes from a world where lightning and thunder, sun and rain clouds live."

In the same way that I do not understand the spark that moves a seed from dormancy into life, neither do I understand the moment that my daughter arrived home within me. I think of her arrival as a sort of blooming. At that moment, I bloomed too. She was at home in me, I with her, and we belonged to each other and to Andrew, and the three of us together to the world beyond. From the moment of that arrival until the moment she was born, I could feel my daughter's light in my belly. Shining in the dark of the womb.

The flutter of little wings.

14

UNRAVELING

In ancient Egypt, the sign of the owl was used to form the word *death* and the phrase *realm of death*. Owls, most of which are nocturnal, have long been believed to be emissaries to and from the afterlife. This is true of barn owls in particular, due to their ghostly appearance, occasional choice of graveyards and tombs as habitats, and their rasping shrieks—often described as a banshee call or a hissing scream. Celtic lore associates the barn owl with Cailleach, the goddess of death. In England, there is a superstition that a barn owl flying past the window of someone who has fallen ill is an omen of their imminent passing.

But there on the webcam sat the barn owls, in the nest box, begetting the next generation of life. One day, an egg appeared. Then another, another, another. Each time, a flurry of emails was sent around among our small cohort of The Land's barn owl fans, all of them with lots of exclamation points. "Another egg!!!"

The incubation lasted just over a month. And then, one by one, small, fuzzy bodies began to appear in place of eggs. (More flurries of emails, even more exclamation points.) The barn owl chicks looked even more haunting and otherworldly than their parents. The hearts that formed around their faces were sunken and skeletal and suggested costumes from a masquerade ball, as if they might pull their faces away to take a sip of punch. We loved them. And as the days went by and they continued to grow, we remained hopeful for their success.

Both parents brought them food: mice and voles. The owlets, I learned, would remain in the nest box for fifty to sixty days, after which they would begin to take their first flights. In the meantime, their bodies were preparing. The development of these barn owl chicks' auditory systems was largely postnatal. As the size and shape of their heads changed, and their external ears developed in those early weeks, so too did their brains' abilities to register those spatial binaural cues. As Susan Volman writes in "Directional Hearing in Owls": "While a barn owl is growing, its auditory system becomes calibrated to its head and ears." As they were preparing to fledge, they were attuning more and more fully to their own sensory worlds.

But the barn owl nest unraveled at almost the same pace at which it was created.

The four chicks were almost always huddled together in one gray-white mass of fluff with eight eyes. We admired them. One parent or the other was often in the nest with them, a rodent or two at their feet.

Then there were three chicks.

Then two.

They seemed to be vanishing without a trace.

✳ ✳ ✳

We reached out to a local owl expert, who suspected the nest was being predated by a barred owl that was able to perch on the nest box's balcony and snatch the owlets out, likely then feeding them to its own hatchlings somewhere nearby.

One morning, I came across a splay of adult barn owl feathers on the ground. Some of the ends were bloody. It seemed like far too many feathers for the owl to have so clearly lost this fight but survived. It was an owl undone. I rushed back inside to check the camera. The two remaining chicks were still in the nest. Perhaps there was still hope.

But several mornings later, the camera showed only the nest box's blank wall. No adult, no chicks. Just an unmoving image that could easily have been a photograph. I took my time going outside that morning, afraid of what I would find. I did the dishes. I swept the floors. I dithered. But I knew I had to go out.

And there, indeed, they were. Everything that remained of the two chicks was scattered in the grass. Their bodies had been taken. Their two heads were lying face up in the sun. Their eyes and beaks were closed. I could not see their extraordinary ears, nor did I move their feathers aside to look. It was surreal to see them. They were larger than I expected. The details of their fine feathers were articulated in the sunlight in a way they had never been on camera. I could make out the rough texture of their beaks, the fine lines that traced their faces—the beginning of their facial ruffs and the early formation of those integrated auditory systems that would have created their world.

In death, no part of them was eerie at all. Only soft and delicate and utterly of this living, breathing, vibrant world.

I stood over them, feeling betrayed. Realizing only then how much I had believed that all of us watching over them should have cast some sort of protective spell. As if our care had been some sort of guarantee.

I dug two small graves beneath a nearby tree.

When I picked them up, they were impossibly light, almost weightless. Like I could have simply released them to the air. But I laid them down in the soil and sang to them, though I don't remember what song. Maybe one of the lullabies I was then singing to Aspen. I put the ground back over them, and they folded effortlessly beneath the soil, as if the same ease of belonging they had held in life was now present with them in death as well.

I stood to cut flowers. The colors of the garden shone too brightly: like staring into the sun, too much life having encountered that final, soft form of death. I wrapped long blades of grass around the bundled stems of two small bouquets and placed them in the grass atop the owls. And I wept.

* * *

Barn owls are known for their ability to fly in total silence, their soft fringe-edged feathers muting the friction between owl and air.

How beautiful the life of the owl who can move through the world so softly.

How sudden a death for the vole struck in the silent dark.

How empty the nest as two bouquets wilt in the grass.

It is a common belief that when the soul of a human departs the body after death, it does so in the form of a bird.

What shape, I wonder, does the soul of a bird take?

* * *

I'm sometimes conflicted about my grief surrounding the death of the barn owls. Not so much the presence of it, but its subjectivity. What if I had instead given my attention to a family of meadow voles who were systematically hunted down in the night? Or to the nest of the barred owl and its own hungry brood of chicks, who also relied on their parents for food and protection?

Though threatened by decline, largely due to habitat loss, barn owl numbers remain stable in Washington state. They are not presently a species at risk of disappearing. And their deaths, too, are common. Across their wide, multi-continent range, less than half of barn owl chicks survive to fledge. The primary causes of nest failure are predation and starvation. From fledging, only 70 percent survive beyond their first year. Adult barn owls in the United States live an average of just four or five years in the wild.

The loss of these barn owl chicks was not uncommon, nor was it going to be any threat to the species as a whole.

But, then again, isn't this an odd way for me to be thinking? Must the stakes be high in order to justify our attention and care? Isn't care for a fellow creature, no matter how ordinary and abundant, enough?

* * *

Birds are believed to move between the realms of life and death. This, perhaps, is part of what made the hairs stand up on my neck when I saw the shadow of the first barn owl that morning. And part of my grief at the lost nest was the realization that belonging does not mean safety. A home does not guarantee any permanent sanctuary.

The pandemic has taken nearly seven million human lives worldwide as of this writing. It is a disease that is believed by most to have jumped from animal to human.

That same number defines this moment in another epidemic: a new strain of avian flu that has either directly caused the deaths of, or prompted the culling of, seven million farmed chickens and turkeys in the United States, and tens of millions of other wild and domesticated birds worldwide. Its effects have been magnified by warmer winters.

And more: A gunman in Maine, a few towns north of where we now live, kills eighteen people. At first, they do not find the shooter, and, as our state stumbles through the first waves of shock and grief, Andrew's school, and many other schools and businesses, are closed for the next two days out of an abundance of caution.

An "abundance of caution" is often my stance as a mother.

For where, without safety, is our ascendance? Where, in fear, is our rooting?

So many—humans and birds alike—are nesting, will continue to nest, at this boundary between vulnerability and safety.

* * *

We ultimately decided to leave the island in Puget Sound. We returned to New England to be back among our families and among the landscape that speaks to us in the language of belonging we know best. This is the language I want to give to Aspen. But it won't be entirely up to me. I'll lay out the first stones of her path. She and this place, with these trees, and this ocean, and these birds, will continue to lay out the rest.

15

HOOPOE, IV

The birds that join the hoopoe on the quest journey through fire. They grow ragged and thirsty. They want to quit. The hoopoe urges them onward, lesson by lesson, parable by parable. Slowly, the birds begin to come undone in the way of the mystic. What they thought they knew is turned on its head. The world ceases to make sense. Everything dis-coheres.

Of the hundreds of thousands that initially respond to the hoopoe's call, only thirty birds make it to the Simorgh's—the great king's—gate. And *Simorgh,* it turns out, is a play on words in Persian: *Si* means "thirty"; *morgh* means "birds."

All along, the birds were destined to meet themselves.

> *You came as thirty birds and therefore saw*
> *These selfsame thirty birds, not less not more;*
> *If you had come as forty, fifty—here*
> *An answering forty, fifty, would appear;*
> *Though you have struggled, wandered, travelled far,*
> *It is yourselves you see and what you are.*

And so, the birds arrive at the divine that has been at their center all along, the division between human and God dismantled, step by step, on the mystical journey. "A myth is something that has never happened, but is happening all the time," wrote Joseph Campbell.

Belonging is both rooted and attuned to what, and who, is beyond. We must keep open our circle of care. We can map our way through sensory worlds with attention to our feet and attention to others. Then we wind our way round and round the circular path, removing the veils where we can.

✳ ✳ ✳

I recently traced a new word, *inscendent,* through three favorite authors—Lucy Jones to Robert Mcfarlane to Thomas Berry (a very good thread to follow indeed)—and thereby stumbled across a word that myself and others had been looking and longing for. Not *trans*cendent—not rising above it all, removed, detached— but *in*scendent, going deeper and deeper into. An invitation into immersion.

My experience with the barn owl that morning in the meadow had been this. An opening into embodied awareness. A dissolution of the bounds of my individual body. A coming home to a truer nature, through relationship to another creature.

Motherhood, too, has been a form of inscendence. An Earthbound, bodily, sensory unfolding alongside another being. At times painful, uncertain, and terrifying—for such immersive relationships require no small degree of letting go and arriving into the unknown.

If the sensory body is the means of our physical inscendence— a way of moving deeper into relationship with the living world— then it can be paired with a spiritual inscendence, through the means of myth and story.

Inscendence is perhaps the defining word of an ecological mysticism: the journey back to oneself as an Earth creature, where self, ultimately, is a condition of relationship, not of individualism. Where belonging comes in response to a sensory experience of place, which grounds us as fellow beings and gives us a glimpse into the mystery beyond ourselves.

This is the path back to ourselves as beings who remember how to see that the sacred is everywhere around and everywhere in us. In the silent, curving flight of barn owls. In our mortal blood, made of oxygen and iron and proteins, the Earth herself running in our veins. In the children who grow in our bodies and then emerge, raw and beautiful in their utter, simple at-home-ness in the world. In their unveiled arrival.

※ ※ ※

A few weeks ago, cleaning some files off of my computer here in Maine, I found the owl cam app. I clicked it open. And there, all the way across the country, on an island in Puget Sound, was a barn owl in the nest box. Waiting for a mate to come, ready to try again. We attend to what roots us.

And then we practice, again and again, spreading our wings.

PART III

ENTANGLED
Tracking Whales

...then over and over slowly revolved like a waning world...
—Herman Melville, *Moby Dick*

16

BODIES IN ORBIT

The arched back of a right whale rises out of the ocean's surface, and the eternal rises through the brevity of a moment. Water cascades down either side of her and reenters the wide sea. Taking a moment to recover my balance as the small boat rocks atop the waves, I bring my binoculars to my eyes in time to see her slate skin part the curtain of winter's bright water, here off the coast of Georgia. I did not anticipate this difference between intellectually knowing such beings exist and the physical experience of encountering one in this mother whale. How fragile a form is abstraction. And how easily shattered.

What remains at the surface when she sinks below: her newly born calf and her sharp puffs of breath. Her lungs new and growing, the calf must breathe much more frequently than her mother, and so she rises and falls just ahead of and above her, ten or more breaths to her mother's one. The sound of the breath of the calf is like distant surf crashing against rocks. I put the back of my tongue to the roof of my mouth and make a sound like *kchsshhhhh*. The mother's breath is fuller, deeper. Though she is capable of diving for thirty to forty minutes at a time, she surfaces much more frequently with a child alongside her. Her breath, when released, carries the shape of a resonant chamber: wind turning a rounded corner in a dripping blue-black cave. I put my tongue in that same position but emit a louder, lower, slower whisper: *ckuuuuu*.

It is the beginning of January, and I am a guest on the *Borant*, a Georgia Department of Natural Resources boat that ventures out on the ocean every weather-permitting day between December and April looking for North Atlantic right whales. The soon-to-be mothers began arriving here in late November from their feeding grounds off the northeastern United States and southeastern Canada, traveling a route known through generations, to give birth to and nurse their calves in these warmer waters.

A North Atlantic right whale and her calf are rarely more than a body length away from each other when the calf is very young, so even when the whale sinks beneath the surface, the presence of the child reveals the approximate location of the mother. In this way, their movements in these early days of their lives together are a perpetual, revolving conversation: two bodies in motion like the moon orbiting the earth, held close by the tether of gravity. An invisible force is at work here, too, defining the interactions of two beings in space and time. The calf rests on her mother's back; she slows to keep her there. She angles her head to the ocean floor and lifts her fluke toward the surface; her daughter drops below to nurse. The calf rolls and arches and spins and always the mother is there alongside, keeping pace.

This tie will continue to exert its gentle force on both of them over the coming months. When the calf's lungs are strong enough, her swimming surer, and winter ebbing in the north, they will travel more than a thousand miles to their feeding grounds in Cape Cod Bay, the Gulf of Maine, the Gulf of St. Lawrence. She will continue to nurse for close to a year. Then, they will most likely part from each other. Though North Atlantic right whales are often seen together in groups, they do not seem to maintain long-term bonds.

But here in this moment, I am witness to their closeness, and I wonder if similar laws of connection are at work between the sand-camouflaged eggs and the plover, the helicoptering seed and the maple tree, my daughter and myself. Who are we as we exist in proximity to our mothers and then to our children? How do we measure the length and strength of those ties? How do we inhabit and move within the connective tissue of kinship?

Only later will I learn that, as I watch this whale and her calf from the boat, researchers are simultaneously tracking an older child of this mother as she swims south. She is four years old and alone. A thick piece of fishing rope is wrapped through her mouth and around her tail, trailing out beyond the length of her body. She is ailing. The length and strength of the tie that has bound itself to her, a product of fixed gear fishing, has likely prevented her from feeding properly. It is cutting into her skin and exerting a dragging force that is draining her energy. She is not likely to become a mother. She is not, in fact, expected to survive.

In these two siblings—one swimming within her mother's protective orbit, the other ensnared in human industry—two parallel and opposing definitions of entanglement emerge. There are lines of care and connection, and then there is fishing rope. There is the invisible, ineffable tether of kinship, and then there is the physics of a line dragging in water, the force that pulls against a whale's mouth.

More North Atlantic right whales are dying than are being birthed into the world. The population is undergoing what is called an "unusual mortality event," or UME. The passiveness of that phrase is unsettling; the acronym feels almost cruel. For these beings are dying at our hands, on our watch. It's an active sort of undoing.

Critically, the population is losing its females of reproductive age—whales that could go on to have another dozen or more calves in their long lives. It's believed that, given the chance, a female right whale could live the better part of a century and remain in reproductive health well into her old age. Because the rigorous scientific study of North Atlantic right whales only began around 1980, it is hard to know how long the natural life of a right whale is. Some of the whales that were cataloged forty years ago at unknown ages are still alive today. What is known: Ship strikes and entanglement are killing females at a disproportionate rate. There are fewer than seventy reproductive females left.

The right whales are losing their mothers.

As this species approaches functional extinction—meaning no reproductive females remaining in the population—as soon as within the next several decades, one must wonder not only about the ways that we inhabit connection but how we move within severance. How is it that we have closed ourselves off from our entanglement in so great a loss?

✳ ✳ ✳

Coastal Georgia is a waterlogged place. Two dozen feet from the sliding doors of my hotel room is one span of the state's 368,000 acres of coastal marshland. I came here after learning about the dwindling population of North Atlantic right whale mothers. I've been weeping for them for weeks now, triggered, in part, by the raw vulnerability of my own motherhood, and also by the growing anxiety and fear of what it means to mother my child in a world that, through blatant violence, is causing other mothers, other children, to vanish.

The first day of my visit begins with the thrum of unknown wings in the dark, the sun a slow-burning ember behind a silhouette of trees on the horizon. The sunrise is a miniature lesson in the relationship of sound and light: different calls come across the brushstrokes of smooth cordgrass, cued by the growing brightness. Great blue heron croaks. White ibis's wingtips buzz. Other songs and calls ebb and flow from species I can neither locate in the dawn nor identify by their voices.

When Clay George, senior wildlife biologist for the Georgia Department of Natural Resources, texts to tell me it's time to make my way to the DNR office building, I'm already in the car, looking for an open pharmacy where I can buy Dramamine. I've never been outright sick on a boat, but I can get queasy, so I follow Clay's advice from our phone call the night before to take precautions. We'll be out on the boat for six to eight hours, and conditions are predicted to be choppy.

The team I'm joining includes Clay, gregarious and philosophical, who, though it's a reductive comparison, has an enthusiastic commitment to his marine work that reminds me a bit of Richard Dreyfus in *Jaws*; Trip, who is quiet until he has something to say, has keen eyes for spotting whales, and eats a peanut butter and dried mango sandwich for lunch; and Ashley, whose primary work is studying nesting site fidelity in successive generations of female loggerhead tortoises, and who teases Trip relentlessly about his sandwich. She helps out with whale work in her offseason.

With mutual offerings of good luck exchanged between our small team and a man in a folding chair who is fishing on the dock ("Nothing's biting!" he says cheerfully), we motor out to sea from the mouth of the Sapelo River. On board, there is no shield from the sun, no bathroom, and just a couple of places to sit, though I'll learn that everyone stands the vast majority of the time—all the better for spotting whales. My companions are well-versed in the marvels surrounding the boat, but I gawk. We pass barrier islands with eroding beaches that have left behind boneyard forests—still standing but dead trees that look like they are walking naked into the rising tide. Bottlenose dolphins arc through the whitecaps, and solitary loons bob on the surface, though they will soon band together to form rafts after a communal molting of their feathers. Brown juvenile pelicans approach the boat hoping for a generous toss of a snack. "It's a tough time of year for them," Clay says.

Despite the blue sky and the midsixties temperature on land—downright balmy compared to January in Maine—I'm surprised by how cold I am on the water. Even with my insulated orange float jacket, bib pants, and two hats, I frequently alternate which frigid hand is balled in my coat pocket and which is holding on for dear life as we bounce over waves.

A four-person aerial survey team buzzes overhead every few minutes in a small spotting plane, flying transect lines. Every day of safe sea conditions, conservation teams like this one, from Georgia, Florida, and the Carolinas, are out, by boat and by plane, searching for right whales in these birthing waters. All births are meticulously tracked and documented. So far, eight whales have been born this season. Today, we are out looking for more. Each new life a step in the direction of salvation.

BLOODLINES, MILKLINES

We are hours on the water without seeing anything. Every few minutes, we travel three miles south to align with the spotting plane's next transect line, kill the engine, wait for the plane to pass overhead, and, if no call comes over the radio to tell us of a whale's location, we head to the next transect.

Clay has as many questions for me as I have for him, and we work our way to the subject of literature, discovering our mutual admiration for Tim O'Brien's *The Things They Carried*, a fictional account of O'Brien's time in the Vietnam War. When I read it during my first year in high school, it was the first time I understood that stories could be truer than facts—that some things are true not because they literally *happened* but because of how they are embodied. After that book, I started looking for such truths in everything I read, collecting them like seeds. They felt like little interior anchors. Later, as a religious studies student in college, I'd learn that such truths are the language of myth.

Trip points off the bow of the boat. "Did you see that?"

Clay nods. "A blow." My heart leaps. I squint in the direction everyone is staring in and see nothing but water, and water, and water. It's only after we've gotten close enough for Trip and Clay to confirm that it is, in fact, a right whale, that she has a calf with her, that I finally discern a distant shape in the water. I lift my binoculars to my eyes.

Her rostrum is angled out of the sea, like a rounded isosceles triangle. The water around her is white and frothy. Even seeing her from this distance, I no longer wonder where tales of sea monsters came from. She is otherworldly. As we get closer and she comes further into focus, I find myself wanting to say that she is beautiful, but she is not this. She is, rather, a being for whom human aesthetics are purposeless. Nonetheless, my mind keeps tugging for the familiar, something known to compare her with. The image that comes is not of another animal but of an island of volcanic rock that has been lifted out of the sea. Her head is not smooth but craggy. Callus-like patches of white skin run up the top of her nose, back toward her blowholes, and give the appearance of a snowy mountainscape in miniature. Her lips curl up to nearly the top of her rostrum. Had I not previously looked at photographs, I would have thought this was where her eyes are, but they are at least six feet below the surface, just below the curve of her deep mouth, in which are enclosed several hundred plates of baleen, some nine feet long.

Waves are breaking over the shallow island of her back. I can't see her full form, but she could be as much as fifty feet long, two and a half times the length of our boat. Her head makes up a full quarter of that length. Underwater, her tail is a wide triangle, notched in the middle. Two paddle-like pectoral fins extend from her lower body, ahead of her belly. (Right whales do not have dorsal fins.) The mouth of a right whale is a pronounced archway, often described as a frown. Hers will likely remain closed while here in Georgia, until she and the calf reach their summer feeding grounds far to the north.

North Atlantic right whales are identified by those craggy patches on their heads, called "callosities." These are patterns of roughened skin that are colonized by cyamids, a species of whale lice, that make these patches appear off-white. Callosity patterns are akin to fingerprints, unique to each individual whale, and make it possible to accurately identify individuals visually.

No one has figured out a method for tagging right whales for extended periods, so scientists rely on photographic or visual resightings of whales to track their movements and survival through space and time. Photo-identification data on North Atlantic right whales has been compiled and continuously updated since the early 1980s. Information on every known whale, alive and deceased—nearly eight hundred individuals—is housed within the North Atlantic Right Whale Catalog, which includes over two million photographs. Within the catalog, each whale is assigned a four-digit number; some have also been given names. A few weeks ago, I spoke with Philip Hamilton, senior scientist at the Anderson Cabot Center for Ocean Life, who is, for all intents and purposes, responsible for the existence and upkeep of this extensive catalog. Critical work. Every plane and boat that is out looking for right whales, every team that conducts right whale necropsies on the beach, carries a partial hard copy of this catalog so that, every time a whale is encountered, they can compare its callosity patterns with the catalog and quickly know who it is. With a population as small as this one, every bit of information—a whale's location, calving history, appearance, behavior—is meticulously recorded.

The catalog has also given scientists a unique means of coming to know and consistently recognize individual whales. "It's intimate to know every individual of a species," Philip told me. "It's this amazing pairing of science and . . ." He pauses. "I don't know what the other word is. But it's not just numbers. It's individuals. Every single one of them has a compelling story." From the way he speaks about the whales, I think the other word he's looking for is *care*.

Clay and Trip launch a drone to get photographs and video of the whale and calf from above, bring the drone back, review the footage, compare it to the catalog, and identify her as Maple. Her callosity pattern is described as "broken"—that is, not in a continuous line—with a pair of symmetrical islands that appear as two bumpy white lines, one occurring on either side of her head. Her other identifying information in the catalog is listed in the form of injuries, scars from fishing gear entanglements and ship strikes: "Memorable mark on back/side/flank; Memorable mark on upper jaw only; Scar in chin between the left and right chin callosities; Significant dorsal or ventral peduncle scar; . . ." The list goes on.

Maple was born in 1987, making her the same age as me. The calf with her is the fourth known to her, and this child is spinning in the sun, waving her fins.

There is a moment when the sound of the mother's breath comes into focus. *Crystallizes* is the word that comes to mind, and it does seem that a shape materializes in the instant that her exhale travels over the water and finds my ears. Not speech but a distinct expression of being. Her breath bridges a distance between us that her body will not. It is only the sound of her that I can directly encounter. This is as it should be. It is illegal to approach a North Atlantic right whale within five hundred yards. And though the *Borant* has a scientific research permit that would allow us to get close, we ought not to unless absolutely necessary, Clay says.

Her calf swims next to her, breathing, breathing, this very same air, and the longing that arises in my mind while watching this child is not to take a photograph but to kneel in prayer.

❊ ❊ ❊

The mother in me can't help but recognize the mother in Maple. Here is a mother resting from childbirth, directing her blubber reserves to her nursing calf. I see how she stays within one body length of her calf, and I think of my daughter hugging my thigh. The whale nurses her child, and I think of how I will later pump milk in my hotel room to keep the supply flowing for when I again hold my daughter to my breast. Bloodlines, milklines: these tether us to our kin. Me to my daughter, this right whale to hers. This has been true for tens of millions of years and beyond for all of us mammals.

Why am I looking for these similarities between me and this whale? I can feel myself reaching. Just as with my untrained eyes on the ocean, I am scanning for something and losing sight, perhaps, of what is real. But I keep searching for connections, for similarities, for echoes of form, because I want to find the node that the North Atlantic right whale inhabits in the web of life. I want to pinpoint the central knot in the pattern and then trace everything that will unravel if this species is cut out.

In one Muslim conception of the universe, the Earth rests on a gigantic rock, which, in turn, sits on the back of a bull, which is atop a gigantic whale. What happens if we take away the whale?

I've been cautioned time and again against anthropomorphizing. Yes, of course, I do not and cannot know the sensory world of this whale. She and I diverged from our common ancestor tens of millions of years ago. There is an interior and exterior distance between us that cannot be overcome. (Though what fun to imagine her sensory world!) But the fear of distortion and projection that can come from ascribing human characteristics to nonhuman beings can serve to make us *too* wary. It can keep us from a fuller experience of empathy. And empathy is one of those anchors of embodied truth, more easily accessed through story and myth than through fact. We live in a time where the facts do so little to turn the tide, to move us into deeper relationship.

But I still wonder if I'm ascribing a human experience of motherhood to this whale in a way that is clouding my thinking. Then again, it is not so much that I am projecting my humanity or motherhood onto *her*; rather, encountering her is helping me to recognize *myself* as an animal. Motherhood has the effect, as Kerri ní Dochartaigh so beautifully writes, of helping us locate our mammalhood. And, indeed, it seems far easier to reach across the species divide as a fellow animal with a child close in my orbit than it does as an individual human being.

Motherhood, thus, is presently one way that I find myself having the energy to attempt to make that reach, from my animal- ness to another's. But motherhood is not the only way. I think of Linda Hogan and the timber wolves. Of sacrifices to the Egyptian deity Thoth, with his human body and bird head. Such reaching will always be limited. I will never know the truth of this mother right whale's experience. Like the Sufis say, we can point to the moon, we can even wade into its reflection in the water, but we can never touch it. There is still worth in the seeking. There are truths to be met in the work of building bridges.

18

SCRIMSHAW

From the 1700s through the mid-1800s, much of the Western world was lit by whale oil.

In the eleventh century, Basque fishermen began hunting North Atlantic right whales in the Bay of Biscay. They developed a practice of launching a boat, killing a whale, hauling the floating corpse back to shore, and processing it for oil that, within a few centuries, would come to be worth more than its weight in gold. In calving season, then and now, right whale mothers and calves hug the coast and are slow-moving, easy targets. It was the success of the Basque hunting of right whales that turned whaling into a commercial industry and gripped the West in a frenzy of slaughter for centuries.

Half a millennium later, in 1690, the town selectmen of Nantucket climbed a hill and, like the Basques centuries prior, they saw right whales (who earned their name by being the "right" whale to hunt) breaching, blowing, and splashing in the offshore waters. According to local lore, it was with those whales in view that one of the selectmen declared the ocean as "a green pasture where our children's grandchildren will go for bread."

Since the arrival of settlers several decades prior, the actual green pastures of Nantucket had become increasingly barren. Persistent attempts at farming and grazing livestock had surpassed the ecological limits of this glacially formed island thirty miles out to sea.

Many of the 2,500 members of the Wampanoag nation who inhabited the island—an Indigenous population of skilled seafarers who had subsisted on the island's sandy soils sustainably for thousands of years—would, over the next few decades, become indentured servants in service to the whaling industry. Their population was simultaneously decimated by epidemics.

Nantucketers embraced whaling with the obsession of a people running out of options. They started out similarly to the Basques, spotting right whales from shore and sending out boats to kill them, then hauling them to shore for processing. As demand for whale oil grew, the process of acquiring it became more efficient. Attention largely shifted from right whales to sperm whales in the early 1700s. The sperm whale had superior oil in greater quantity and swam in pods in deep ocean waters around the globe. By the mid-1700s, the local population of right and sperm whales around Nantucket had nearly been extirpated. The industry kept pace as the years rolled on. Whaling sloops, outfitted with twenty-one-person crews and brick tryworks that enabled processing whales at sea, ventured further and further afield, gone for as many as three years at a time.

Upon sighting a whale on the high seas, six-man crews set out in whaleboats. The whale was harpooned, at which point it would often flee, dragging the boat in a "Nantucket sleigh ride" until it tired itself out. The boat would then pull alongside the whale and the boatsteerer would plunge a twelve-foot lance into it, targeting a coil of arteries near the lungs. When struck, the whale would die, choking on its own blood and vomit. A whaling voyage would bring home as much as forty to fifty whales' worth of oil.

The lucrative nature of the work outweighed the known dangers. Whalemen were drowned, killed in accidents, succumbed to disease. By 1810, historian Nathaniel Philbrick writes, "there were 472 fatherless children on Nantucket." In 1846, a fire raged through the waterfront, fueled by whale oil, and consumed four hundred buildings, spiraling Nantucket into economic depression and contributing to the permanent decline of the whaling industry on the island.

The International Whaling Commission did not ban commercial whaling until 1986. Over the course of one thousand years, the commercial whaling industry is estimated to have depleted the world's populations of whales by as much as 90 percent.

For close to two hundred of the West's whaling years, Nantucket had dominated this industry.

My brother and I moved from Oklahoma to Nantucket with our father when I was eleven years old. Because of my then-stepfather, my mother's home had become unsafe for me and my brother. And so the legal and emotional rift that already existed within our family suddenly became geographical as well. Our flat, hot, suburban neighborhood in Oklahoma gave way to fog and gray shingled houses and pitch pine forests.

I understood, and in many ways welcomed, the move. Yet in each quiet moment of that year, I felt every one of the 1,774 miles of distance between my mother and me. Our former home was least of all safe for her, and I felt we had abandoned her. I developed a near-obsessive practice of praying for her safety.

It was 1998, more than six decades since the last North Atlantic right whale had been intentionally hunted and killed, in 1935—that whale had been a calf, shot and harpooned by sport fishermen. Its mother stayed by the calf's side for more than six hours, despite more than a hundred of her own bullet wounds, until her child was dead and its body lashed to the side of the men's boat. Only then did she swim away. Later that year, the League of Nations granted right whales international protection. The mother would live for another sixty years, when she would be struck and killed by a boat.

My sixth-grade class in the island's middle school had a long unit on the history of whaling. I don't remember much of what I learned, but I can still feel the pride that lifted my preteen shoulders when I learned how this new island home of mine had a long history of high seas adventure and once supplied the Western world with its lamplight.

Years later, in a pile of old homework assignments and dusty trinkets, I found the piece of scrimshaw I had carved that year. Men aboard whale ships practiced this form of folk art, in which intricate scenes are carved into the teeth of sperm whales and the ivory of walrus tusks. When our class took a field trip to see some of these artifacts at the local whaling museum, I was surprised at how beautiful and delicate the engravings were. The fine lines depicted whaling ships, or valiant battles at sea between man and beast, or ornate portraits of beautiful women, many of whom would die widows. I liked the images of the women best. And I liked the idea that, because photography was not yet invented, if whalers wanted an image of a loved one, they had to painstakingly transfer that image from their memory onto a tooth wrenched from the very thing that had necessitated their distance.

I do not remember thinking much about the whales then. I did not know, for example, that sperm whales practice a communal form of childcare. Calves do not have strong enough lungs to dive, long and deep, with their mothers. So when one mother dives below, other females will stay at the surface and protect her calf until she resurfaces.

Into my own piece of bone—in truth, a piece of PVC pipe which had been roughly sawed into the shape of a large tooth—I remember simply wanting to make something beautiful to show to my mom. My whale tooth was adorned with a series of unpracticed wiggly lines, so clearly the work of an eager child's hand, coming together to outline a bouquet of flowers.

FLUKEPRINT

Flukeprint: a mark on the ocean's surface that a whale leaves behind with its tail. These patterns appear as buttery-smooth ovals of water, while the surrounding ocean remains choppy and variable. A print can linger for several minutes. The hydrodynamics are such that when a whale is swimming at the surface or descends for a dive, its fluke generates a "vortex ring" that creates a breakwater that dampens the waves inside the print. If you don't know what you're seeing, you might think you've encountered a portal into an underwater world.

Flukeprint: Captains of whaleships used various stamps in their logbooks as a code or shorthand to track progress. The stamp of a whale's fluke meant a whale was sighted. The stamp of the entire body of a whale meant a whale was slaughtered. Whaling logbooks are littered with prints of flukes and prints of whole whale bodies. It's a haunted sort of transference: a whale vanishes from the ocean and reappears as ink on a page. As oil in a barrel.

Flukeprint: the marks on the surface of the ocean that a mother right whale in Georgia is making, forming a noticeable pattern, a path like footprints in the sand, because she is swimming near the surface, alongside her calf. In addition to distant splashes and blows, flukeprints are what Clay and Trip are scanning for over the bright surface of the water as the *Borant* motors miles out to sea and onward.

20

DREAM

Before my trip to Georgia, I dream of standing in chest-high water, far from land, in the open sea. In the dream, I sense a right whale near me and then sense the direction I must move in to meet her. Though I'm moving toward the distant shore, the water grows deeper, not shallower. I wait. A whale finally approaches—a calf. She does so slowly and gently. I know that she is coming over to nurse, and so I present my breast to her. Somehow, I know, too, that breastfeeding this whale might make me pregnant, though with a human or with a whale I'm not sure. The calf nurses for a long moment and swims away.

URBAN WHALE

Right whales have been nicknamed the "urban whale" because their habitat—the coastal shelf-waters of eastern North America, extending from Florida and Georgia through the Bay of Fundy and the Gulf of St. Lawrence—brings them into direct contact with concentrated territories of human fishing and shipping industries.

Bear with me here. This is a painful learning, but it is important to understand the means and the extent of our entanglement with this species and its loss of its mothers.

Let's begin with fishing. The fixed-gear fishing industries in the United States and Canada rely on traps or nets set on or near the seafloor to collect their catch. The two most consequential of these industries as they pertain to right whales are snow crabs in Canada and lobster in New England—primarily in Maine. Fixed-gear traps are "fixed" because they are left on the seafloor for extended periods of time and connected to buoys on the surface via vertical ropes. That way fishers can later locate their gear, pull up the trap, and retrieve the crustaceans that have crawled inside. It's estimated that on their migratory routes between the southeastern United States and Canada, right whales must swim through a maze of one million such vertical fishing ropes. Entanglement in fishing gear is a chronic problem for baleen whales—a category that includes, among others, right whales, blue whales, humpback whales, and fin whales—and is a primary cause of death for large whales.

Right whales feed by swimming continuously with their mouths open, a feat of energy worth the expense when it's feeding season and food is plentiful. They have around 250 baleen plates on either side of their upper jaw, made of keratin and some more than nine feet long. Water flows through their mouths as a type of zooplankton called "copepods" are filtered through the bristle of their baleen plates. The water is not so much sieved as pulled: in cooperation with the deftness of her tongue, which weighs up to three thousand pounds, the whale pulls the water out of her mouth through what David W. Laist calls an "elegant dewatering mechanism."

When a right whale swims into a rope, she panics and spins, often wrapping herself further. Rope is frequently found wrapped through a right whale's baleen. It is a cruel fate. If an entangled whale does not free herself, or is not freed by a dispatched disentanglement team, two possibilities grow increasingly likely the longer she is entangled: that she will die from drowning; or that her death might be dragged out for months due to stress, increased energy demands, and slow starvation from the inability to feed or from infection. As veterinarian Michael Moore painfully recounts, during a necropsy he performed for one right whale, a fishing line that was wrapped over the whale's back was found to have embedded itself in the animal's back muscles. When the whale was pulled to shore, part of the left shoulder blade fell from the body, having been severed by the rope, while the bone in the whale's right shoulder had managed to grow around the line, like a tree around a fence.

Nine decades since hunting North Atlantic right whales was made illegal, an estimated 85 percent of these animals have been entangled at least once in their lives. "What is worse for a whale— an explosive harpoon or entanglement?" writes Moore, who has performed dozens of North Atlantic right whale necropsies, in his book *We Are All Whalers*. "One of the biggest surprises of my life is that the answer to this question is neither obvious nor clear-cut."

Then there are the vessel strikes, which account for a little over 40 percent of North Atlantic right whale deaths. Mothers and calves are especially susceptible to being hit by ships. Their coastal distribution exposes them to areas of high-density traffic, and mother-calf pairs remain close to the surface and move slowly in their first year together. In general, right whales do not tend to avoid vessels, and vessels, especially as they grow larger and larger, often do not see the whales, especially as the density of ships grows ever higher. In terms of tonnage, an estimated 90 percent of the world's traded goods are carried over the oceans. By 2050, maritime trade volumes are expected to increase threefold. As demand rises and ships grow larger in size and quantity—including what are literally called "ultra large container vessels" that measure up to four hundred meters in length and span as much as sixty meters in width—shipping lanes expand, encroaching further and further upon others' habitats. And it does not take a ship anywhere near this large for an encounter with a whale to be fatal.

Measures for reducing ship strikes in whale populations have included education campaigns, providing the real-time location of whales to all ships in an area, establishing speed restrictions, and modifying shipping routes. The International Maritime Organization has implemented some such mitigation measures and guidelines. There are also federal measures in place, such as the 2008 "ship strike rule" in the United States, which set speed restrictions within defined marine mammal management areas. In an effort to reduce collisions of right whales and ships, the rule requires all commercial vessels longer than sixty-five feet to travel ten knots or less in ten seasonal management areas. Such speed restrictions, when complied with, are at least partially effective. But collisions have not ceased. Enforcement is limited, and success is contingent on widespread compliance.

Success is also contingent on whales showing up in the same place and at the same time of year, such that existing regulations coincide with the location of significant portions of the right whale population. But in 2017, the whales showed up somewhere unexpected.

Which leads us to the impacts of climate change. As more CO_2 enters the oceans and the atmosphere, the ocean is changing. The Gulf of Maine, one of the whale's traditional feeding grounds, is warming as fast as, or faster than, any other area of ocean on the planet. Sometime around 2010, the distribution of abundant concentrations of copepods crept north, from the Gulf of Maine to the Gulf of St. Lawrence in Canada.

It takes time for copepods to aggregate in a new place, and it then takes time for right whales to locate and learn where their food has gone. This gap in time between copepod scarcity in a known place and its abundance in a yet-to-be-known place carries a direct correlation to the number of right whale calves being born. Females who are recovering from childbirth and nursing, with their depleted reserves of blubber, need time to replenish the energy reserves that would enable them to become pregnant again. These females are thus especially susceptible to being impacted by a limited availability of prey.

With copepods no longer in high enough numbers to facilitate this replenishing in the Gulf of Maine, 2010 saw the beginning of a significant decline in the calving rate. But that, in itself, would not have posed a significant threat to the species.

I spoke with Scott Kraus—a marine conservation biologist who has worked with right whales for decades and was the one who coined their nickname: the "urban whale"—about whether this species would still have a strong chance of recovery if we could curb direct human-caused mortality, given the severity of climate crisis. Absolutely, he told me. Right whales are long-lived, and females can give birth well into their old age. Even if it took the right whale population a decade to locate a new source of food, their blubber reserves (even those of new mothers) would likely see them through those lean times. Yes, the calving rate would slow for that time, but it would rebound when the whales rediscovered where the copepods had gone. Additionally, the zooplankton they eat is the most abundant species of plankton on Earth and has previously endured and survived extreme climate scenarios.

Climate change alone, therefore, is not believed to pose an extinction threat to these animals. Their ability to be patient, Scott tells me, "gives them a resilience to environmental changes, to ecological changes, even to ecological catastrophe. They can wait it out. They will do fine." But not if human impacts continue.

In 2015, five years after the copepods had migrated out of the Gulf of Maine, the right whales showed up in the Gulf of St. Lawrence, having found where their food had gone. But there were no fishing or shipping restrictions in place in the Gulf of St. Lawrence, because no one expected the whales to be there. The toll was steep: seventeen right whales were killed by human activity in 2017—twelve in the Gulf of St. Lawrence and five in the United States. There were ten more deaths in 2019. Between 2011 and 2020, there were 51 known deaths (though, given that an average of two-thirds of mortalities are undetected, it is more likely that there were closer to 150 deaths) and 113 known births.

Between 2012 and 2020, an average of only ten calves were born per year, a decline attributed to less food availability and to human-caused injury and mortality. At the same time, calving intervals for reproductive mothers have gone from three years to close to ten years between births.

Calving must outpace mortality to stop the decline of the species and permit recovery. Thus began the unusual mortality event for North Atlantic right whales. And with it, predictions that the species could be functionally extinct within three decades.

In researching population recovery for marine mammals, scientists use a calculation called "potential biological removal": the number of individuals that can be taken from the population, due to human impact, for the species to sustain or recover its population. The PBR for North Atlantic right whales is currently < 1. *Less than one.* In other words, a single human-caused mortality per year is enough to threaten the recovery of the entire population.

✳ ✳ ✳

The day before I arrived in Georgia, a right whale calf, believed to be just days old, was sighted swimming alone near a pier in Beaufort, North Carolina. No one was able to find the mother. The calf died the morning of my second day on the water, January 7. At this age, they cannot survive without their mothers.

✳ ✳ ✳

There are people, including Clay, Trip, and Philip, who have been trained to disentangle whales. It is dangerous work. A member of a Canadian disentanglement team, Joe Howlett, who had dedicated his life to cutting whales free from rope, died in the process of freeing right whale number 4123 from thick fishing rope and a heavy metal crab trap. It was that disastrous summer of 2017, when so many whales were dying. Joe had only just successfully freed the animal when the 150,000-pound whale dove and thrashed his tail, striking him in the head.

Ironically, entanglement responders have had to use methods informed by whaling techniques: coming alongside a whale in a small boat, grappling onto the fishing line that is wrapped around the whale in order to add drag so that the whale will tire and slow down. Much of the work of cutting the rope must be done around the whale's head and face as fishing gear is often trailing from a whale's mouth, wrapped through baleen or digging into the whale's rostrum. Often, the best that a disentanglement team can hope for is to simply cut the rope shorter to decrease the drag on the whale, giving him a better chance of surviving long enough to eventually free himself.

Disentanglement, in other words, is not a sustainable approach. The whales have to stop becoming entangled in the first place.

In October 2022, the National Marine Fisheries Service (NMFS)—a bureau of the National Oceanic and Atmospheric Administration (NOAA) that is responsible for upholding and implementing federal environmental laws intended to protect whales and marine mammals—met with Maine fishers to update them on the need for further restrictions to the lobster fishery and to hear their ideas and feedback. Right whales are well-documented feeding in and migrating through the coastal waters of the northeastern United States, where there are an estimated 920,500 vertical fishing lines, 912,300 of which are from the lobster industry.

It was an angry, distrustful audience. The common refrain was that no right whales are known to have been entangled in Maine lobster gear since 2004, and none have been known to die as a result of entanglement in Maine gear, and so further restrictions on the fishery are unreasonable.

Maine's governor, one US senator, and two congressional representatives were present at the meeting and quickly placed themselves on the side of the lobster industry, which is the second largest fishing industry in the United States, economically speaking, valued at more than $725 million dollars. Maine lobster draws thousands of tourists to the state every summer and contributes an estimated $1.5 billion a year to the state's economy.

During the more than three hours of public comment, anyone who suggested modifications or any further regulations to the industry was loudly booed. No one in the audience spoke for the whales.

Several months after that meeting, Senator Susan Collins, along with a congressional delegation from Maine, inserted a provision into a $1.7 billion spending bill that put a six-year delay on new fishing regulations intended to protect North Atlantic right whales. One environmental attorney said, "this rider will doom the right whale to extinction."

And then, in late January 2024, a young female right whale, number 5120, washed ashore on Martha's Vineyard entangled in what was confirmed to be Maine gear. Born in 2021, she had been entangled for seventeen months of her short life. By the time of her death, she had grown increasingly thin, and the rope had come to be tightly wrapped around her tail.

Back during that long and painful meeting, one lobsterman spoke what felt to me like the deeper truth that was simmering in the audience. "I am angry and hurt," he said, his voice wavering. And anger and hurt are understandable responses. As Michael Moore writes, "Fishermen have been burdened and fatigued by years of whale conservation–driven mandatory gear modifications, while the problem of whale trauma has continued to get worse." Many of these fishers came to this work through generations spent on the water, hauling traps. They have worked in other ways to successfully make the industry more ecologically sustainable. None of them set out to entangle whales. Most of them say they have never even *seen* a right whale. So why, they want to know, is their way of life being threatened?

Because, the science says, repeatedly and with ample evidence, the rope needs to come out of the water. Ropeless gear is being developed. There are whale-safe ways forward for the industry. The price of a species is far too high a price to pay to opt not to do the hard work of change.

And still . . . it is easy to look at the lobstermen and demand they make sacrifices in order to save these whales. Though, to be clear, I do. But the harder part is pointing that finger back at myself. The harder work is not allowing myself to simply blame the lobstermen, and the ships, and the politicians, and then stop there. It is finding all those places within my own life that are entangled with harming the world, and the whales. It is locating my own fear of change and sacrifice. All the ways I am entangled in those lines of extraction. And it is finding the courage, again and again, to cut myself free.

DEVOUR

In one Jewish legend, a young man goes daily to the shore in order to feed a fish. Over time, the fish grows huge, begins to create chaos among the other creatures of the sea, and eventually eats the man himself, then spits him back out. From then on, the man understands the language of birds.

In another myth, Jonah (in Hebrew, Yōnah; in Arabic, Yūnus—both meaning "dove"), is commanded by God to bring a prophecy to the city of Nineveh, foretelling God's impending wrath. Jonah attempts to flee this mission. He boards a ship, is thrown overboard in a storm, and is swallowed by a "large fish." He spends three days and three nights in the belly of the whale before he repents and is delivered, spewed out on land.

In North America, the Unaliq people of the Bering Strait have ancient stories of Raven entering the belly of the whale. Inside, he sees a lamp that he is warned not to touch. But he does touch it, and the whale dies. Similar stories are told by the Inupiaq and the Nunivak.

In Celtic lore, an ocean beast called Oilliphéist, thought to be a dragon, once swallowed a piper named Ó Ruair. Ó Ruair, drunk, kept playing his music nonetheless, until the beast spat him back out in irritation.

In the Kathāsaritsāgaraḥ, written in eleventh-century India, a man named Saktideva falls into the sea after his boat encounters a storm, where he is swallowed by a great fish. When the fish later passes by an island, it is captured, and the king orders it cut open. Saktideva emerges in good health, "having endured a second wonderful imprisonment in the womb."

As anthropologist Jean-Loïc Le Quellec writes, there are many of these myths—dozens and dozens of them—from around the world. The devoured hero often emerges from the belly of the whale by cutting his way out or by being cut out by someone on the outside. He is usually unharmed, though often he has undergone another sort of transformation: emerging with no hair or with his skin turned white like a ghost. The cutting almost always kills the whale.

Le Quellec goes on to explore how these myths were later analyzed. In the late nineteenth century, the anthropologist Edward Burnett Tylor came up with a theory to account for such similarities in whale myths across cultures, for they presumably arose independently of each other across great spans of time and distance. He attributed their likenesses to the "evident regularity of mental law," suggesting that even geographically far-flung human beings will create the same stories due to some universal mechanism within the human imagination.

Others theorized that these mythical whale monsters were examples of the mother archetype, specifically "the devouring mother." Similarly to Tylor, Jung concluded that there is a common mythical function in the human brain, such that the "the regressing libido continues back to the intra-uterine, pre-natal condition, and leaving the sphere of the personal psychology altogether, irrupts into the collective psyche where Jonah saw the 'mysteries' in the whale's belly." A Freudian analysis similarly suggested that Jonah had fled the father (God) by reentering the womb of the mother (whale).

I don't know enough to accept or reject any of these analyses, though I don't feel particularly interested in any of them, especially the psychoanalytical. Especially since another universal human truth that spans time and distance is that no pregnant woman has ever enjoyed men making the unimaginative comparison between them and excessively large mammals. But in all seriousness, my interest flags because I don't particularly care about the *why* of these similarities—whether these parallel myths are a universal function of the human psyche or stories passed from one group to another through ancient migrations.

What I find much more interesting and disturbing is what it means to be swallowed whole, and what it means to devour.

*   *   *

Psalm 69 found me in a stone church in Norwich, Vermont, at sunset. The service that evening was a liturgy of Tenebrae. Traditionally held during Holy Week in early spring, this is an ancient ceremony to prepare participants for recounting the suffering and death of Christ on Easter. *Tenebrae* is Latin for darkness, obscurity, shadows.

This was summer, not spring, and the service this evening was not about the crucifixion of Christ but about species extinction and the crucifixion of the Earth.

The lights were out. Candles burned on an altar. A choir in the back of the church chanted a Litany of the Extinct—species either declared to be or believed likely to be extinct—in polyphonal Renaissance a cappella, interspersed with psalms of lament.

The service began with the antiphon of Psalm 69: *Zeal for your house has eaten me up.* Something in those words pinned me to my pew. It was, in part, that particular English translation from the Hebrew: *eaten me up.* Other versions I have read use "consumed me." But it was especially visceral to think of the psalmist being gobbled.

I sat there in the candlelight, longing to be devoured, too. Jewish by birthright but having not yet found a spiritual home in any particular faith tradition, some part of me had always been kneeling in prayer, hands folded, head bowed, waiting for some revelation from God.

Zeal for your house has eaten me up. I sat there and longed for the light of the divine to consume me. I wasn't yet paying attention to why we had all come.

The sun sank and darkness fell. After the reading of each psalm, a candle was extinguished. And the names of the dead were chanted from the choir in the back of the room. *Dutch Alcon Blue Butterfly, Golden Toad, Ascension Night Heron.* Not dead. Vanished. Disappeared. The *words* of them were all that remained. Fleeting embodiments, like a last escape of breath, their articulations haunted the air. A harpooned whale stamped in a logbook. The room seemed at once to expand and contract in this unceasing flow of species that had been turned into harmonized syllables.

The small congregation was instructed to say, together: "Save me, O God, for the waters have risen up to my neck."

Then we said: "Deliver me, my God, from the hand of the wicked."

Then the names continued. I could almost make out the shapes of each of these creatures curling gray and transparent in the candlelight. A fan of wings. A swishing tail. The sloping curve of a back. What was it for an entire species to turn to smoke? I found that I could not move my body. I wondered if I was breathing. *Upland Moa, West African Black Rhino, Tahiti Sandpiper.* I longed now only for the chanting to stop. I did not want this weight.

But there were so many, many more names to say. *Zanzibar Leopard, Madeiran Large White Butterfly, Tecopa Pupfish.* Creatures obscured. *To obscure:* to veil, to conceal. The truth of them now forever hidden, exiled to the realm of shadow.

Pyrenean Ibex, Round Island Burrowing Boa, Black-faced Honeycreeper, Passenger Pigeon, Javan Tiger, Formosan Clouded Leopard, Cape Verde Giant Skink, Sri Lanka Spiny Eel, Northern Darwin's Frog,

Zestos Skipper Butterfly. They blurred together and their forms dispersed, and after the last name was sung, they hung in the air and then together descended with a slow finality, a rain of ash too light to feel but coating every exposed surface, a burial shroud that billowed and came down to rest upon all of us who were now held fast within the throat of an unbearable silence.

It was only when the candles were all extinguished, night descended, and my personal longing for God retreated that I realized we were here in this church because it was us—we with our faces now hung in slanting curtains of shadow—who, in all our zeal, were eating up the world.

WHALE CHASE

On my second day in Georgia, when we've almost cleared the surrounding salt marshes on the *Borant* and have emerged again into open water, the aerial team radios in the coordinates of a mother-calf pair spotted twenty kilometers off the coast. We head to the location. No whales are in view, and for the next hour, we alternate between slow forward movement through the water and cutting the engine, everyone taking a cardinal direction to look in as long, silent minutes roll by on the waves. I'm having trouble simply discerning fact from fiction as I stare out at the brutally bright water. I keep seeing a streak of deep blue where the ocean meets sky, thinking it's a spit of land, but it's only my eyes losing track of color. Even shutting my eyes for long moments hardly offers relief: the glare of the sun remains a fiery streak across the black canvas of my eyelids. The rocking of the boat makes it nearly impossible for me to hold my binoculars steady against my eyes. I will not be the one to spot these whales.

Finally, nearly five kilometers from the original coordinates, Trip finds the pair. The drone is sent out again. This, we learn, is Spindle, number 1204. She is at least forty-one years old, and this is her tenth known calf, the most children any living right whale is known to have brought into the world. Her callosity pattern is continuous—unbroken—with four symmetrical peninsulas. She has a propellor scar on her flank, a scar around her blowholes, a scar on her tail, and is missing the tip of one of her flukes.

A small pod of bottlenose dolphins has joined the mother-calf pair in what very clearly seems to be a playful intention.

In a long-term effort to better understand right whale genetics and to keep track of the past, current, and possible future populations, scientists biopsy every new calf of the season. In addition to callosity recognition, genetic data provide invaluable information about the age, sex, and reproductive status of an individual right whale. Additionally, a calf will not have permanent, and therefore consistently recognizable, callosities until he is around a year old, and by then he will no longer be traveling with his recognizable mother. Genetic samples also help researchers to keep track of the survival rate of right whales from calf to juvenile to adult.

If the *Borant* manages to retrieve a sample today, it will be processed into four parts. The blubber will be frozen and stored. Two samples will go into a fixative for preserving DNA and be sent to Saint Mary's University, where there is a lab for right whale genetics work. The final part will be stored as an archive.

The process of obtaining such a sample from a right whale calf is at once delicate and brash, requiring both a special permit and a special crossbow. The *Borant* has both. Today we will get close to the whales, close enough for Clay to get an accurate shot. The arrow he'll fire is hollow, with a stiff piece of orange foam attached an inch back from the tip. The foam keeps the arrow from going too far into the calf, ensures that it will rebound off, and makes the arrow and its genetic sample retrievable, as it will float in the water. If he shoots accurately, we will retrieve a cylinder, one centimeter in diameter, of skin and blubber. Another piece of the puzzle will be put into place in this coordinated effort to save a critically endangered species.

The boat picks up speed; we approach.

Trip drives. Clay is standing, bracing himself against the side, crossbow ready. The idea is to be with the whales for as little time as possible; it is quickly clear that our presence is not a welcome one.

The mother and calf are relaxed at first. Spindle is at the surface, her head and back in view, the calf rising and falling, breathing and diving next to her. But we get closer, and the sound of the boat is roaring underwater, and then they are both down beneath, vanished. Flukeprints in the water, but not whales.

We begin to circle them, cutting off their forward movement. They start to circle, too. A fin rises, runs through the blue, and falls. Gone again below, but their presence is now clear in the waters just off the starboard side. A vague movement of black beneath the chopping sea.

There is a primal fear welling in me. An old sort of corporeal knowing that sends the reaction through my body before my mind counters, with logic, *you're safe in the boat, you're safe in the boat.* It's rare for me to notice the presence of raw instinct, perhaps not since giving birth to Aspen. But strangely, this black shape emerging from vast open waters has the effect of making me feel part of a *species* rather than like an individual. It doesn't seem like something *I* am afraid of, but something my body knows that *we—Homo sapiens—*are afraid of. In this way, I am both terrified and oddly comforted.

Another fin breaks the surface, races through the water. Spindle is on her side, circling protectively around her calf. Gone again below. And then, there—*there*—she rises. Head and an arc of back and then fluke. An old wound, a boat scar, is briefly revealed on her hip. The calf follows and surfaces to breathe next to her. Clay fires. Misses.

We retrieve the arrow, reload, try again. The whales have had a chance to flee, but their flukeprints linger in the water when they go below, marking out their path. We follow.

We come near again.

Where will they emerge? We're all looking, all of our bodies tense—human and whale.

They rise and breathe, once, together.

I feel her vulnerability. Her protectiveness. I wonder if they carry the genetic memory of whaleboats, and I fleetingly think again of the painful irony: because we once so ruthlessly chased them down, because we now unintentionally continue to kill them, we are chasing them down still.

I sense the mother's fear and think that it is not just the shared connections of blood and milk that tie both of us to our children but a deep, visceral vulnerability.

Starboard side again. Flukeprint. Then nothing.

Farther off the boat again, the mother.

Motor closer.

Here she rises again.

So, too, does the fluke of the calf. The fluke is already colonized with cyamids that he inherited from his mother and that are concentrated in the notch of his tail, a spongy off-white marking. Again the fins of his mother. She is turning, turning. Protecting what is hers. But we are close now. Then the calf is up to breathe. This time, he rises between his mother and the boat. Clay fires again. The arrow finds its mark.

I release my breath. Clay retrieves the arrow floating in the water.

The motor goes quiet. We can leave them be, although I feel a prickle of fear about the fate we are leaving them to.

When a right whale calf is struck by a ship, I am afraid of how quickly that ineffable, uncrossable distance of mystery between a human and a whale collapses in on itself.

I am afraid of all that is at stake in extinction.

Did the whalers of Nantucket know they were driving a species to the brink of disappearance? Herman Melville would say no, they did not. He writes in *Moby Dick*: "[The whale] swam the seas before the continents broke water; he swam over the site of Tüileries, and Windsor Castle, and the Kremlin. In Noah's flood he despised Noah's Ark; and if ever the world is to be again flooded . . . then the eternal whale will still survive, and rearing upon the topmost crest of the equatorial flood, spout his frothed defiance to the skies."

Then again, I'm not entirely sure, even now, that we believe in extinction. At least not as an embodied truth. We do not feel the weight of it.

"First they came for the coral," Jenny Offill's narrator thinks to herself in her novel *Weather*, "but I did not say anything because I was not a coral."

* * *

The truth? Sometimes I do feel like the sea monsters in all of those myths. Sometimes I am tempted to play the role of the devouring mother. Sometimes I want to swallow my daughter whole and put her back where I can best keep her safe.

WHALEFALL

I carry forward a habit, formed when Aspen was days old, and I was terrified of the tender fragility of her new life. I would repeatedly check her breathing when she was asleep, placing a hand lightly on her stomach, relief coursing through me when her warm belly rose against the palm of my hand. I suspect this is a ritual of many new mothers. I still do this. Every night before I go to sleep, I feel for her breath. I imagine a halo of light around her, keeping her safe. These are the quiet moments in which I unequivocally know myself and my daughter as mortals. As I learned about the plight of the right whale mothers and calves, my understanding of Aspen's safety took on new dimensions, like a many-sided, shifting shape. Faces other than hers began to appear on that shape: other beings whose presence is required to satisfy the conditions of my own child's well-being.

What is at stake if the mothers of the North Atlantic right whales cannot endure? How do we measure what would be lost in the extinction of this species? Would we, would the ocean, would Aspen's world fifty years from now truly notice the absence of 350 whales?

Along with right whales, the fourteen species of baleen whales are known as the "great whales": they are among the largest animals in the history of life on Earth. Because their numbers were already so depleted by the time serious scientific study of them began—compared with their historical numbers, blue whales have been reduced by an estimated 99 percent—and because of the ongoing logistical challenges of studying large, rare, and constantly on-the-move marine mammals, comparatively little is known about them.

What *is* known about the great whales is that their presence alters the topography of the seafloor, changes the water column (humpback whales, for example, exhale underwater to create "bubble nets" that concentrate their prey), sequesters massive amounts of carbon, and transfers vital nutrients like iron and nitrogen from areas of high productivity to areas of low productivity. This redistribution occurs not only within the ocean itself, but—via the bodies and movements of other animals like salmon and seabirds—whales contribute to the recycling of nutrients from saltwater to freshwater, and from sea to land.

The term *biological pump* refers to the various marine processes that work to fix carbon dioxide into organic matter and transport it to the ocean's depths, where it can stay sequestered for hundreds of years. Such sequestration plays a significant role in regulating atmospheric carbon dioxide. Reducing baleen whale populations is known to lower the rate at which marine ecosystems sequester carbon. This is, in part, because whales store massive amounts of carbon within their living biomass and transfer that carbon to the seafloor in the form of a whalefall.

When a whale dies, its corpse sinks to the ocean floor. As it does, it feeds and provides habitat for many hundreds of other lives, working through the hierarchy of the food chain as it descends into the lightless depths. First, the soft tissue is consumed by sharks and other animals that feed on the flesh of the dead. Then, the invertebrates arrive to feed on the bones and on the rich sediment that hovers around the whale like an edible aura. Lastly, the whale enters the phase of anaerobic decomposition, in which microorganisms break down organic matter in the absence of oxygen. This phase can last for decades. More than

200 unique species can inhabit a single whale skeleton. Whalefalls transfer an estimated 190,000 tons of carbon annually to the seafloor. That's more than 2,000 years' worth of average carbon flow to ocean floor sediments.

In her book *Fathoms*, Rebecca Giggs writes, "what message should we, who never venture to these depths, take from the whalefall—what does this story boil down to? What I carry forward is this: Nothing ends without adding vigor to the conditions under which new beginnings are conceived. No state is condemned to be changeless . . . the death of a whale can prove not a tragedy but a turning point."

Is this not also a charge of motherhood? That when we dare venture to the depths of our own mortality, we might see new ways of adding vigor to the conditions under which new beginnings are conceived?

A North Atlantic right whale embarks on her final descent just as an ancient tree falls in an old growth forest. The layers of the body are recycled. New life is made possible. There is redemption and comfort in the naturalness, the wild dispersal, of death.

But the ongoing, sharp decline in the ocean's populations of megafauna is like a butterfly effect of sterility. The possible extinction of North Atlantic right whales is akin to a different kind of descent: a species-wide, human-caused whalefall.

What particular shape does a fall as great as this take, as it descends from the sunlight into the dark?

In extinction, there is not nourishment. In species-death, there is not redemption. It is far harder to see the meaning in my own mortality when I imagine leaving my child an emptier world to inherit.

The shape of a right whale entangled, dead, washed ashore, body taken from the sea, is something hollow, devoid, like the negative space around an image. It is only an erasure.

CHIMERA

There are dangerous ways of being entangled: a rope wrapped into a whale.

And there are positive, mysterious, sometimes ambiguous means of entanglement: a child orbiting a mother.

There are countless tethers that wrap us into each other's lives.

This tethering begins for many of us when we are in the womb.

When I was pregnant, Aspen inhabited her own ecosystem, a micro-sea. But there was a conversation between her body and mine, not only as mediated by the placenta but also in our very genetic material. In the womb, some of Aspen's fetal cells crossed the boundary of the placenta and entered into my bloodstream, where they then circulated and eventually lodged into my body's tissue. My cells did the same to her. Science has dubbed this phenomenon *microchimerism.* Science writer Elena E. Giorgi writes that this "new school of thought in biology claims that we are not individuals, but rather symbionts—distinct organisms living with one another." It is a phenomenon that is widespread among mammals.

The definitions of *chimera* include "a fire-breathing she-monster in Greek mythology having a lion's head, a goat's body, and a serpent's tail" and "an imaginary monster compounded of incongruous parts." A chimera can also be "an illusion or fabrication of the mind." And a chimera is also "an individual, organ, or part consisting of tissues of diverse genetic constitution."

Chimeras in the living world include slime molds and corals, beings who are made up of multiple, genetically distinct creatures, existing as one. Mothers and children, it turns out, are also this. Fetal cells are similar to stem cells in that they are *pluripotent*: they can grow into many different kinds of tissue. With chemical cues from my neighboring cells, Aspen's fetal cells grew into the same type of tissue to match wherever they had lodged themselves. Beyond this, microchimerism is not well understood. Some studies suggest that fetal cells play a role in the mother's milk production, and that fetal cells may also be transferred postnatally through nursing. There is speculation that fetal cells could, in some cases, increase risk of cancer, but mostly these chimeric presences seem to have positive effects. In one study, fewer fetal-derived cells were found in the brains of women with Alzheimer's, suggesting that the presence of *more* fetal cells could lower the risk of degenerative brain disease. One study tracked fetal microchimeric cells in a mother rat with a damaged heart. The fetal cells migrated to her heart, where they became heart cells and helped her heal.

Peripartum cardiomyopathy, a form of heart failure, is a condition that affects thousands of pregnant women or newly delivered mothers. For reasons not yet understood, approximately 50 percent of women seem to, miraculously, simply get better—a recovery rate higher than for any other form of heart failure for any demographic. Microchimerism has been suggested as a possible reason. Fetal cells, it's thought, migrate to the heart, multiply, and come to resemble "full-fledged heart muscle cells," contributing to the health of the mother's heart.

Which is all really to say: there is still so much mystery to all of the ways we intersect and inhabit each other's lives. This is true of mothers and children, of women and whales. We will never fully know when and how we tug upon each other, how entangled we truly are.

26

KNIFE'S EDGE

Back on land in Georgia, surrounded by the calling birds of the marshes and surprised at the extent of my exhaustion given that I had essentially stood still on a boat for eight hours, I recall again the shape of Spindle's head—how it looked at first like volcanic rock.

And then I recall how the Hawaiian Islands began as an eruption on the ocean floor and climbed their way into the open air, forged from fires in the deep. When, I wonder, can it be rightly said that one form echoes another? What physics are at work on both the emergence of an island and the rostrum of a right whale; on both the first spouting breath of a calf and the eruption of fire from a seam in the Earth?

Rock is different from flesh is different from cosmology is different from fetal cell migration. Geological and biological and mythological forces operate according to their own laws. But I am reaching, I think, for a common physics of *creation*, a refrain that is heard within emergences. I want to understand how things both distinctly *begin* and also how, then, it is possible that they can disappear.

I want to carve out a space from which to consider how that swimming child, that whale calf, is also a convergence of creative energies. And I want to practice not turning my face away from what is at stake in his death.

Though perhaps I'm searching, in truth, for a way to understand how motherhood has situated me on a knife's edge between ineffable love and unimaginable loss. I have never in my life been more vulnerable than in these last three years. I feel my entanglement with Aspen viscerally, in ways large and small. I have, countless times, woken up between thirty and sixty seconds before Aspen wakes up, somehow sensing that she is about to stir. I am perpetually haunted by her mortality. This, her mortal life, is the monster under my bed, the ghost in my closet, a bottomless well of thoughts that claw their way to me in the dark.

It is easy to become paralyzed when asked to face the possibility of unbearable grief. This is something I have felt acutely in motherhood. And it is not all that different from something it seems we are asked to do all the time: to look at how the world is burning and then look down to see that we have only been given a one-gallon bucket, and it is empty of water.

And yet something has also activated within me from this precarious place. The flip side of that coin is a flourishing—a veritable ongoing riot—of love and care. And it is when balancing between the light and the dark that I seem most able to discern a new path forward.

"On the last day of the world I would want to plant a tree," W. S. Merwin famously wrote. Diligent, active care, even at the end of the world. I wonder: is this the same place from which to be in service to my child, to the whale, to the world?

✳ ✳ ✳

"Mama, get me the moon."

Outside around the fire in our backyard in Maine, we're pretending to fill our coat pockets with stars. The days have grown short, so by 5:00 pm, Aspen is reaching up to pluck distant lights from the sky. It is the same motion she used to pick July raspberries.

The frank expectation of her request is what moves me: no sense that she's asked the impossible. She asks, rather, with the same tone of "more noodles" over dinner. Andrew and I exchange smiles.

I reach up and cup my palm around the crescent moon, thinking I would love nothing more than to bring the impossible down to my child's waiting hand.

I'm thinking, too, about one of my own requests of late, one I haven't uttered aloud but repeat again and again to myself. It's a request that sends me reaching for something that, at moments, seems as impossibly distant as winter stars:

"God, save the right whales."

As I speak to Clay, Philip, Scott, scientists who have spent decades working to save these animals—searching for them, documenting them, physically disentangling them from hundreds of feet of rope, testing ropeless fishing gear that won't wrap itself through a right whale's baleen, prohibiting her from feeding herself—I am moved to hope. Here are people who might find a whale they have known for thirty years literally torn apart by a ship's motor. And then they are back on the ocean the next day, pulled over the water by the knowledge that there are more whales out there, that there is still more to be done.

They are pulled, too, by love.

All of them tell me they have hope for this species. And all of them qualify their hope.

Philip Hamilton, the scientist who works on the right whale catalog, volunteers as a hospice worker in his local community. He told me that helping individuals and families navigate the transition between life and death is connected to his work with the right whales. "We don't have control over what's happening, but we do have control over keeping our hearts open," he said. "And that's not small. If you can keep your heart open with all of this happening, with all of this pain and hurt and loss of beauty, and see that beauty is still here. . . ."

Hope can seem such a frivolous word. Light as a feather, never touching the ground. But this hope on behalf of whales is not passive. It is a lifeline. A way of continuing to move through darkness. Hope in the face of unimaginable loss can forge a tie that connects the best in ourselves to the best in others. It can enable us to decenter ourselves in service to other forms of life.

No, hope alone will not save the right whales. But as much as we ought to be wary of frivolous hope, we ought also to be wary of the passivity that comes with assuming there is no hope to be had. "We are all potentially at risk of a fair amount of hubris if we make these assumptions about what is going to happen with such certainty," Clay tells me. "Right now, there's a lot of scientists talking about [right whale] extinction."

But, he says, twenty years ago, the whales were at another critical moment. Back then, when he started working with them, many assumed they couldn't recover. But then the whales turned it around, and the population rebounded. The whales are at such a moment again. "If we can get the human causes of mortality under control," Clay says, "these animals could go back to living fifty, sixty, seventy years; they would be able to almost certainly weather these cycles in low calving. I find some amount of hope in that."

An active, embodied hope might help us envision and then bring about a future in which the whales are present. But such a hope must span times and tenses. It must at once point our attention to the future and be rooted in understanding—and reckoning with—the past. And its *doing*—its embodiment—must always be in the present tense. For here are the whales, swimming and feeding and nursing, now.

Now, they are still here.

And here, too, is my daughter. Here she is: listening, seeing, touching, learning language in a world both burning and beautiful. I hope for her a healed world, and so I must do my part in the healing.

And in writing this, I realize I have to look closer at my prayer: *God, save the right whales*. I have to dare to look at the other prayer that sits and glows at the very center of my heart, a place I sometimes hardly dare look for how tender it is: *God, watch over my daughter*.

I have to look closer at these supplications, because these phrases can carry their own troubling passivity. It is not always enough to pray.

On one long night in December, I imagined a world where I could reach up and pull the moon into my daughter's hand.

Every night, night after night after night, I lie in bed and imagine another world: one where my daughter thrives on a thriving Earth, where a right whale is giving birth to a calf, nursing him for one turn around the sun, teaching him the old migration routes, and, eventually, ushering him forth to his own long life in the vast sea.

That world is not yet impossible.

27

FAREWELL

Coastal Georgia:

The *Borant* rocks on quiet waves as Spindle and her calf depart, the biopsy now safely in the cooler. Tomorrow, I will fly home, into my daughter's waiting arms. But here, for a moment that stretches long and low like the light from the sun that is setting beyond the ocean's horizon, I watch this mother and child as they swim away, together. I have a sudden urge to call something out to them, a warning maybe, but no words take shape, and I stay silent. They swim away to the southeast, disappearing into the orange light.

Their lives their own.

PART IV

COMMUNITY
Imagining Trees

Years and distances, stars and candles, water and wind and wizardry, the craft in a man's hand and the wisdom in a tree's root: they all arise together.

—Ursula K. Le Guin, *A Wizard of Earthsea*

28

MYTHICAL FORESTS

The magnificent forests of my early childhood first sprouted in the pages of books. There were plenty of trees in the suburban Oklahoma neighborhood where I grew up, but never a spanning, interwoven community of wooded giants that I could walk beneath and among, as I longed to do.

For years after we could read on our own, our dad continued to read aloud to my brother, Nathan, and me before bed. The books I remember most clearly: *The Dark Is Rising* series; *The Ear, The Eye, and the Arm*; *The Hobbit*; and the *Lord of the Rings* trilogy, which we read through at least twice.

The last time my father read Tolkien's words and worlds to us aloud was the year we moved with him to Lost Farm on Nantucket. It was an Audubon sanctuary, fitted with a small house, where Dad would spend the bulk of his career. I was eleven, Nathan nine, and in the waning evenings of autumn, the three of us would sit together in the light cast out from the bronze floor lamp. The words and the voice that spoke them were comfortingly familiar in a way that our new home was not. Our living room was small and fitted with bunk beds, doubling as Nathan's and my bedroom. Dad sat in the reclining chair; Nathan and I sat on the floor or the bottom bunk.

I spent a lot of time reading silently and alone, too, but when I attempted to read Tolkien's books, my young mind stumbled over many of the words, which pulled me out of the fantasy and into the mental acrobatics of deciphering symbols on the page. Sometimes this was an enjoyable challenge. But I preferred, any day, hearing the story through the vessel of my father. Delivered orally, it was as though Tolkien's world arrived directly into my imagination, and I could float along the story like a leaf in a river. My mind was free to inhabit and explore, and I lingered in my favorite scenes as Dad read on. I ducked again through Bilbo's round door. Kept bobbing with the dwarves in their barrels. Climbed once more into Treebeard's branching crown. Grew drowsy with Frodo and Sam in the foothills of Mordor. Apart from the barren land of Sauron, the entire series took place, in my mind, in an unending forest— not so different from Tolkien's intention, perhaps, but lacking any sophisticated topography of valleys and mountains. I was content imagining a world of ubiquitous, uniform trees.

In addition to reading us books, Dad required that we spend the daylight hours primarily outside. If there was not a hurricane or a blizzard, we biked to our destinations. We learned to identify edible mushrooms and trim the trails around the house. We carried jugs of water to his research plots, mowed meadows, and, often, simply played.

Being outdoors in the daylight and reading in the evening didn't feel entirely like separate experiences. I brought the stories with me out into the world, not by playacting specific characters or scenes but by a continued experience of the land as the place where stories could *happen*. We played a lot of games in the pitch pine forest that grew around our house: capture the flag, fort-building, hide-and-seek. But mostly I remember simply carrying around an undefined but certain sense of possibility when outdoors, like there was a myth or two draped in the trees with the bearded lichen or scurrying away just out of the corner of my eye.

After dinner, I brought the land back inside with me as I listened to my father read. Tolkien's forests took on more subtlety and clarity as I increasingly came to have my own experiential vocabulary of the woods, even though I lacked the words to express it. The place where the books and the land met was my imagination, not the alphabet.

Perhaps it's not a coincidence, then, that a few months after our arrival to Nantucket, and a few weeks into enjoying evening immersions into Middle-earth, I was claimed for the first time—to use the verbiage of mythologist Martin Shaw—by a mythical forest in my own world. On the trail that narrowed into the woods beyond Lost Farm's homestead grew a stand of hawthorn trees. That spring, they bloomed. But they didn't just bloom; they bloomed all at once, like a string quartet inhaling a simultaneous breath and meeting their bows to the strings so that the voices of their instruments sound, not with four voices, but with one voice. A breath and then a harmonic manifestation: pink-white petals, a cathedral ceiling masterpiece between me and the sky. In my memory, I see myself standing beneath this canopy, not as if I'm at the portal to another world but already transported.

Standing amid the petals flipping and drifting to the understory, I felt myself to be, quite literally, under a story. I didn't have the knowledge or the words to tell it, scientifically or otherwise. I knew nothing of the ecology of hawthorn trees or their relationship to the seasons or the reason for their thorns. Nor did I have any vocabulary of the sacred. No wordy narrative spelled itself out in my mind. I don't recall that any descriptive words at all rose to the surface, nor do I recall missing them. There was a simple and silent conversation, or composition, at work between the trees and me.

Not long after that spring, a winter storm whipped through the stand. Heavy snow and high wind bowed the trunks. Thorny branches either snapped off or snagged into each other and held fast. Afterward, the trees were irreparably snared and tangled, an illegible cursive scrawl. Though most of the trees survived, the canopy never recovered to what it had been. But I can still return to the moment of that spring. When it surfaces in my mind, my physical body still responds, here in the present, to an infusion of awe. And only with the space of the intervening twenty-five years can I now say that what was there in that moment was an invitation. And that without being fully aware of it as a child, I accepted. I said yes to being imprinted by this community of trees.

29

CULTIVATING ROOTS

Children easily flow between imaginative landscapes and physical ones. These terrains might be separate one moment, seamlessly merged the next. Just as Aspen said "Hi!" to all of the beings around our house at twelve months old, now, at two-and-a-half, her conversations continue. Her world remains deeply animate, primed for story. At any moment, anything might speak to her. She will unhesitatingly speak back.

One of Aspen's favorite books of the moment is *Old Rock (Is Not Boring)*, a story about a very old, stationary rock who convinces a skeptical pine tree, hummingbird, and beetle that his life is not, in fact, boring. He tells them how he was spewed out of a volcano, took a ride inside a glacier, and was sat upon by a mastodon.

Not long ago, on our way to northern Vermont, we stopped to stretch our legs at a community garden with large boulders placed throughout. One of them, I noticed, looked exactly like Aspen's favorite story character. "Aspen!" I called. "I think I found Old Rock!" She ran over to see.

"Hi, Old Rock!" she said, patting the rock on its "head." "Brrr! You were in a *glacier*!"

✳ ✳ ✳

More than twenty spring seasons after I stood beneath that bloom of Hawthorn flowers, I shared the emergence of another spring with my daughter. Aspen and I were in the backyard looking at last year's maple seeds, revealed in mid-March by melted snow. They were brown and brittle, scattered about in the grass and moss. I held one over my head and dropped it to show her how it helicoptered, but she was more interested in holding it still so she could take a close look. In the palm of my hand, we noticed a little green shoot growing out of one end. We peeled off the outer coating, and she held the seed in her hand. It was pea-sized, flat and round, the color of coffee with a dash of cream.

I explained to her what this seed was. "This will grow into a maple tree," I said. She fixed me with a questioning look, as if waiting for me to laugh and say, "No, no, not really!" For it *is* almost unbelievable, isn't it, that we can hold what will be a tree in our hand? I could see this information play across her face: disbelief to belief to looking at this seed and then imagining a tree. I could almost see it rooting in her mind. In that moment, I wasn't sure what was more miraculous: that this tiny seed did in fact hold the potential of becoming an enormous tree, or that this tiny seed grew, right then, into a tree within my child's imagination.

We decided to plant it. I retrieved an empty yogurt container from inside and scooped up some soil. Aspen put the seed in. She gave it too much water, so that mud swirled at the top. She admired her work and wanted to plant more. Many of the other casings were empty of their seeds, which had been eaten by squirrels and birds over the course of the fall and winter, but we easily found two more with green shoots.

"This seed's perfect," Aspen said of the third one, in her own palm, before pushing it into the soil alongside the others. I never would have used that word about that little burst of life, with so many others like it everywhere around us that would soon be growing in every raised bed, in the flower garden, in the gutters, in the cracks in the driveway. But seeing *this* seed in my daughter's hand, I had to agree.

Several weeks later I was weeding the garden, surrounded by maple seed after maple seed, each with two crumpled green leaves that had shaken off their brittle coats, spreading in the sun like butterfly wings. Their green-white roots already reached an inch or two into the soil. I pulled most of them up, but with several of their sisters growing on our windowsill, I admit to feeling conflicted at choosing our garden over their forest.

But then again . . . spring was here, and there were northern cardinals and house finches in the trees, and the irises were rising, and I felt so at home kneeling at the edge of the garden beds in spring's abundance, which was everywhere like a promise. I, too, looked around and imagined the shape of what was to come. Lobelia and lilac, weeping cherry blossoms, and daisies. Pulling up the maple seedlings felt less like a removal and more like making room, leaving openings for others.

After weeding, my hands were covered in dirt. I spread them before me—and then . . . they were not my hands, but my mother's. Just as a tree had sprouted in Aspen's mind, my hands had manifested a presence: my mom. I turned them over. Yes: the same thick fingers and wide, flat fingernails. But it was the dirt that gave them away as inheritance. My mother's hands are those of a woman who labored for years in gardens—not our own but other people's. She landscaped for nearly two decades, and I remember how she always came home caked in dirt, dog-tired, and sunburned in the unforgiving Oklahoma sun. This was so she could feed and clothe and shelter us.

There were lean times at the beginning of this career, when she was newly divorced and in her late twenties, with little professional experience. We subsisted on what were then still called food stamps. Our oft-broken-down car meant walks to the pay phone because, also, the phone bills were overdue, and they had cut off our landline service. There were times when, if my brother and I wanted a treat—usually a McDonald's Happy Meal—we collected cans from the neighbors' bins to raise the four dollars. And another time, in the middle of the school day, when the counselor excused me from my third-grade class and brought me to Salvation Army to pick out winter clothes, along with several other students. I didn't understand, and didn't ask, how we'd all earned this special outing, thinking that what connected us must have been good behavior or good grades. It didn't cross my mind that what the school recognized in all of us was poverty. That winter, our Hanukkah/Christmas presents arrived in two large paper bags—"from an angel," my mom said. I can still hear her stifled sob of gratitude and the crinkle of the bags as she set them down on the floor. A woman at the bank where my mom had asked for an extension on making her car payment, also a mother, had purchased these gifts so my mom would have something to give to us. Learning later who that flesh-and-blood woman was did not dispel my belief that she was, indeed, an angel.

But times often didn't *feel* lean with my mom. Even when we once ate Hungry Jack pancakes three meals a day because pancake mix was all she could afford. Even though I have since learned the extent of her shame and guilt and the daily presence of a gripping fear that she wouldn't be able to support us, that the courts would take us away.

She had ways of creating abundance.

This was, in part, a function of her love and her innate tendency toward joy and creativity. She is someone who has managed to hold onto a childlike imagination, far more than most adults. I don't mean that in a derogatory sense; rather, that she has easier access to wonder and laughter. There is always a new world at her fingertips. She was, and is, an artist. She makes wire sculptures, and she begins, always, with a roll of black wire that you could find in any hardware store. Pliers in one hand, she begins to bend and twist and loop and wrap. What emerges are large, archetypal creatures, built of spirals and stars and motion. Women dancing. Giraffes with bowed heads. Wriggling lizards. She mostly does not work from photographs or real-time observation. The beings emerge from the imaginative world she inhabits, through the shaping movements of her hands.

As a mother, she conjured whimsical worlds and made space for our imaginations to fill them. Once before bedtime, after Nathan lost a tooth, she covered the green carpet between our bunk beds and the room's only door in a generous dusting of baby powder to prove to us that the tooth fairy existed, because, she said, any other creature would leave footprints overnight, but the tooth fairy could fly. In the morning, there were human footprints through the powder because—I now understand—she did not leave herself any other way to cross the room to leave a quarter beneath Nathan's pillow.

Our felt abundance was also a function of the community she built around us. She's the sort of person who could show up in a brand-new city and, several hours later, be greeted warmly by name on the street. She tended to friendships the same way she mulched and watered and pruned and fertilized.

She took pride in her landscaping, slowly earning her recommendations and new clients. Early on, she made the decision to work primarily with native, perennial plants, which required less water, drew pollinators, and could weather the extremes of the Southern climate. The plants she placed into the soil thrived.

So did the community that sprouted up around us. It was rooted, reliable, adaptable. People showed up when we needed them. Not always perfectly, but consistently. When cancerous cells of the same disease that killed my grandmother showed up in my mother's thyroid, and the radiation treatment caused her to miss a full season of work. When she hosted our annual neighborhood latke parties. When Nate and I needed backpacks and books. Even when, during the 2008 financial crisis, many of her clients could no longer pay her, and she missed several mortgage payments, and the bank gave her the option of either selling our childhood home or being foreclosed on. People showed up. And my mother, like her warm season grasses and her roses and her black-eyed Susans, was resilient—partly because she did not have a choice to be anything else. Mothering, I'm learning, is like that.

Just like the hawthorn trees and Tolkien's forests overlapped for me in some internal way, the plants and the community of my childhood with my mom also remain connected in my mind. I see their faces; I see her gardens. Perhaps I subconsciously understood that both were the result of care and cultivation.

And isn't it odd that I did not know I had my mother's hands until I was sitting there with earth curved beneath my fingernails and nestled in the cracks of my skin? Until my own daughter was digging in the raised beds with a small blue shovel?

I am wondering how to best put these hands to use. How to tend. Not only to my daughter, and to the perennial garden beds my mom helped us put in last year around our home, but how to cultivate sustaining relationships with people and birds and trees and tides. How to bring a fertile, open imagination into these networks of community. How to make them resilient.

I am privileged to be raising my daughter with the means to ensure that she is fed and clothed and sheltered. This does not release me from responsibility to others in our community; nor does it shield Aspen or me from the bigger changes that are arriving as the climate crisis finds its way into all of our places of home and refuge. Mothering requires that we nurture not only children but resiliency in the communities around us. And resiliency cannot be achieved alone. It is both a communal undertaking and an imaginative one.

Motherhood is changing my understanding of what this resiliency looks like. Before Aspen, I was more focused on personal choices, individual action, writing as a persuasive—and often lonely—vehicle for telling stories. But I am beginning to see that resiliency entails place-based practices of community.

I am working to define more thoughtfully the bounds of the communities I inhabit, their function and their meaning. So that in times of abundance, and in lean times, and in times of pain and loss, and in all of the uncertain times to come, we can be there for each other, especially in the places where we are rooted in the same home ground. So that, as that ground shifts and changes, we can imagine and enact ways forward.

We can help each other to keep reaching for the sunlight.

Community is rooted in the Latin *munus*, meaning a duty or an obligation. Also: a gift or a service. At first, those definitions seemed at odds with one another, but it only took thinking of being Aspen's mother for me to see how those functions are not mutually exclusive within relationships. As Aspen's mother I am bound to this tie of kinship. I am obliged—my presence is required, as is my patience, as is my heart. I am often burdened: I dare not calculate the hours of sleep lost, nor can I any longer keep count of the new gray hairs, or the number of times I've wanted to do something else, something independent, but have errands to run or a hungry child to feed instead. I am forever in service—whether measured in ounces of breast milk or books read or songs sung or tears wiped away, Aspen's and my own. I am the daily recipient of the gift of a renewing, familial love. This unceasing, terrifying, wonderful love. This, always.

And as someone who is learning what it is to mother the bit of Earth that we reside upon, I am, again, obliged, burdened, in service, and increasingly in love. We are learning, slowly, on our small bit of land around our house, which flowers draw the bees, which critters eat the squash, where the sunlight lingers longest, which birds like which trees.

And then there are all the bits of Earth beyond our fence line and the people who reside upon them. This is what I mean by community: the unique assemblage of beings who coinhabit a place—a particular ecological region—and the dynamic, shifting network of relationships that define that coexistence. Thinking about community in this way reminds us that we are mutually dependent on both our shared humanity *and* our shared ecology.

In *The Unsettling of America*, Wendell Berry writes: "We have given up on the understanding—dropped it out of our language and so out of our thought— . . . that our land passes in and out of our bodies just as our bodies pass in and out of our land; that as we and our land are part of one another, so all who are living as neighbors here, human and plant and animal, are part of one another, and so cannot possibly flourish alone."

Who are your human and plant and animal neighbors? There are so many iterations. Here is one: Andrew, Aspen, our extended family, the wealthy residents of the beachfront where we visit the piping plovers; the unhoused people who have pitched tents along the busy intersection at the end of our street, the oak and spruce trees who offer them shelter and shade, and the people in passing cars who, sometimes, offer them dollar bills or bottles of water. Our neighbors include the ladybug on the windowsill and the red maple trees growing along our fence, who scatter hundreds of their children into our lawn. The cattails around the local pond, and the invasive phragmites that are beginning to crowd them out, and the red-winged blackbirds who alight on both. And planted carrots and wild black-capped chickadees.

What does it look like for this community to flourish? What does it look like for it to flounder?

Steve Blackmer, a conservationist and Dartmouth-trained forester, in addition to a woods priest, once told me that place is land overlaid with story. What, then, are the stories that arise from a shared, inhabited landscape? Where do these stories converge, diverge, contradict, collide? Contract? Expand? Here in Portland there are overdoses, and there are soup kitchens. There are multi-million-dollar development projects, and there are more and more people failing to pay rent. There is a thriving farmers market, and there are concerning levels of PFAs in local agricultural soils. There are refugees fleeing violence, and there are doors that open to them upon their arrival in Maine. There are gardens, and there are fences between them.

Community, then, is not uniform, never a single story, but an evolving, shifting expression of diverse and changing patterns of coexistence in a place. Community is a shared, lived expression. And being *in* community is a reminder that we do not act alone: our lives touch the lives of others, and others' lives touch our own. Through these relationships, we can strive toward a vision of a shared inhabiting.

We hold the maple seed in our hand, and we imagine a tree.

30

CUTTING DOWN THE WORLD

We own twenty acres of land in northern Vermont. In the context of Western property ownership, it is not a valuable piece of property. Neither would the casual visitor be likely to think that it was remarkable in an ecological or geological sense. From the road, the land immediately begins to rise at a grade that requires switchbacks to ascend, and even then, the going is rough. It is home to a typical forest community for the region in the present day: a beech–red maple–hemlock hardwood forest, interspersed with pockets of birch, and several magnificent white oaks with black-brown hollows split into their wrinkled trunks.

Exposed granite cliffs jut out in places, too steep for soil and roots to have taken hold but covered in carpets of spongy green moss. Here and there, thick knuckles of quartz glimmer from the leaf litter. There is a flat spot at the northern boundary, the highest point of the property at 915 feet, where sunlight pours through a gap in the canopy onto ferns growing in their fractal fronds. To the east, a brook fed from springs and snowmelt tumbles down the hillside, traveling a rocky cascade of falls and pools, through a culvert beneath the road, and into the Lamoille River.

There is one structure on the land: a single-room cabin built by the previous owner. It has a damp floor, ringed with growing circles of dark mold as it takes in water that seeps from the slope behind. It is not cheery and snug like a hobbit-hole but gloomy and dank. And yet it has the trappings of love. A peace sign was hand-painted above the door; birch trunks serve as pillars supporting the overhang on the front porch. A bird's nest was left in the windowsill, and ceramic mugs were left carefully arranged in the cabinet. The woman who was here before had lived here alone, off-grid, even through the long Vermont winters. She was well into her eighties when her family insisted that she could no longer support herself. We got the sense that she parted from the land reluctantly. We never met her, but we marvel at what it must have taken for her to make a life here: an intimate reliance on the natural and human communities of this place. The brook delivered her water through a long black hose that she ran from one of the small waterfalls, down the hill, to a PVC pipe that drained into the cabin's sink. Neighbors helped her with repairs. The sun powered two tiny solar panels, each enough for just one dim light bulb. Wind-felled trees, chopped and fed to the woodstove, provided her heat. What a strong woman she must have been. We imagine she liked her self-sufficiency, and that she did not feel lonely in the company of the forest.

We've tried sleeping inside the cabin a few times, but between the mold and all that is continually left by the mice who nest in the ceiling's insulation, we woke with sore throats and red, puffy eyes. Now we set up a tent outside. We've had several professionals come out to take a look at the structure, hoping to salvage some or all of the little house, but the consensus has been unanimous: it needs to come down.

Thankfully, it's not the cabin that makes the land feel like home.

We call this place Earthsea, named for Ursula K. Le Guin's book series of the same name—a fictional world of many islands and the many shapes of water between them, a world inhabited by wizards, dragons, and an ancient magic rooted in the land.

Though it's technically a young adult series, I did not discover *Earthsea* until I was well into adulthood, when Andrew was on a mission to read every word Le Guin ever wrote. I read the *Earthsea* books as I was trying to get pregnant, and I often imagined a child by my side as I rode along in Ged's boat, "Lookfar," or deciphered runes in the spell books. Reading *A Wizard of Earthsea*, the first in the series, was the first time in a long time that I felt like I was seated by my father, a parallel universe arising around me. The book arrived to a fertile soil in my mind, like I had cleared a garden bed, unknowingly waiting for this very story to take root.

Around the time I was reading Le Guin's words, we visited the land in Vermont for the first time, drawn to the location because we had previously lived in a town nearby. It was early spring: mud season, arguably the least desirable part of the year in New England. Crusty, discolored snow lingered in places. The barren trees rattled. We slipped and stumbled up the "driveway" that was far too steep for our car and were panting with wet socks and cold feet just ten minutes into our arrival. But then, spontaneously and independently of each other, Andrew and I were swept into a long moment of joy. We began to run and leap. I was dizzy and lightheaded and utterly delighted. *How silly!* I thought. *I feel like a child.*

The realtor arrived a few minutes later. Even at its low cost—being an undesirable and largely unbuildable piece of land without major excavation into the hillside—we couldn't afford it. But we both felt like we had already made a commitment. Our families helped us get a loan, and we signed the papers a week later.

❊ ❊ ❊

A Wizard of Earthsea follows Ged, a mage from the land of Gont, from boyhood through his becoming a wizard, and tells of the trials he endures along the way. The story is in many ways a classic hero's journey, as Ged becomes entangled in the perpetual struggle between light and dark, outwits dragons, sails around the world pursued by an evil being, and comes out the other side transformed. But Le Guin subtly brings the land into play, too. The power of a great mage of Earthsea lies in knowledge of the true nature and names of things and in understanding how the world's beings and its elements—waters, rocks, creatures large and small—exist in relationship to each other. Everything is bound together by the magic that infuses the land. There is, thus, a communal ethic at play in the narrative: a way of being in Le Guin's imagined world that is grounded in understanding that one always acts and speaks in relationship to others. As such, speech and action become increasingly circumscribed as the wizard grows wiser: he comes to understand and therefore restrain his power to influence the world.

As the Master Hand cautions a teenage Ged, who is impatient to work his magic: "You must not change one thing, one pebble, one grain of sand, until you know what good and evil will follow on that act. . . . [I]t is dangerous, that power. It is most perilous. It must follow knowledge, and serve need. To light a candle is to cast a shadow."

✳ ✳ ✳

The story of Vermont's present-day forests begins twelve thousand years ago with the retreat of the Laurentide glacier. Spores of pollen unearthed in the newly exposed glacial till took root and covered the bare land with shrubs and grasses. The trees came next.

The Alnôbak, or Abenaki, arrived in the world from the trunk of the ash tree and have lived in Wôbanakik—the place now called Vermont—continuously since the disappearance of the ice. Here, they have been managing and subsisting for all of those millennia.

Neither Vermont's forests nor the people who lived among them have been static; rather, they have shaped and guided each other, alongside the long cycles of climate and short cycles of the seasons that are continually at work in the wider landscape. As Dr. Frederick Wiseman, an ethnobotanist and member of the Abenaki tribe, writes in his book *Voice of the Dawn: An Autohistory of the Abenaki Nation*, around eleven thousand years ago, the land converted to open woodlands consisting of spruce, fir, birch, and poplar. Young conifer forests were home to a small species of mastodon, moose-elk, and caribou—all hunted by the Abenaki using an atlatl, or spear thrower. The people lived in homes built of spruce and fir covered with hides or waterproof birch bark.

The climate warmed further, and the larger mammals migrated north with the shifting tundra, while deciduous trees migrated up from the south: white oak and hickory among them. Blueberries, strawberries, and currants became part of the people's diet. Sugar maple groves, where sap was collected in baskets of elm or birch bark, were inhabited during the spring. Spruce and hemlock roots were used for cords and lacing.

The interglacial period set in several thousand years later, warming the land further. Wiseman names this era "the Years of the Log Ships." During this time, the Abenaki lived in villages dotted through river valleys, consisting of wigwams and council houses. They built seafaring ships that greatly expanded their range and trade network. They developed an intricate practice of woodworking. "The spiritual world and the world of the common became tightly bound during the Years of the Log Ships," Wiseman writes. "We knew that the Earth and its components were connected and cyclical. Birth, puberty, death, woman's menstrual cycle, the migration of waterfowl, and the cycle of the Moon and Sun were the heartbeat of creation. This cycle was reflected in the birth and childhood of an Alnôba youth. At birth, *dzizdiz*, the child was shown to his relatives and the world, then strapped to a joyously carved wooden cradleboard." Celestial observation and understanding advanced during this time, as well as healing and medicinal traditions, which were intimately tied to the seasons and what the forests provided. "The spirit of leaf, bark, and stem became a source of our living and health," writes Wiseman.

From one thousand to four hundred years ago were the Years of Corn, marked by the development of agriculture and settlements along river valleys during the growing season. Crops included corn, beans, squash, and artichokes. But in the 1530s, "a series of afflictions washed over Wôbanakik, carrying away the knowledge of our elders, the potential of our young, and the strength of our adults," writes Wiseman. "Whole regions had to be abandoned. This biological assault is still remembered with a prohibition to discuss it in detail, an interdiction I will follow."

This affliction was colonization, and it marked the systematic dismantling of both the people's communities and their forests. Let's pause for a moment here to honor Wiseman's silence. Let us acknowledge this gap in narration and honor this refusal to put detailed words to the decimation and the totalizing loss, because sometimes an interdiction to speak brings us closer to the horror of a thing.

By the mid-1600s, the forests of New England had become a key force of sustenance for the British navy. White oak was harvested for the planking of British naval ships, while white pine was taken for the masts. In the early 1700s, royal surveyors were dispatched into forests to blaze potential mast trees with the mark of the broad arrow. Pitch pine supplied the pitch and turpentine. Beyond shipbuilding, entire forests were clear-cut and then burned to make way for agriculture. More forests were cut down for fuel. The average New England household required thirty to forty cords of firewood per year—more than an acre of forest. "It is probable," writes William Cronon in *Changes in the Land*, "that New England consumed more than 260 million cords of firewood between 1630–1800."

Apart from very few pockets of old-growth forest that escaped the saw, the vast majority of New England's trees disappeared with white settlement. Cronon writes: "The imperative here was not just the biblical injunction to 'fill the earth and subdue it.' Colonists were moved to transform the soil by a property system that taught them to treat land as capital." The permanent arrival of settlers in the region was the beginning of trees as commodities on American soil.

* * *

In *A Wizard of Earthsea*, a young Ged, challenged by a rival classmate, weaves a dark spell that is built from his limited knowledge of ancient books, the fire of magic that resides within him, and his boyhood ignorance and anger. But the spell wields its own will, appearing in Ged's mind as if he has opened a book that he is compelled to read, giving him a false sense of control: "Now he understood what he read, speaking it aloud word after word, and he saw the markings of how the spell must be woven with the sound of the voice and the motion of body and hand."

By bringing the words of the spell into the world via his voice and his body, fueled by rage and pride and a power he does not understand, Ged's spell becomes too powerful. It rips the seam between the realms of life and death. Through this tear crawls a darkness—"a clot of black shadow"—that comes to haunt and hunt Ged, pursuing him across the world.

There is a dangerous power, Le Guin seems to be saying, lurking within our intentions, brought into the world when those intentions are embodied. The words we speak can work not only our will but the will of that which is beyond our limited, or impoverished, understanding.

* * *

Mothering, too, is an embodiment of intention and imagination. And there are terrains of mothering that destroy rather than create.

In 1911, Mrs. Matthew T. Scott, president of the Daughters of the American Revolution, spoke aloud these words: "We must conserve the sources of our race in the Anglo-Saxon line . . . We, the mothers of this generation . . . have a right to insist upon the conserving not only of soil, forest, bird, minerals, fishes, waterways in the interest of our future home-makers, but also upon the conservation of the supremacy of the Caucasian race in our land."

The eugenics movement, which became a hallmark of Hitler's Germany, sought, in part, to apply Charles Darwin's theory of natural selection to the human race by intentionally selecting for the human "germ plasm" that held the greatest potential for mental and physical fitness—meaning, broadly, of European descent. Among the means to this end was forced sterilization. Tens of thousands of these acts of violence were committed against women, and, to a lesser extent, men—primarily poor, Black, Latinx, and Indigenous—across the nation. It's notable that Nazi Germany was influenced by American practices of forced sterilization in the early 1930s.

Meanwhile, the urgent need of America's early conservation movement to rescue and preserve America's "wilderness" came only in the wake of the American destruction of prairies and old-growth forests; the damming and pollution of rivers; the extermination of buffalo . . . the list goes on. That destruction, in turn, was undertaken in ignorance of the ways in which diverse Indigenous peoples not only successfully lived among but actively managed and stewarded healthy, resilient, and biodiverse ecosystems. These ecosystems were not pristine, untouched wildernesses at all, as many whites wrongly assumed, but functional ecological communities that included people and land together.

Though the two movements were largely held to their own spheres, there was nonetheless a narrow and unsettlingly influential overlap between eugenics and the early environmental movement in the United States. In this context, eugenics was a particularly evil branch of the ongoing efforts to safeguard what remained of America's "pristine" landscape and to wage a long project of ethnocide against Native Americans.

The eugenics movement had its greatest hold in the United States in the early twentieth century. While it was met with disgust and derision from many, some influential thinkers considered it inseparable from both social progress and the goal of securing a future for America's diminishing wild landscapes. Some prominent American eugenicists, such as Madison Grant and Charles Goethe, were celebrated naturalists of their time who shared a dual obsession to purify land and humanity alike. The implementation of eugenics laws in the United States coincided with many of the efforts to preserve America's natural resources and wild places from rapid industrialization and urbanization.

Like Ged's spell, colonization ripped the seams between worlds: the eugenics law severed mothers from their possible future children, from the ability to pass on knowledge, wisdom, and tradition. Genocide, treaties, boarding schools, and bans on cultural practice and language severed diverse Indigenous peoples from their homelands. Rampant felling severed trees from the landscape. The people were parted from the forest. The forest was parted from its people. It's hard not to draw a line between the fact that eugenics went into effect as law in Vermont in 1931, just decades after 80 percent of Vermont's forests had been clear-cut.

In all, 253 documented sterilizations occurred in Vermont (only the twenty-fifth highest number of sterilizations in the nation), most of them between 1931 and 1941. Two-thirds of them were performed on women identified as being poor, "mentally deficient," or "unfit." The Abenaki in Vermont, as well as other

Indigenous communities across the nation, were deemed to represent a persistent threat to the projects of colonialism. The last sterilization in Vermont occurred in 1957.

But these atrocities continued elsewhere. As Jane Lawrence writes, "Native Americans accused the Indian Health Service of sterilizing at least 25 percent of Native American women who were between the ages of fifteen and forty-four" in the 1970s alone. An estimated seventy thousand people in America endured forced sterilization in the twentieth century.

In our world, too, clots of shadow have crawled through places where worlds were ripped apart. The human imagination has sought to impose its intentions and words onto others in disturbing and cruel ways—ways that continue to haunt and hunt us. "There presently the yumens came and began to cut down the world," Le Guin writes of her fictional colonizers in *The Word for World Is Forest*. "They have left their roots behind them, perhaps, in this other forest from which they came, this forest with no trees."

RESTRAINED GROWTH

Here at Earthsea, there is ample evidence of logging: cleanly sawed, decaying stumps; overgrown logging roads; half-buried, rust-red cable winch systems that would have tethered logging equipment to the steep slopes; and stands of birch that, as a pioneer species, favor highly disturbed sites. These places are healing. The birch are working to reestablish the soils, creating fertile ground for other, longer-lived trees to grow. Hemlock and red maple will find their way back in as the birch, a tree with a comparably shorter lifespan, falls away, having done its job. It will take decades beyond our lifetimes here for the forest to grow back into a healthy, mature forest, and even then, there is no guarantee that it will. The world around and within the forest continues to change and shift. Warmer winters, pests like the hemlock woolly adelgid, invasive plants, and forest migration all leave a pall of uncertainty hanging over New England's forests and their future.

Two summers ago, we invited forester, conservationist, and woods priest Steve Blackmer to come out to take a look at Earthsea. We walked the property together as he narrated what he was seeing in this community of trees. When we arrived back at the cabin, I asked, "So, what can we do to take care of this place?" I was in action mode, ready for a list of timely tasks. Did we need to remove any living trees? Clear away any of the fallen ones? Rake away the leaves? Plant anything new?

"You can love it. The forest knows what it's doing," Steve said.

Where the standard practice within the timber industry is often to manage forests for rapid growth, a healthy forest left to its own devices can manage itself, in part on the principle of slow growth and restraint. Growing slowly, especially when a tree is young, contributes to the structural integrity of the inner woody cells within the tree's trunk. A tree that can take its time is able to keep these cells small, with little air contained inside. This makes them flexible and more resilient to weather, and it also makes it more difficult for harmful intruders like fungi to spread internally. Trees that experience restrained growth early in life are much more likely to live for a long time. And a forest that is populated with old trees stores more carbon, has healthier soil, fosters more biodiversity, keeps the surrounding air and water cleaner, and becomes more and more resilient to change.

Young trees accomplish this slowness in relationship to their elders, but especially in relationship to their mothers, who provide for this restraint through something very simple: shade. Take the eastern hemlock, for example. Hemlocks are highly shade-tolerant, and young hemlocks thrive in the cool understory of their parents, where limited access to sunlight keeps them small for a long time. Because they are known to grow slowly— it is not uncommon for a one-inch-thick hemlock sapling to be eighty or one hundred years old!—the presence of large hemlocks in a forest is generally a positive indicator of the forest's health. That's not only because sizeable hemlocks demonstrate a lack of intensive disturbance that has given these trees the decades, or centuries, they need to grow, but also because hemlocks are a foundation species. They help create and sustain the ecosystems around them. Their shallow roots filter and clean water. Their canopy shades streams and keeps them cool. They provide winter food and shelter to deer, porcupines, and moose. And they help to ensure the health and success of the next generation.

In her book *Finding the Mother Tree*, Suzanne Simard, the scientist responsible for bringing the wood wide web into mainstream Western consciousness, writes about the importance of conserving the largest trees—Mother Trees, she calls them—in forests. These elders store carbon, provide habitat, clean the air and the water, and, crucially, have endured substantial changes around them that have altered their very DNA—meaning they pass greater genetic resiliency onto their offspring.

Through Simard's scientific experiments with birch and fir, she demonstrated that Mother Trees—"majestic hubs at the center of forest communication, protection, and sentience"—recognize and support not only their direct descendants but other trees (even other tree species!) within their forest community. By passing them carbon via the mycorrhizal networks that connect the trees' roots beneath the forest floor, she writes, "these old trees were not only favoring their kin; they were also ensuring the community in which they were raising their kin was healthy."

Today, northern New England's forests have largely been allowed to grow back, and states like New Hampshire, Vermont, and Maine boast between 78 and 89 percent forest cover. Many of the Northeast's forests also continue to be working forests. In such places, trees remain commodities, but harvesting timber can be—and in many places very much is—carried out with an intent to minimize harm to a forest community and with genuine respect and care for the land. The evolving understanding and forestry practices that go with such intentions are finding their way into practices of forest management and extraction, thanks in part to the work of Simard and others who are bringing the communal nature of forests into forestry science.

We are learning more and more, too, about the ways in which the resilience of any one forest entails a complex, shifting, and in many ways uncertain set of questions, which unfold across a long arc of time as forest communities recover, respond, adapt, and compete in a context of historic and present-day land use and ongoing changes in climate. Even in forests that are not being managed for timber, questions of human management are present, as they have been for thousands of years. People can—and in many cases, increasingly must—be active participants in a forest's resiliency, keeping invasive species at bay, protecting land from development, helping to keep resident species in balance. To do this work, to participate in a forest community, we can begin, again, upon a foundation of restraint. We can slow down, step into tree time. Scientific study in a forest context, in the case of tree migration for example, often occurs on the scale of decades.

And what of those of us who are not scientists, seeking to care for or be in relationship to a forest community? As stewards of this land we call Earthsea, we, too, are finding ways to practice restraint. We are holding in our minds the vision of a healthy forest that knows how to heal itself, and we are working to learn about ways that we may be able to participate, now, in the forest's future health. As a human mother, I do not have the luxury of growing centuries old alongside my daughter, or alongside these trees. I will not get to keep my child close by, shaded and shielded. But I do have the ability both to think generationally and to act as a member of a community that both includes and extends beyond my human family. As German forester Peter Wohlleben writes in *The Hidden Life of Trees*: "A tree can be only as strong as the forest that surrounds it. . . . Their well-being depends on their community." This strikes me as being equally true for a tree as it is for my child.

Peter Wohlleben has been criticized—rather intensely—by some members of the forestry science community who have cast serious doubt on his scientific methods and lambasted him for his anthropomorphizing of trees and his claims of nonhuman sentience in idealized forest communities. As a lay reader, I neither doubt that these criticisms hold some water, nor do I dismiss Wohlleben's invitation to—with rigor—think about and experience trees differently. I prefer an approach to the world where sentience, for example, is not presumed to be absent until proven present. Where the possibility of a tree's ability to feel and perceive is a living question—especially where such an ability is assumed to occur in ways we do not fully understand. This strikes me as neither an idealistic nor a romanticized approach but a respectful and humble one.

Human language is so limited that perhaps we should permit such words as *feel* and *perceive* to exist in ways we do not fully understand. Perhaps trees "feel" and "perceive" via carbon transfer, chemical reaction, and evolutionary adaptation. Through both competition and community, through the passing on of genetic knowledge to kin via fungal networks. Allowing for the possibility that a forest "perceives" brings us, yet again, to restraint. It demands that we consider what it is to act, as feeling, perceiving beings, upon other feeling, perceiving beings.

Intending to pass Earthsea along to Aspen when she becomes an adult, we are working to keep our impact on the forest to a minimum, to always arrive as guests and as part of a wider network of relationships. In small ways, we hope to earn our keep. We are learning. We are listening.

Every summer, Andrew clears away the invasive knotweed that is growing further and further into the property from the roadside, crowding out native trees and shrubs. I clear leaf litter from a stretch of a tiny, hemlock-cooled creek so that we can fill buckets with water. If we ever rebuild the cabin, we plan to keep it to the same small footprint. We are making a few short, gentle trails that zig and zag up the easiest grade of the hillside, raking leaves away in pathways wide enough for our feet. But there is also something nice about, for the most part, not having any human-made trails here. We often follow deer trails, as the deer know how to find the best ways across and through. The predators, too, seem to know where the deer traverse the steep grade, and often along these trails we find bones and tufts of fur, though most of the evidence of these violent endings has been dispersed by the time we come across them. Removed by creatures who, bellies full, have flown or crawled or loped on to another site of death and decay. For this, too, is a truth of forests.

The land both guides us across itself and keeps us oriented. If we're ascending the hill, we're going north. The brook marks the eastern boundary. The road and the river across it are to the south. Walking with no trails allows us to wander and follow our curiosity, not as a deviation from a marked path but as the path itself.

And mostly, we try to simply let things be. We also try to simply *just be* when we are here. We are learning what is asked of us—and what is not. Neither of us is a forester or an ecologist. I won't pretend we know all that much about what we're seeing or observing on the land. But one thing I've now learned: when we find the young hemlocks growing beneath their parents, and among their kin, we are reminded of the importance of taking our time and of the immense, mysterious nature of time within a forest.

When we take cues from the trees, the terrain of mothering within a wider community becomes one of slowing down, of cooperation, of attentive presence. Giving Aspen and ourselves the time and space to explore, imagine, and play. Giving the forest time and space to do the work it knows how to do. This forest has its own story to tell. It's a story being told in ways both visible and invisible to our eyes, both audible and inaudible to our ears, both felt and unfelt by our bodies, both within and beyond the timescale of our own lives. It is being written in soil and creeks and the patterns of decaying leaves and needles. How do we listen to this story as best we can? And how do we, in turn, *arrive* to this place with the stories that we inevitably bring with us so that they are not imposed upon the land but woven through this community of beings?

We do not get to simply brush away the harm that was unleashed, is still being unleashed, in projects of control. Those legacies are alive in the world, still growing among the trees, and they affirm all of the ways that stories can become distorted and dangerous when we speak and act without true knowledge.

As he confronts the shadow he released into the world, Le Guin's Ged confronts the shadow part of himself. He learns that in order to vanquish this shadow, he must discover humility and surrender his belief that he can exercise control over the ancient forces at work in the world: "From that time forth he believed that the wise man is one who never sets himself apart from other living things, whether they have speech or not, and in later years he strove long to learn what can be learned, in silence, from the eyes of animals, the flight of birds, the great slow gestures of trees."

Part of our work at Earthsea is not only learning how to be with the forest but working to understand the layers of human stories that reside within the land. These, too, are the stories that Aspen will inherit. As her parents, and as caretakers of this land, we have to acknowledge and do our work to learn, confront, and then unravel the shadow narratives that have shaped this place and that live within us, too. These are practices of mind, body, heart, and spirit. These are practices of listening. We must be mindful of our intentions and how we enact them. We must work to be aware of the places those intentions come from.

Simard writes that when Mother Trees die, "they pass their wisdom to their kin, generation after generation, sharing the knowledge of what helps and what harms, who is friend or foe, and how to adapt and survive in an ever-changing landscape. It's what all parents do."

We must listen—to the trees, to the land, to the histories entwined there—before we speak and act. We must be willing to act on the principle of restraint.

CREATION STORY

How can we tend to and embody our imaginations in such a way that the land thrives? How can we bring the land into each of our own Earthseas—wherever those places are for each of us—so that our imaginations, too, thrive?

Ursula K. Le Guin's creation of the world of Earthsea began with a hand-drawn map of the islands of the archipelago, which, according to writer Julie Phillips, "offered her the freedom to imagine who might live there."

First a world, then its beings.

This is not so different from the arc of so many creation stories, including the theory of evolution. Deep speaks unto deep. First the raw winds and wide waters, then life emerges, finds land. Plant and animal beings arrive. Then come the humans and their capacity for imagining and creating infinite iterations of worlds. Eve eats the apple. The Abenaki emerge from the ash tree.

That human cultures since time immemorial have told origin stories—cosmogonies that tell us of the cosmos and beginnings—perhaps speaks to our inherent understanding that we once emerged and continue to emerge into a story that is always being written, always being read aloud to us, if we choose to look and listen. The story of an Earth in the throes of an ever-unfolding creation.

Creation stories, too, are the terrain of mothering. Beyond the literal creation of life within our bodies, our children are born into a place and its histories—geological, biological, ecological, and sociological. By inhabiting places, we and our children are participants in this creation story as it unfolds in our particular place.

And there is a word for how we inhabit, and how we read, our parts of this universal story: home.

In a 2002 lecture that became her essay "The Operating Instructions," Le Guin said: "Home, imagined, comes to be. It is real, realer than any other place, but you can't get to it unless your people show you how to imagine it—whoever your people are."

How do we foster a robust imagining of home as a community of fellow beings, brought together by forces largely beyond our control, with the ancient magic of creation humming in the soil? How can we nurture and support this web of life? If you were to imagine the map of your home in paper and ink, and all the lines of kinship extending from it, how might you then draw it?

We've given place-names to locations at Earthsea that have a special quality or feeling to them, most of them references to Le Guin's fictional Earthsea world: Roke Knoll, the North Reach, the Tombs, Lookfar. Others are names we came up with that describe a feature of the landscape: Three Oaks, Thousand Bend River, Window to the Sky, The Crossing. Andrew hired an artist friend of ours to draw a map of the land that features these names. The map is geographically accurate: it shows the correct property lines and the shape of the river and brook. But it also features drawings of bears and caves, distant mountains and dragonflies. It is a layering of land and story, place and imagination. So one informs the other, informs the other, and so on.

We map imagination onto the land. And the land maps itself onto our imaginations. We are beginning what we hope is a decades-long process of getting to know this land, grounded in the knowledge that the land's story came before us and will continue after. We are learning to weave, keeping ourselves open to the storied moments when the boundaries between land and imagination dissolve. And certainly, Aspen will notice such moments far more often than we will.

In the same 2002 talk, Le Guin said: "A child who doesn't know where the center is—where home is, what home is—that child is in a very bad way." As parents, we hope to give Aspen one possible imagining of home here at Earthsea: a place that she belongs to but does not own; that she acts in concert with but only very selectively upon; that she can grow up with and that will grow beautifully beyond her.

It will be a good few years before we introduce Aspen to Le Guin's *Earthsea* series and the stories of Ged and his life in the archipelago. Then, the three of us will sit down in the last of the daylight and read the adventures aloud, evening by evening.

Interestingly, this means that, for the moment, Earthsea is not a book for Aspen but a real place. Tolkien came first for me, and then the imprint of the hawthorn trees. For Aspen, perhaps it will be reversed. Earthsea, first, will be the place where we make bunny houses (her preferred alternative to fairy houses) out of fallen twigs and leaves. The place where she helps Andrew tend the fire. Where she says hello to the trees and kicks her legs in the river as we hold her afloat. Where she sleeps poorly—but oh so enthusiastically!—in the tent after making us imagined bowls of "night night soup," served atop books. The place where, as we leave, she says "Goodbye, Earthsea! Come back soon!" And on the way back to Maine she asks, repeatedly, "Which way is Earthsea?" as if wanting to remain oriented.

I wonder what it will be like for her: for the rooted, "real," forested place to come first, and then the imagined world that inspired it. We will have to wait for her to tell and embody that particular story.

But then, the human imagination is a bit like a tree in a forest, isn't it? It exists not only in itself but within an ecosystem of communal knowing, history, and within a web of stories that whisper to and shape each other, that together evoke shared experiences of being.

"And the world changes wholly," writes Le Guin, "when a man holds in his hand the fruit of that tree, whose roots are deeper than the forest."

TREE SEED

It's near the end of April, and I'm walking with Andrew and Aspen on the Bradbury-Pineland Corridor Trail in Pownal, Maine. It's a gently hilly, shady loop that crosses a river and winds through a forest that hums with a chorus of birds. We usually turn right at the first fork in the trail because we sometimes see a pair of pileated woodpeckers at work in a small island of trees that intersects a wide meadow, a grassy expanse that we cross before the path winds into the forest.

The last time we were here was nearly a year prior, and I was nearly full-term, Aspen kicking and turning in my belly as I panted up even the shallowest inclines. At that time, the meadow was full of shrubs and short trees, many of which had fluorescent pink flagging tied to their branches with the word *invasive* scribbled in black Sharpie. The meadow had grass, too, but it was clear that the grass was losing ground.

This spring, Aspen is seven months old and riding in a carrier on Andrew's back, fighting the sleep tugging at her eyelids, insistent on taking in her new surroundings.

These surroundings have changed since we last saw them: all of the shrubs and trees are gone from the meadow. In their place is a uniform layer of new, vibrantly green grass, just an inch tall, climbing up into the daylight from charred, blackened soil.

"This was a prescribed burn!" I say, excited because I've been researching the use of fire as a land management tool in the prairies of the Great Plains and didn't expect to see evidence of a controlled burn here in southern Maine. But the signs of a planned fire are all right here at my feet: the clean line of the firebreak around the perimeter of the new growth; the absence of the encroaching woody plants; the plant and leaf litter cleared from the ground; the grass now blanketing every square inch.

The meadow is being returned to a meadow.

The image of all that new grass stays with me over the ensuing days, and though I want my mind to stay focused on the pollinators that will return or the redtail hawks that will circle above looking for rabbits and mice, I inevitably find it wandering to the meadow's edge, to the firebreak: the line that has the blackened, rich soil on one side and the road, and homes, and snaking interstate on the other. That border between an act of restoration and the status quo.

A few weeks later, we attend our local city council meeting, held—like all meetings in this pandemic moment—over Zoom. The council is considering the adoption of a tree ordinance, which would largely prohibit cutting down any tree in the city limits that has a diameter of ten inches or greater. Andrew and his fifth-grade students have prepared a presentation for council members, having spent several months researching the benefits of urban trees and interviewing local conservationists—facts and testimonies which they include in a short video. After their presentation, each of them takes a turn speaking during the public comment period.

One student, Miles, has technical difficulties when it's his turn. He looks panicked when the city manager tells him that his sound isn't coming through. Miles holds up one finger to the camera, indicating he needs a minute. The councillors smile. Miles exits the frame, leaving us to view a puppy yawning on the couch in his living room. He returns after a few seconds, his mother's hand in the frame for a moment, adjusting his newly fitted headset and microphone.

At the end of his short speech, he reads a haiku he'd written:

Grab that tree seed now
Plant the seed in the moist soil
You just saved the world

A local developer speaks shortly after. "Look," he says, "I love trees." But he goes on to outline all of the ways that this ordinance would hinder development, place an undue hardship on homeowners and businesses, and get in the way of affordable housing ("affordable housing" was a phrase often used at the time to get building permits, even though the subsequent houses and condos were often anything but). It's an argument repeated by many callers over the next hour: "I love trees, but. . . ."

But the burden of protecting them is too inconvenient. But they would result in too much lost income.

Many people speak in favor of the ordinance, too. But as citizen after citizen speaks, I can't help but think how surreal it is that the fate of thousands of trees in our city is being left to a bureaucratic process in which trees are not trees at all but itemized components of a human landscape to be put in or taken out accordingly. An estimated twenty-three acres of Maine forest is converted to other uses every day. I can't help but think: even if this ordinance passes, what about all the trees beyond the city limits?

My mind wanders to the forest's edge: trees on one side, a bulldozer on the other.

This is how much of the work of conservation is done in our country: patchwork projects that restore land or maintain natural resources where such measures have been delineated and permitted. A municipality can save some of its larger trees within the bounds of the city. A controlled burn can restore a few acres of grass. Our society can curb its hunger in bite-size pieces—protecting some woodlands, some waterways, some wetlands—as long as much of the rest remains available for our use. Conservation is the exception, not the rule.

I want to see new rules enacted in the world my daughter will inherit. I often feel at a loss as to how to do this.

Fifth-grade Miles says something else in his comments that stays with me, that stuns me: "Trees are the flowing balance of life on this inhabited spherical ecosystem in the midst of the universe. Knowing this, I'd want to propose a tree ordinance on the world so that, many millennia from when I pass, people are still living and enjoying the shade that the trees give."

Hearing this, my mind wanders to its own edge. I come up against the limits in my imagination. I come to the border between the present and a future that I can't conceive of. I come to the darkness that is arriving in our wake, that is already here.

I peer over that edge and am surprised to hear Aspen's voice and Miles's voice and surprised to find that something like trust, something like love, flickers there in the dark.

* * *

The grassland ecosystems of the Great Plains evolved with—depended upon—fire. Prairies are wildernesses that would not exist without fire's powerful disturbance.

Here's what I love about wildfire: over the last eleven thousand years, some of the prairie fires were started by lightning, but others were started intentionally by Indigenous people who understood fire's regenerative power on the landscape. Human participation helped to prevent the prairies becoming crowded out by trees, helped to keep their biodiversity intact.

This fact counters a definition of wilderness that still stubbornly roots in my consciousness: that wilderness is only pristine when humans are absent. For prairies are wildernesses that depend upon human participation. Even now, with 96 percent of the tallgrass prairie lost to the plow, the small fraction that still exists relies on human intervention. When the relationship between human and grassland is well understood, humans become agents of biodiversity: we become a function of wilderness.

Here we come to another edge, another boundary: when wielded with understanding, fire is restorative; when misunderstood and misapplied, fire is monstrous. In California, where most ecosystems are fire-adapted, the widespread suppression of fire from the landscape—even the suppression of prescribed burns set with an understanding of conditions, seasons, and timing—has meant that when fires start, they rage. They spin out of control, consuming everything in their path: trees, homes, lives, entire communities.

There are no clean edges to such wildfires, no firebreaks—just smoke, loss, fear.

✻ ✻ ✻

I think what has stayed with me about what Miles said is that it invites us into a space that is both narrowly delineated and utterly grand: engage in the simple act of planting a tree; allow yourself to imagine that a thousand years from now one of your descendants will pause under the shade of a descendant of that tree.

Many would likely call this naive. I'm inclined to think that what is naive is thinking that we could ever do anything *other* than this; thinking that it is enough to permit conservation and restoration only to the extent that it allows us to maintain our lifestyles; thinking that we can always turn a blind eye to the harm those lifestyles inflict on human and nonhuman communities.

Grab that tree seed now.

May those trees thrive.

May those restorative fires burn.

May we learn to see, grow, and imagine beyond our edges.

PART V

EDGE WORK
Traversing Salt Marshes

It is the elusiveness of that meaning that haunts us, that sends us again and again into the natural world where the key to the riddle is hidden. It sends us back to the edge of the sea...

—Rachel Carson, *The Edge of the Sea*

VULNERABLE NEST

There was a small nature preserve near our former house in South Portland made up of mature birch and hemlock trees and a two-acre pond filled with native cattails. Andrew and I walked there weekly after the pandemic started and lockdowns began; our usual trails had grown overcrowded. Though the preserve was less than a quarter mile from a trafficked road, and there were a number of houses that abutted the boundary, it remained a quiet place.

We brought binoculars and watched the black-capped chickadees chattering in the scrub brush and the downy woodpecker at work on the trunk of a tree. We hardly ever came across any humans on this trail, which extended just a third of a mile, the pond on one side, woods on the other.

Several weeks into these walks, we began a habit of turning off the trail to step out onto a narrow peninsula that extended twenty feet into the pond. It was barely eight feet wide, built of spongy moss and damp grass. To get to the far end, we had to crouch or crawl beneath the young trees and bushes that had taken root on this strip of land.

There, at the cusp of land and water, was an oasis. The cattails grew free from the encroachment of invasive phragmites and knotweed that were elsewhere crowding into wetlands and marshes. Red-winged blackbirds swayed on reeds, and turtles poked their heads above the surface. Mallards plunged their heads into the submerged weeds.

We were away from the news and out of view of the nearby houses. If the sky was clear, I rolled up the bottom of my shirt and turned my rounding belly to face the sun. I took deep, clean breaths.

One day, we saw another couple across the water. We would see them daily at the preserve from then on. We kept our six-plus feet of advised social distance, and they kept theirs. All of us seemed to prefer silence.

They were Canada geese.

* * *

One late evening, a warm sun set over the water. One of the geese was directly across from the peninsula, seated atop a small mound of grass and reeds, inches above the water. The early shapes of fiddleheads curled out of the ground around her. Behind her was a shelter of reeds and tall golden grasses.

She turned slowly in place, adjusting her stance and stretching her wings along her back. She sat and rocked herself a couple of times side to side and then used her beak to arrange bits of down, tucking it carefully around her copper body.

I instinctively put my hand to my belly.

She, too, was going to be a mother.

The next night, I felt my child move for the first time, subtle and fluttering.

* * *

One morning, it was raining lightly, and the surface of the pond was soft with movement. The goose sat on her nest, her long neck turned, her beak tucked into her back feathers. The gander stood in the shallows around the reeds, thirty yards away.

I'd been reading: Mothers generally begin to feel the fetus move between eighteen and twenty weeks, indistinct flutterings. Soon I would feel them all the time, and Andrew would be able to feel them too.

I'd also been reading: A Canada goose makes her nest atop a slightly raised mound into which she makes a bowl-shaped depression. She will be near a water source, with an unobstructed view of what is around her. She will line the nest with cattail, grass, reeds, and down that she plucks from her own breast. She will lay between five and twelve eggs over the course of as many days and then incubate them for four weeks. The gander will always be nearby, keeping watch. They'll defend the nest together, if need be.

❊ ❊ ❊

In those months that the pandemic shrunk everyone's world, as a new world bloomed inside of me, I kept my head above water, stayed calm, found things to smile about. I tried to keep the anxiety at bay by taking deep breaths, by limiting the news, by leaving the window open as the cold rain came down with a steady thrum that made our home feel like a cocoon.

I didn't feel that I had much of a choice. My pregnancy books told me that a fetus could experience some echo of their mother's stress and worry. I wondered if this was true, and then, like so many of my thoughts that inevitably drifted to include this other being growing within my body, I thought that even the *possibility* of its truth meant I should take heed. And since I had the luxury of finding ways to keep calm—I was not sick, I had a home, plenty of food—I kept trying to quell my fear.

It's not that I was in denial. I don't think it was ignorance. It was more like an ongoing practice of joyfully inhabiting a shrinking world: my home, my husband, a growing baby, and the edge of that peninsula where I had a view of the only other mother that I could visit, sit with in the middle of a global pandemic.

At the pond one afternoon, three great blue herons flew overhead, long necks bent to their chests, wings steady. I'd never seen three together before, and this small, airborne community seemed a good omen. Below them, the goose was quiet and alone and on her nest, as always.

I wrote in my journal: *How small her world is! How gracefully she inhabits it!*

∗ ∗ ∗

I wanted to see my mother and my friends, show them how my belly had grown.

I learned that the number of confirmed novel coronavirus cases in the United States had reached nearly half a million (a number which is almost laughably small now that you are reading this . . . except who could laugh?)

Ahead of my next prenatal appointment: the nurse called and told me to come in, this time, with a mask. They would take my temperature in the lobby. Mothers around the world were giving birth alone, without loved ones by their sides.

Several weeks later: heavy rain turned to heavy snow as the sun sank into a dull sky. There was an inch of icy white on the ground by the time I went to bed, and it was still coming down fast. I thought of her there without shelter in the dark, snow collecting on her feathered back.

∗ ∗ ∗

The storm passed. There was a paper-thin skim of ice over the pond in the places that had yet to meet the rising sun. The goose had her neck stretched in front of her, prone on the ground. Her right eye was unblinking in the lens of my binoculars. The gander was nowhere in sight.

I handed the binoculars to Andrew. "It doesn't look good," he said, and a knot tightened in my stomach. But then she raised her head and looked around, tucked her beak into her back feathers. Stayed put.

∗ ∗ ∗

A few days later, I passed the gnarled, old white pine at the foot of the peninsula and crawled along the damp ground, arrived again at the meeting of land and water. Here I sat, hands on either side of my stomach, this growing edge between womb and world, and watched her, thirty feet away.

Both of us in the sun. Both of us quiet. Both doing our needed work, in needed solitude.

"How was she?" Andrew asked later as I hung my jacket and binoculars on two hooks by the door, removed my shoes, and stepped into the warm kitchen.

"She was good," I say. "Content."

* * *

Several weeks into the third trimester of my pregnancy, the goose's nest failed.

The first time I saw that she was not sitting on the nest, I rejoiced, assuming that the eggs had hatched, and she and her chicks were tucked away somewhere in the reeds. The next day, I saw her and the gander swimming alone. Maybe they'd temporarily left the goslings somewhere safe? But when I looked toward the nest with my binoculars, I could make out the white curve of an egg a meter from the nest. It had rolled down to the water's edge and was alone, untended, unhatched. I knelt in the grass and cried.

I cried for the goose and her eggs, but I cried, too, for the weight of things that don't go the way they should; for all of the lives that come into this world carrying more of that weight than they ought to and that exist in a more dangerous world than the one my daughter will because of it; for our failure to share and ease that burden or to make this world safer for all; and for the sometimes unbearable uncertainty that claims so much, even the quiet eggs in a goose's nest.

A week later, I rose early and went to sit on a damp bench beneath the big elm tree at Pleasant Hill Preserve in Scarborough. At the headwaters of the Spurwink River, the preserve is part of a wildlife corridor that connects a long band of tidal salt marsh, forming a bridge between the Scarborough Marsh and the Rachel Carson National Wildlife Refuge. That morning was overcast and misting, and the meadow beyond the tree was full of birds: swifts, song sparrows, goldfinches, red-winged blackbirds. The air smelled soft, of recent rain and the marsh and the last wafts of the multiflora rose, which had almost finished blooming. I sat as still and quietly as I could, wondering if the child growing in my belly, still then without a name, could hear the birds singing. I imagined the day when I would get to bring her to see them and smell the meadow, how I would place her small fingers on the ridged leaves of the elm.

She was close to sixteen inches long and weighed up to four pounds. She was most active in the evenings, kicking much faster and stronger than I had imagined possible.

We had just finished a birthing class that temporarily quelled most of my anxieties about labor. We learned how to recognize early contractions, how to breathe, what to expect at home and in the hospital, what would happen right after the birth. Most helpful for me was the reassurance that my body would know what to do when the time came—and so would my child. That surprised me again and again throughout my pregnancy: that my body and child knew exactly what to do. My growing belly, her stretches and kicks, the sound of her heartbeat at every appointment—all felt like blessings that occurred without any active doing on my part. I could only marvel.

Everyone I knew who had gone through labor prepared me for the possibility of the unexpected occurring in the midst of it all. That was all right. Perhaps it was only the comfort of ignorance, but I didn't feel afraid of the uncertainty of birth. Most often what I imagined was not the birth itself but the long-awaited moment when they would place my child on my chest and our hearts would beat side by side, and I would get to touch and hold her.

But the image of that goose egg alone by the water, of that untended nest, stayed in my mind's eye. Within the egg was a nearly hatched chick. Within the egg was all that I would not be able to control once my daughter was in the world.

The apple trees, whose early buds I held in the palm of my hand in the snow in late February, never bloomed, never displayed their pink-white flowers. Too many late frosts, and so no apples would grow in our yard that season. But the trees nonetheless came to be full-leafed and green and growing taller, and there was next year to look forward to. *The Earth is resilient*, I told myself. *It knows how to mend.*

Then a close family friend died. He fell from a ladder at his tree farm in Oklahoma and hurt his back. His wife brought him to the hospital and left him seated in a chair while she parked the car, and when she came back, minutes later, he had died of a heart attack. Just like that, in the time it takes to park a car.

As my pregnancy progressed, I returned again and again to a line from a sermon that a friend of mine gave to her Unitarian Universalist congregation. She was speaking about how, when her own daughter—now a young woman—was so small and so new, she would hold her and think, "This is as safe as I will get to keep you."

In those final weeks of pregnancy, I think this was the real root of my fear in imagining the world my daughter would come into: that this was as safe as I would get to keep her, there in my womb, where she was warm and protected.

Andrew and I had daily conversations about how to raise a child who watches geese and plants seeds and eats apples off the tree and listens to birds. Who respects and holds space for others who are different from her. We wondered about how to help her be aware of and address the privilege of white skin as we continue to educate ourselves about our own privilege and complicity. We talked about how to raise her to listen, especially to those whose voices have routinely been silenced or dismissed, and the richness that listening brings.

When I started to feel fear creeping in—when I thought about what it would mean to labor in a face mask, to quarantine for several weeks after the birth, without visits from our parents and other family members, and from there to navigate a pandemic with an infant; when I smelled the emissions from the oil tanks up the road from a company that routinely flouted EPA emissions caps; when I read reports on how quickly the Gulf of Maine was warming, faster than almost any ocean water in the world— then I tried to remember that the goldfinch that morning at Pleasant Hill Preserve knew just where to land on a tall blade of grass so that the grass bent *just so*, just enough to hold his weight a few inches above the ground. And how that bright little bird stayed balanced on the grass for a long moment, and when he departed, the grass righted itself again and the bird was gone in a flash of yellow in the mist.

I tried to remember that my body would know what to do to bring my daughter into the world. The goldfinch knew what to do. And the goose and the apple tree. And there are so many in the world who know to listen deeply, who are working to heal wounds. Who gracefully inhabit that narrow edge: a rooted awe on one side, the painful unknown on the other.

POROUS BOUNDARIES

From the moment I learned I was pregnant, I began losing track of the boundaries of my body. My pregnant body had a growing edge. I'm taller than average, with a wide frame, and my body, with child, wanted to expand. It did so effortlessly and inevitably, the way gravity draws a dropped orange.

It was a wonderful feeling, expansiveness. A reaching out. Not just my belly, but every part of me. I grew out of my regular clothes and then most of my maternity clothes. My wedding ring. Then the larger, fake wedding ring. Then my shoes. Even my thoughts puffed out of my mind and floated away like soft clouds you could sweep a hand through. I stopped trying to contain any of it.

My daughter, enwombed, was encased in a saltwater ecosystem. "And as life itself began in the sea, so each of us begins his individual life in a miniature ocean within his mother's womb," writes Rachel Carson in *The Sea Around Us*. I like to think that my spreading body then was like the waxing tide, a running edge of ocean.

There was both comfort and fear in knowing that the growth would be finite, that it had a limit. My body, and my child's within me, knew that the time would come to make the transition. She would make her entry from the water to air, my belly would wane, and we would navigate a new, redefined boundary

between mother and child. Andrew and I would witness the shifting relationships at work between child and world.

After Aspen's birth, I thought that I would begin a slow
return to my individuality and come back into the solid bounds
of myself. But, approaching three years with Aspen, I have only
grown increasingly porous.

Porousness is theoretically beautiful and practically uncomfortable. Sometimes I am drowning in vulnerability. My love for
my daughter is often tightly wrapped around a suffocating fear.
My individuality can feel like a knitted sweater with one loose
thread tied round Aspen's ankle as she sprints away and unravels
me. Sometimes I weep at my inability to contain any of it still.

And then there is the almost unfathomable: that this child,
this now two-year-old girl is coming into a world that, no matter
what I do, I cannot guarantee will be okay. Not far from our front
door, the ocean is rising, and the maps are changing. Where can
we look for models and teachers of navigation?

I was longing to know more about the shifting border
between land and sea and about ecological edge-places when
I picked up Rachel Carson's *The Edge of the Sea*. And there was
my invitation, just several pages in. "It is the elusiveness of that
meaning that haunts us, that sends us again and again into the
natural world where the key to the riddle is hidden," Carson
writes. "It sends us back to the edge of the sea, where the drama
of life played its first scene on earth and perhaps even its prelude; where the forces of evolution are at work today, as they have
been since the appearance of what we know as life; and where the
spectacle of living creatures faced by the cosmic realities of their
world is crystal clear."

Two and a half years into motherhood, I am haunted by
that elusiveness of meaning. So often, I still want resolution. A
few weeks ago, I stopped looking for recent articles about North
Atlantic right whales, because they are still dying, and it became

too much. I started reading science fiction at night, immersing myself in worlds far away until I could barely keep my eyes open and would fall straight to sleep, because I wanted to stop lying in the dark while shadows crept across the walls.

I wanted assurances. The world kept reminding me that there are none.

Which is to say: I am a mother in a time of rising seas.

Which is to say: motherhood necessitates the acceptance of endless transformation.

Which is to say: Mother-work is edge work. It must be done in and from a liminal, transitional, shifting, uncertain, utterly porous space. Victor Turner wrote of the "autonomy of the liminal": being in a liminal state, he said, relentlessly threatens us but is also the only path forward.

Mothering through ecological crisis is not the work of building walls and barriers. It is the work of tearing them down.

Mothering is a tidal practice.

And so I've come, at last, to willingly place my feet at the edge of certainty, at the edge of guarantee. I've come to the place I will have to step beyond in order to learn how to exist, how to mother, within transformation and change, not against it.

BETWEEN THE TIDES

The tide is out when we arrive at a sheltered cove on the south-western end of Southport Island, tucked along a tidal saltwater river called the Sheepscot. If you look at a map of Maine, the coast from Portland to Eastport is the place where the land appears to drip and run off of the mainland and into the sea like thick, wet paint running down canvas: islands and peninsulas with snaking estuaries, smiling bays, and pooling coves between them.

We have come to stay at Silverledges, purchased by Rachel Carson in 1952. She had a cottage built and spent some of her most contented summers here. Aspen is two-and-a-half years old, and it's past time for her nap, but the blue cottage with white trim infuses her with an almost frantic energy, and she runs back and forth across the large rectangular room that includes the living and dining areas, peeking into the bedrooms that branch off. She repeatedly confirms with us that we'll be here a while. "We get to stay here *two days* and not even go home, Mom!" She arranges her stuffed animals—a bunny in red pajamas, a dinosaur puppet, a fox that is really a deer—on the bench in the living room. Andrew and I pull back curtains and open the shades. Amber slants of sun fall into the house from the western-facing bay window that looks out over the bright sea. A simple space is revealed: wood paneled walls and ceilings, wicker furniture with faded cushions, a large fireplace, full bookshelves, a table lamp affixed with wooden cups that are filled with shells and sea glass.

I've come here to Rachel Carson's summer home because in my striving for mothering-beyond-biological-kinship, I have come up against a wall. It's a wall built of fear and despair, of self-doubt, and of questions I know I cannot answer but am trying to force answers to. Perhaps worst of all, it's a wall built of apathy, in the form of the small, poisonous thought that whispers in my ear: *Why bother? Wouldn't it be easier to turn away?* That question is the cement holding this wall together. I am seeking a way to chip through it.

I've come to Silverledges to learn from Rachel Carson, who was not a biological mother and who dedicated herself to the flourishing of life—a dedication that is, by definition, wall-destroying.

Flourishing: deep, vigorous growth. Thriving. To orient oneself toward the flourishing of life—human and more-than-human life—is to acknowledge that those lives exist and have inherent value, that we are directly and indirectly connected to those lives and have some responsibility to them, and that we are therefore called upon to act on that responsibility not for our own benefit but because it is the moral thing to do.

The flourishing of life, importantly, is not an idea rooted in capitalism, which is oriented toward the limitless accumulation of profit and the forward, linear trajectory of human progress. Neither is the flourishing of life an idea rooted in patriarchy, which is oriented toward structures of power and hierarchy and often maintained through physical, psychological, and ecological violence. It is not an idea bound by gender, which is oriented toward sharp delineations of identity, aspects of which are, in turn, rooted in both capitalism and patriarchy. No, the flourishing of life operates outside of those ideologies at the same time that it dismantles them. To work toward mutual thriving is to remember that the dominant ideologies of our time are just that: ideas, seemingly omnipresent but thin as air. While those ideas are presently affecting every being on this planet, they have no hold, no sway over the essence, the inherent *beingness*, of our companion kin. Human systems will not change the wild nature of the right whale, even if they pollute and dissect its habitat. To orient toward the flourishing of life, then, is to begin to peel away those ideologies from ourselves. Rachel Carson was one of many whose work and words sought something different, sought to tear down walls.

Carson is best—often exclusively—known for *Silent Spring*, the work that helped launch the modern environmental movement, contributed to the founding of the EPA, and drew public alarm at the spread of chemicals being indiscriminately and widely released into the environment. Most notable of these was DDT, an insecticide that was decimating bird populations, including bald eagles, osprey, and brown pelicans, through bioaccumulation in the food chain that, in birds, caused reproductive failure through eggshell thinning. DDT also found its way into the bodies of human beings, including in breast milk, where it was then off-loaded to nursing infants. Possible side effects of human exposure to DDT include cancer, effects on reproduction, changes in menstrual cycles, "uterine alterations," and how long it takes to conceive a child. Even though DDT was banned in the United States in 1972, three decades later, the CDC found detectable amounts of DDE—a metabolite of DDT—present in a majority of blood samples collected in the United States.

As Rachel Carson's great-nephew Roger tells me when I speak with him over the phone after we've arranged our visit to Silverledges, *Silent Spring*'s legacy has often been equated with the ban on DDT, or more broadly with concerns about pesticides. But "that's kind of missing the point of the book," he says. "I've always felt the book served as a specific example of a much larger point. That point was in her mind all the time."

From speaking to Roger and from reading Carson's books, essays, and posthumously published letters, I take that point to be that she was driven by a deeply ingrained, deeply felt sense of responsibility to the beings she came to love and care for. She embodied an expansive, bold, uncompromising belief in the exquisite mystery of life, in all its myriad, crawling, swirling, patient, interconnected forms. Through this embodiment, she undertook a radical sort of mothering.

Rachel Carson saw different ways of being and different ways of knowing at work in the world and saw them to be worthy of our attention. She was willing to make sacrifices: not because she was a woman, but because she took the time to see inherent worth in the lives of others and saw that self-evident worth was in need of defending. Her success in bringing this Earth-consciousness and the ways human beings were wreaking havoc on the planet into the public eye came at a price. *Silent Spring* pitted her against the petrochemical industry (and they came at her, hard). It had her testifying in front of Congress, even though her life was nearly at its end, the breast cancer hard at work against her ailing body.

What I take Roger to mean is that beyond Carson's environmental activism was a persistent sense of wonder and unquenchable curiosity. Both of these are present throughout her sea trilogy: *Under a Sea-Wind, The Sea Around Us,* and *The Edge of the Sea.* All are sharply focused, meticulously researched, carefully articulated works. All of them are also brimming with awe.

Carson's fascination with the ocean is what brought her to revel in the tide pools here on the coast of Maine. In *Always, Rachel,* the compiled collection of letters written between Carson and Dorothy Freeman, an entry from Carson on February 3, 1955—written while she would have been writing *The Edge of the Sea* from this cottage—begins: "Darling, Two small paragraphs only, before I go back to my barnacles."

I wonder what has remained here in the cottage since the last time Carson was here, sixty years ago. I imagine her at this window, watching the tides ebb and flow on the beach below. Carson's written words transfer her palpable marveling to the reader, and that awe becomes something like an inheritance: something you feel responsible to pay forward. Creatures you have never imagined become profoundly interesting, because she has brought them to life for you. The swaying kelp forests. The periwinkles "grazing on the intertidal rocks."

This making of space for expressions of awe is a practice of mothering, too. In *The Sense of Wonder* Carson writes about ways of being outdoors with children, based on outings with Roger. Carson was approaching her fiftieth birthday when five-year-old Roger's mother died of pneumonia, and Carson adopted him as her son. The two would have just seven years together before Roger lost his adopted mother, too. As the year was preparing to turn from 1963 to 1964, as *Silent Spring* was rising in the public consciousness, and as she was agonizing over Roger's future without her, she was longing, too, to return here to the coast of the Sheepscot. But time was against her as the cancer spread. She would not come here again until Dorothy scattered her ashes.

Carson felt a deep love and concern for the human and more-than-human life that she encountered. She treated the beings around her with care, curiosity, and sustained attention. She cared for her family members, even when it took away from her time to write and research. And she wrote and researched on behalf of birds and minuscule sea creatures and human communities, even when, at the end of her life, her body was failing her.

Those are the acts of mothering I mean: embodied in the person who inhabits a sensory world, who seeks to be *a part of* rather than *apart from*, and then, crucially, takes the generous time to kneel down beside us, whatever age we are, and say, "Look here, do you see how wonderful this is?"

Roger still comes here every summer with his wife Wendy. They rent the cottage out on weekends when they can't be here to help pay for upkeep and taxes. The colorful set of sci-fi novels lining the shelves of one of the bedrooms is, I suspect, his. And he and Wendy certainly are the ones who left on a side table the spiral-bound *Tide Log* that informs us that the tide was lowest two hours ago.

I head outside and down the short pathway that is bordered by bayberry scrub and red spruce trees, the star flowers blooming, the scent of brine and salt on the air. I step carefully down steep, slanting slabs of granite and gabbro that lead to the meeting place of land and sea. Here, the Sheepscot is flowing inland on the tide, rising up from Sheepscot Bay, beyond which is the Gulf of Maine and the Atlantic Ocean. The sea is ever-churning in and through such delineations.

I've come here, in part, to get a better sense of Carson's embodiment of mothering. But I've also come to sit with her tide pools, to learn more about edges. I've come to suspect that this—the edge of land and sea—is the place where the walls come down.

The beings who inhabit this edge make a home in a porous space. There is endless transformation in the littoral zone between high and low tides. It is a thin strip of landscape that alternates between inundation and exposure as water rises and falls twice daily. Within this narrow, fluid edge, forms of life and pathways of movement are possible that are not possible elsewhere. What do the plants and creatures of these liminal ecosystems have to teach us? What can we learn of resiliency? Of adaptation? Of loss? Of change?

The New England landscape still seizes me with bursts of wonder. Just as snow and ice in winter mean the ability to move atop water, low tide means walking on what was, and will soon again be, the seafloor. High tide is several hours away. The many rounded stones that sit at this shoreline, few of them taller than my calf, are hidden beneath thick drapes of black seaweed. I look closer and see that it is black and dry only where exposed to the sun. Lifting one frond, I see and smell that the seaweed below is still green, wet, slimy, immersed in saltwater. Where the stones are submerged on the seaward edge, the seaweed is upright and swaying, thickening the movement of the water, a submerged forest.

Two long spits of rock extend into the sea on either side of the little cove. Between them, there is a concave sweep of pink-gold made up of millions of empty periwinkle shells intermixed with coarse sand, their sheen dulled by the sun. The shells crunch and shift underfoot as I walk along the shore. Oblong pools of left-behind seawater magnify purple fans of sea-leaf no bigger than my pinky; bright red algae; the bleached jewels of barnacles. Common terns, tireless little birds, are fishing a dozen yards away. They chirp and whir, hover then spiral down, plunge into the water, white wings angled into finely drawn w's, orange beaks thrown spears. They reemerge with their catches, shake themselves off midair, repeat. Their colony must be nearby, eggs soon in the nests. A goldfinch sings somewhere in the spruce trees behind me.

In one tide pool, I pick up a white rectangle no bigger than my thumbnail and several millimeters thick. At first, I think it's a piece of plastic because its corners are so smooth and square. But it's a broken piece of shell. I look at it through the jeweler's loupe I carry with me. Magnified, it has the delicacy of lace. There are four columns running vertically across its face, with dozens of tiny holes between each of them. The columns are composed of raised circles that look like the tops of spiraled seashells. I cannot fathom what creature or creatures made this. It is inscribed with a language I do not know.

I came here to Silverledges to begin my exploration of what is possible at the edge, and to peer at what is held within fluid boundaries.

I came to the tides to ask: what can be learned from the beings who inhabit the edge—the creatures who do not resist the ebb and flow of water but exist as part of it, who live because of it?

The tide is coming in. Soon these tide pools, these shells, this sand, will be underwater, and the sea will reconfigure the patterns before revealing them again.

The daily ebb and flow of the ocean is still present here at Silverledges, just as it was more than a half century ago, when Rachel Carson would carry down a mattress and lie still, with a pair of binoculars set to her eyes, watching birds for hours, perhaps ancestors of the terns that are fishing here now, as Roger ran along the beach.

But there are new stories to be read in this meeting of land and sea.

Our lifetimes, and those of generations to come, exist in this moment of a prolonged incoming tide, a long arc of changing patterns, thousands of years of inundation.

The boundaries between land and sea are changing. "We live in an age of rising seas," Carson wrote in *The Sea Around Us*, published in 1951. Others knew that this and other changes to the oceans and land were happening, too, but did not yet fully know what they meant. Systematic measurements of rising CO_2 in the atmosphere would not begin for another eight years. There was not yet an understanding that the ongoing influx of seawater was not solely due to geologic or cosmic forces beyond our control, but, in fact, we had become one of the forces that was pulling the water further onto the shore.

What can be learned from these shifting lines? What can be witnessed?

The elusiveness of meaning "sends us back to the edge of the sea," Carson wrote, "where the spectacle of living creatures faced by the cosmic realities of their world is crystal clear."

It is to the boundaries, to the edge-places, that we must go to get a clear view of the realities that are at work in the world right now.

So it is with the types of stories we need now: edge-stories. Wild stories. Myths that come from and hold space in the margins. Stories where the human and nonhuman worlds can be fluid. Stories that make us porous. Stories that stir us up and take down what we have built between the world and ourselves.

I can hear Aspen and Andrew up on the deck. I find a periwinkle shell, smooth and white. A tiny, abandoned shelter, the snail that once lived here now gone. I'll bring it up for Aspen to see.

From Silverledges, I'll be journeying to several of the East Coast's great salt marshes: ecosystems that are mediated by the tide, that have evolved because of the conditions that exist at that vulnerable, changing interface between land and water. In Maine and in Louisiana, I'll venture further into that fluctuating edge, to the place where the water is advancing.

For now, I am going to rejoin my family. While we're here at Carson's cottage, Aspen will repeatedly confuse the word *cottage* with *village*. "Let's go back to our village now," she'll say when we are out on a walk, at the local market, or grabbing dinner.

We'll come down here together to peer at all of the life that exists between the high and low tides—not one home, but many.

A village indeed.

EDGE EROSION

It's the day after the summer solstice, and the dock at Wells Harbor is vibrating with summer energy. A man in khaki shorts is hosing down a charter fishing boat in much the same motion as a mother is spraying her daughter with sunscreen. Floppy-hatted tourists make their way to the beach.

I meet Rachel Stearns, a biological science technician for the Rachel Carson National Wildlife Refuge, at the mouth of the Webhannet River. The refuge runs along fifty miles of Maine's southern coast, from Kittery to Scarborough, and includes roughly three thousand acres of tidal salt marsh. Rachel is close to my age with a frizz of curly brown hair sticking out from beneath her hat and the unselfconscious authority of someone who has been doing her job well for many a field season. She and an intern, Sam, are both dressed the way I suddenly wish I were: long-sleeve, high-necked shirts for sun and bug protection; fast-drying pants; tall wading boots. I'm wearing some of Andrew's old hiking pants with a fly zipper that keeps falling down and rain boots that barely reach my ankle and have at least one major leak.

I join the two of them aboard a small, open boat. We motor carefully along the shallows of low tide. Today we'll be measuring salt marsh edge erosion.

The questions I'm holding with me: What does a healthy salt marsh look like? What are the complex functions of such ecological margins? If liminal ecosystems can teach us about inhabiting and navigating constant change, if they can reveal new ways of embracing our wild edges as mothers, then what do the integrity and resilience of such edges look like? And, conversely, what happens if these in-between places erode, vanish, into the sea?

* * *

Tidal salt marshes are among the most productive of Earth's ecosystems, frequently cited alongside coral reefs and tropical forests. They are meadows of salt-adapted grasses that smell sweet and briny in hot sun, set above the sea on platforms of peat. In the salt marsh meadows of New England, saltmarsh sparrows lay their eggs in grass-woven nests. Indigenous peoples—among them members of the tribes of the Wabanaki Confederacy in Maine—gather sweetgrass along the marshes' landward borders. Great blue herons stalk the pools. Muddy banks are home to mussels and to barnacles that spray water as the tide comes in. Estuaries wind through the meadows, draining and filling twice daily, feeding and growing the fish—the migratory striped bass, for example, which have, in turn, long fed and grown people, bald eagles, osprey.

These marshes are wave absorbers, carbon storers, sediment trappers, toxin filterers. They are a wild sort of edge: not carefully delineated, but the homes of the in-between. They are shaped by the constant flux of the tides and, therefore, by the moon. They have the infinite sea on one side, the land that climbs up and away on the other.

Salt marshes are places where natural disturbances are routine, expected, and, by and large, necessary to the marsh's resilience and ability to respond and adapt to change.

Such an adaptive, resilient, ever-changing edge has come to serve as the defining symbol to me of an ecological motherhood. As I come further into my understanding of salt marshes, two things have occurred: I've grown increasingly invested in their well-being as inherently valuable landscapes that are, first and foremost, literal, physical, living places. And I've met more and more faces of the archetypal edges of mothering.

* * *

It is their adaptation to the tides that make salt marshes unique ecosystems. The oldest existing salt marshes in the United States date back to around five thousand years ago, formed by running meltwater that came together in streams and rivers, which eroded the foundations of forests and carried the soil, made up of rock flour and sand, down to the end of the land. The soils settled and mixed with mud at the cusp of land and sea, creating a fertile environment for vegetation. Birds arrived along shorelines, carrying seeds. Grasses and forbs took to the soil.

Salt marsh vegetation is dominated by grasses. *Spartina alterniflora*, smooth cordgrass, is found between high and low tide lines across the East Coast marshes of North America, from Newfoundland to southern Florida, and around the Gulf of Mexico to Texas. Here in New England, smooth cordgrass grows most often on the seaward edge of marshes. It has broad, flat leaves that taper to a fine point. If you run your fingers along a blade of cordgrass and then along your tongue, you taste salt secreted from the grass's cells. *Spartina patens,* salt hay, tends to blanket the mid and higher elevations of the marsh in thin blades of grass that grow thick and soft, forming windswept cowlicks over the marsh platform.

Salt marsh resilience is, in part, a function of both accretion and migration—both made possible by their resident plants, the *Spartina* grasses in particular. Even as sea levels have historically risen and continue to rise, salt marshes can often keep up with these changes through vertical accretion. As organic plant matter decomposes, the roots of the grasses bind it together, continually forming it into new layers of peat. Marshes also gain elevation as suspended sediment flows in and out on the flooding tide, and as freshwater enters the marsh on the landward side via rivers, streams, and creeks. In both of these movements of water, the plants trap silt, sand, and clay. These sediments settle into the soil, lifting the marsh platform further.

And then there is marsh migration. As sea levels rise, or as powerful storms blow saltwater inland, the seaward edges of a salt marsh may erode or drown (even the highly salt-tolerant cordgrass cannot survive sustained submergence in saltwater). But if given enough time, the rhizomes of the *Spartina* grasses will retreat from sites of increasing salinity and send new shoots uphill to drier ground. In this way, a marsh will start to take root farther inland.

Rates of plant growth and decomposition, sediment supply, rates of sea level rise, historic and present-day land use, and tidal restrictions in the human-built environment combine to determine the ways in which salt marshes expand or shrink. Where marsh migration and elevation gain are possible, many a marsh can keep up with rising seas. But only to an extent. Prior to 5,000 years ago, for example, the seas rose quickly. The salt marshes of an older time were drowned. When the rate of sea level rise slowed again between 5,000 and 2,500 years ago, marshes began their return. Many of those marshes have flourished and are still with us today, and new marshes have continued to form over these last few millennia.

Today, the balance is shifting again.

The degree of relative sea level rise between 1970 and 2009 was three to four times higher in the northeastern United States than the global average. NOAA's Sea Level Rise Technical Report stated that "relative sea level along the contiguous U.S. coastline is expected to rise on average as much over the next 30 years . . . as it has over the last 100 years."

Salt marshes are cooperative and competitive, adaptive and resilient, productive and biodiverse ecosystems, all parts of which function to make their edge-life possible. But whether or not marshes will continue to keep pace is an open, complex, and site-specific question.

This is part of the research occurring at the Rachel Carson National Wildlife Refuge.

✳ ✳ ✳

The boat bottoms out just once on our way to the first research plot when low tide runs us into a sandbar. Rachel and Sam, sparing my leaky boots, get out to push. I use the moment to take in my surroundings. To the east: a green stretch of marsh and then a thick line of white and beige beach houses that rise between the grass and the ocean, obscuring the view of the sea. To the west: the visible buildings are farther away, with a wider swath of marsh grasses between infrastructure and the river. The other major barrier to marsh migration: human development and shorelines armored against flood. A marsh cannot travel through a concrete wall.

We anchor alongside the marsh bank, which, at low tide, is taller than me, the peat crumbly and wet, slate-black and muddy. We climb up to the marsh platform.

In the last few years, Rachel has set up ten research plots along the Webhannet, each a triangle formed by six pieces of PVC pipe standing vertically in the marsh—"triangle arrays" that provide five transect lines from which to measure the distance from the plot to the defined edge of the marsh (the "defined edge" being the place where the vegetation stops growing or where the channel bank drops vertically). She takes measurements at each of the ten plots once a year to monitor whether the seaward edge of the marsh is holding its ground, expanding, or eroding, and how quickly. Though she cautions that a conclusion requires long-term data and nothing definitive can be said yet, she tells me that it's already quite clear that the edges are retreating.

At this particular site, they think the erosion is, in part, due to the Army Corps of Engineers dredging upriver near the harbor and then dumping the collected material out to sea, thus removing large amounts of sediment from the bottom of the channel. Meaning: the salt marsh will be exposed to a higher volume of water between high and low tide. If data from this erosion study can help show that this is the case, the refuge might be able to make the case for reapplying the dredge material to the marsh platform instead of hauling it away.

At each plot, Rachel and Sam make note of what vegetation is growing, all of it still young and low to the ground at this time of year. At this first plot:

Puccinellia maritima, seaside alkali grass: blooming now in the delicate, subtle way of grass.

Triglochin maritima, seaside arrow grass: Rachel hands me a blade of it and says, "If you break it apart, it smells like cilantro." It does. I'm tempted to taste it. "Don't eat it though; it's toxic," she adds, just in time.

Distichlis spicata, spike grass: both living and present as thatch (last year's growth that will decompose into peat). "You can tell it's *Distichlis* thatch," Rachel instructs Sam, "because its leaves curl."

Salicornia seedlings, pickleweed: a succulent. "You can eat this one," Rachel says, handing me a stout green tip. It tastes bright and salty.

Plantago maritima, sea plantain: stem in the shape of a crescent moon.

Limonium nashii, sea lavender: soon to burst into purple and white flowers.

Measuring tape in hand, Rachel backs two meters away from the edge and then measures another meter to the right, parallel with the marsh edge. Here, she presses a metal rod into the soil, twists a knob at the top, pulls it out, and gives Sam the reading: 2.1. She does this twice more. She is measuring the shear strength—the ability to resist tearing—of the peat in kilopascals.

Her hypothesis is that the higher the reading (i.e., the greater the shear strength), the more roots and organic material are present within the peat, and, therefore, the healthier and more resilient the marsh edge. Conversely, peat that is hummocky and soft—a low shear strength—is a sign of a marsh in distress.

* * *

Between 1300 and 1850, sea level rise in New England occurred at a rate of one millimeter per year. In 2007, the IPCC predicted that it could get as high as nearly six millimeters per year this century. Others have predicted rates as high as sixteen millimeters per year, which would drown today's healthy, intact salt marshes.

The peat-based marshes of New England are some of the least likely to keep pace with rising seas, because they have comparably low sediment accretion rates, relying primarily on peat buildup from plant detritus to gain elevation—a slower process. Marsh migration may help them persist where such migration is possible. But there are many human barriers. Casco Bay in Maine, for example, has already armored a fifth of its shoreline against sea level rise, therefore armoring it against marsh migration as well. And across the northeastern United States, shifting vegetation patterns, widening channel networks, marsh pool formation, and changing sediment structures are evidence that marshes may be lagging behind rising oceans.

At another plot later in the day, the kilopascal reading will be zero after the instrument meets a large pocket of air beneath a thin layer of peat. "This one isn't looking good," Rachel will say. That wild edge is falling into the sea.

PASSAGEWAYS

In the face of the complexities of the interplay of forces at work on marshes, and the grand scale on which they are operating, scientists have turned to a tiny creature for help, one who is able to live within what is called the "extreme marginal environment" of the littoral zone. These creatures have endured many millions of years of change within the ocean, and within the shifting borders of salt marshes.

Within a salt marsh's layers of sediment, down deep in the peat, these microorganisms, and the ancient fossils of their forebears, have something to tell us about living on the edge in a time of rising seas.

Foraminifera—*forams* for short—are single-celled microorganisms, protists, that inhabit almost all marine environments, from deepest water to shore. The first record of them in the human canon dates back to the fifth century BCE, in Herodotus's *Histories*, when he makes note of shell-like fossils embedded in the limestone blocks of the Egyptian pyramids.

Like us—and like all animals, plants, and fungi—forams are eukaryotes, meaning they have a cell structure with a clearly defined nucleus that contains distinct genetic material. This is about as far as the similarities go.

One of the almost impossible spans of difference between us and this organism is in the form of time. While we *Homo sapiens* have been around for as many as 300,000 years, according to recent fossil evidence, forams have been here since the early Cambrian days: 545 million years ago—when all manner of life was still confined to the sea, and hard structures like shells and skeletons were relatively new evolutionary inventions.

To read even several sentences about forams is to come into a new vocabulary of what life is capable of. Forams build shells, called "tests," around themselves, which they can do in multiple ways, including by secreting a calcareous substance of their own creation or by collecting minerals from the waters around them and cementing them together in a process called "agglutination." These shells are single- or multi-chambered and shaped either like a spiral or like a whorl, and most often are between half a millimeter and one millimeter long; salt marsh forams tend to be smaller, ranging in size from tens of microns to a half millimeter. The word *foraminifera* is derived from *foramen*—"openings or passages"—referring to those that exist between the chambers of their shells.

If you search for an image of a foram, you will likely see what looks like a rudimentary shell with a series of ethereal lines shining around it like the sun's corona. These are *granuloreticlose pseudopodia*, or *rhizopodia* (*rhizo* meaning "root"). They function as an organ of the cell and are made up of the cytoplasm, a substance that exists between the nuclear membrane and the cellular membrane. Forams extend and retract these cytoplasmic threads as needed for moving, feeding, and constructing their shells. These arms feature "bi-directional cytoplasmic flow" and are in symbiotic relationship with other strange, tiny creatures like dinoflagellates, which are photosynthesizing algae.

Forams are highly site-specific. Each species has evolved within a narrow set of conditions, such as the temperature and oxygen content of the water or the mineral makeup of the surrounding sediments. These site conditions are not preferences but rather nonnegotiable bounds of survival. The successive generations of a species of foraminifera—of which there are thousands known—subsist within the exact same set of narrow environmental constraints, across millions of years. Thus, when a particular combination of site conditions is present, researchers know which species of foram they will find. Conversely, if the fossil of a certain known species of foraminifera is found in a sediment core from the bottom of the ocean, scientists can infer what the sea conditions must have been like when that foram was alive.

It is their shells that keep the record of these conditions. The shape and structural content of their tests, as determined by their depositional environment, gives precise indications of which environments they exist in today, or existed in millennia ago. Forams also evolve rapidly across generations, which means their shells are not only indicative of an environmental setting within the seas but of a moment in *time* as well. These qualities, in addition to their being some of the most common and abundant microfossils within marine sediments, means that they have been used extensively in geological reconstructions of deep time marine conditions. Forams have become a crucial tool in marine biostratigraphy, the use of the fossils within sedimentary rocks to correlate them and determine their relative ages.

In this way, the impressive list of foram-fossil-informed discoveries includes changes in sea levels during the Carboniferous (more than 300 million years ago), variations in the oxygen content of water during the Jurassic (201–145 million years ago), changes in water salinity during the Cretaceous (145–66 million years ago), and glacial freezing and melting during the Quaternary (beginning 2.5 million years ago). Writes one earth scientist: "Foraminifera is both the clock and the recorder of the Earth's history. It has played a crucial role in developing our understanding of the evolution of life and the environment on Earth."

Foraminifera can be planktonic—floating—but the vast majority are benthic, meaning bottom dwelling or occurring within marine sediments. There are roughly ten thousand known species of benthic foraminifera living today. Of these, a small subset is known to occur in the intertidal waters of coastal salt marshes.

Many of these foraminifera that live in salt marshes are *agglutinated*, meaning their tests are built of rock debris that the foram cements together around itself (rather than organic material that the cell produces itself).

Salt marsh forams live both on the water's surface and within sediments. As forams do elsewhere, salt marsh forams occur very specifically within zones that are delineated, primarily, by elevation. Oxygen levels, salinity, organic content, pH, and the type of sediment also factor in to where these creatures dwell. And similarly to their usefulness in other marine environments, the living and fossilized forams that exist within marsh peat—an anoxic environment where other organisms are not well-preserved—are like a code that, when cracked, has helped us understand changes in sea levels in coastal marshes over time.

The shells of forams keep the record.

The record becomes something like a prophecy. By examining assemblages of foram fossils within salt marsh peat cores—which are akin to time capsules, each layer of peat preserving traces of the marine environment in which it was laid down in a marsh—scientists can get a sense of how quickly sea levels have risen at various points in time, across the five-thousand-year life of our oldest salt marshes.

For example, the foram species *Trochammina inflata* is known to live within a narrow vertical range in the intertidal zone of Maine's salt marshes, inhabiting an area between twenty-eight centimeters below to eight centimeters above mean high water. Thus, if a fossilized shell of *Trochammina inflata* is found within a salt marsh peat core that has been radiocarbon-dated to four thousand years ago, researchers can extrapolate where mean high water was—where the ocean was on that particular coast—four thousand years ago, based on the presence of that shell, and then extrapolate the marine conditions that must have been present for it to have lived. And with thousands of species of forams across nearly all marine environments, scientists have been able to paint a very clear picture of not only where the world's oceans have been for millions of years but how ecosystems like salt marshes have responded—including when a marsh drowned, when it migrated, when it flourished and expanded.

This way, we can get an idea—a guess, really—of how well a salt marsh might do with the changing oceans of today and of the future. Might a marsh drown? Might it keep up via migration and accretion? What barriers could we remove to provide it with the chance to do so?

The living forams, meanwhile, keep to their strange worlds. They are born, they build, they give birth, they die. They evolve, adapt. They leave behind their stories.

Why look to foraminifera, a being who has so little in common with us, who shares almost no function or mode of being other than the spark of life itself, for ways of mothering at the edge? Perhaps precisely because of that great chasm of difference. Because strange forms of life can shake us up, make us see things differently, help us realize there are other ways to find connection.

Because foramen are openings, passageways.

Because rhizopodia might help us imagine how to extend our own ethereal roots, help us see that we are beings who are not confined within a solid form but inherently capable of reaching out and joining in symbiotic relationship.

Because navigating the edge also requires the creation of shelter and responsiveness. This is a way of weathering storms.

Because even a half-millimeter-wide home is a story-keeper, a preserver of a moment in the life of the sea, to be read by future generations.

Because that home is built through agglutination, an aggregation of minerals and sediments that are cemented into a shell.

Because agglutination has another definition, a linguistic one. *Agglutination* is also the process of aggregating morphemes—the smallest units of language that retain distinct meaning—and cementing them into a word, such that a single word conveys what might otherwise require a complex sentence. There are agglutinative languages, including Turkish, Japanese, and Swahili.

Agglutination is a way of building and expressing complex meaning in a simple, elegant way. The word *agglutinated* itself is derived from the Latin, *agglutinare*, meaning "to glue together." And that leads me to another meaning.

Agglutination could also be the practice of being present where we are—within the specific environment in which we find ourselves—and extending our arms to sense and collect the various pieces of what is happening. It could mean stringing those pieces together, cementing them into a story.

Part of the work of the edge is witnessing what each of us is uniquely placed to witness. As Donna J. Haraway writes in *Staying with the Trouble*: "We need stories (and theories) that are just big enough to gather up the complexities and keep the edges open and greedy for surprising new and old connections." Is this not agglutination? Is this not also a description of a foram shell? Gathering up the complexities into an open-edged, passageway-ed form.

We need to build these stories: stories that witness, stories that are both sticky and porous, stories that are spiraled and whorled and that lead us through openings between chambers. We need whale stories. We need microorganism stories. We need salt marsh and seabird stories. We need the stories of the beings who open us up, beckon us down new and old passageways of being.

RECLAIM

In attempting to tell such sticky, porous, open-edged stories, there is unlearning to be done, *un*sticking to do. The conditioning of my Western brain tells me, again and again, to place myself at the center of stories. See: in the two sentences I've written so far in this chapter, I've already used "me," "my," "myself," and "I." So let's be honest: I am not a master foraminifera-storyteller. I am, rather, a mother seeking a way back to this knowledge. Trying to reclaim something. The foram shells I build will be misshapen and rickety. Practice, practice, practice.

To make mother-work successful, to ground it in the Earth, we must simultaneously do the work of not only weaving stories but of striving again and again to understand that there is more than just ourselves within the meaning of these stories. To build stories with open passageways, with the possibility of deeper connection, we must strive to include the landscapes themselves as autonomous voices with agency.

* * *

Atop the marsh platform at the Rachel Carson National Wildlife Refuge, Dr. Susan Adamowicz, a salt marsh biologist, is working with two interns on a project to measure marsh elevation change. As Rachel Stearns and I approach them, Susan—silver hair in a ponytail, eyes peering closely at the ground behind tinted prescription glasses—glances up at us and raises a hand, cautioning us not to get too close. "The measurements here are on the scale of millimeters," she explains to me. "Your footprint could obliterate a decade of data."

Sue walks a wide circle around the plot and gestures Rachel over to a creek running through the marsh, pointing out two large wooden beams in the creek bed. There's a third one, half-eroded out of the peat. Though the wood is likely at least a century old, it only emerged out of the peat in the last few months. It means there's likely a lot more of it buried beneath. If they knew exactly where all of the wood was, it could help explain why the elevation of this marsh seems to be sinking in places. Sue shakes her head. "I want X-ray vision, Rachel," she says. "You can get it for me for my birthday."

Rachel turns to me, nods down at the exposed wood. "We learn new things every year about what the farmers did."

❊ ❊ ❊

Land reclamation—"the cultivation of waste land or land formerly underwater"—is the term used to describe the transformation of a landscape whose functions are altered and molded to benefit human needs. European land reclamation practices date back to the installation of diking systems in the Netherlands, which were well underway by the eleventh century and which included raised tracks that permitted the expansion of farming into marshland and protected the land from floods. By the mid-sixteenth century, reclamation was prospering in England as a way to create productive agricultural land, achieved by draining wetlands.

Major land reclamation projects came to America's shores with European settlers. Larger reclamation efforts began as early as 1675 in salt marshes along Delaware Bay. The US Federal Swamp Land Acts of the mid-1800s passed authority over large areas of wetlands to the states, who sold much of the land to farmers and encouraged them to drain marshland so that they could grow freshwater crops.

A special report issued by the USDA in 1885, entitled "Tide Marshes of the United States," states: "When our marshes shall be wrested from the tides, our political, social, and industrial conditions will warrant as well as demand the conquest, and its methods will be American."

The numbers vary widely due to a lack of historical data, but somewhere between 37 and 80 percent of the salt marshes that existed in New England prior to European settlement are estimated to have been lost to human use and development, a process mercifully slowed at last by the Clean Water Act of 1972, which protected the nation's salt marshes from dredging and filling except by permission of the Army Corps of Engineers.

Today's salt marshes continue to be affected by previous reclamation projects. Along the Webhannet River, the exposed beams that Sue pointed out are, she thinks, from a drainage system the farmers of long ago put in to keep the marsh platform drier, knowing that valuable salt hay preferred fewer tidal inundations. The infrastructure would have facilitated the water flowing out of the marsh in ways that likely shifted the ecosystem's hydrology, and, therefore, its plant composition and assemblages. Sue thinks the wooden beams that made up the infrastructure have since collapsed beneath the peat, and what was originally intended to drain the marsh is now having the reverse effect: piles of wood are causing water to back up and pool within the marsh, creating the possibility that living roots will rot, effectively drowning a ribbon of vegetation.

Everything we can see here across the marsh platform is still responding to historic land reclamation practices, Sue tells me.

* * *

David Abram writes that it was, in part, phonetic writing that broke the animistic bonds that had kept us in constant dialogue with the more-than-human world around us. Through this form of written language, we came increasingly to express ourselves in ways that only we could understand, thus closing ourselves off from that wider conversation. "By denying that birds and other animals have their own styles of speech, by insisting that the river has no real voice and that the ground itself is mute, we stifle our direct experience," he writes. "We cut ourselves off from the deep meanings in many of our words, severing our language from that which supports and sustains it."

Just as salt marshes underwent a long era of reclamation, alterations meant to serve human ends, did not the same sort of co-optation occur within our Western language, stories, and myths? How then do we ensure that our stories are not beams of wood, shoved into a salt marsh? Is it possible to see what lives and processes our stories might ignore or disrupt, despite our best intentions? I'm not sure. But this uncertainty calls us to another practice within the ecological terrain of motherhood: to not only bring landscapes into our stories but to bring ourselves fully into landscapes. We practice translating landscapes into words on a page, employing them in service to a story, but we must also become students of place—not for the sake of the story but for the sake of the place itself—seeking to decipher what is there.

The patterns among the plant communities of a salt marsh—where one plant grows, where it doesn't, who it grows next to—can be read in this way by someone with well-trained eyes. It's a language written in many subtle shades of green that gives clues to a marsh's past and future. "Each species is telling you about their local conditions," Sue says. Each plant has its own tolerance for salt, its preferences for moisture, and its adaptations for when it expends energy during the growing season. Several inches of elevation change can completely shift species composition. Just a meter from my feet, in an almost too-perfect illustration of this point, the land dips down a mere three or four inches. Abruptly, the salt hay gives way to cordgrass, which entirely spans the meter-wide, micro-valley. Salt hay takes over again on the other side as soon as the land lifts.

All of these factors, and therefore the makeup of plant communities, shift alongside shifts in the larger landscape. The laws governing those shifts are both natural and imposed. Primary succession is the first inhabiting of a bare landscape by a plant community, usually in a regular, predictable pattern. (There is little recorded knowledge of what North America's salt marshes looked like before European settlement.) Secondary succession is what a plant community does after a profound or prolonged pattern of disturbance, such as ditching or dredging.

Prolonged human disturbances are ongoing in salt marshes. Among them: contamination with hazardous materials; infilling in order to build roads or highways atop marshes, often with culverts beneath them that fail to allow for natural tidal flow; dredging and stream channelization; installing dikes, dams, and levees for flood control and storm protection; invasions of phragmites, which are spreading in part due to human-caused nitrogen loading of ecosystems. And, of course, human-caused sea level rise.

This is part of what makes salt marsh research and management complicated. The gap in historic knowledge, combined with present-day sea level rise and uncertainty in predictions of future sea level rise, combined with ongoing human disturbance, makes it difficult to know what the goal post is and how to achieve it for any individual salt marsh.

A week prior to my visit to RCNWR, Slade Moore, a salt marsh ecologist, brought me to a marsh thirty minutes north of the refuge. This marsh is far too wet, pooling everywhere with standing water—an early warning sign of a marsh's conversion to open water. It was easy to see why this was happening: on the far side, the railroad runs directly across the marsh. On the side where we were standing, the marsh runs up against a mammoth industrial building and then a highway. Both severely disrupt the in-and-out flow of the tide. Knowing how to fix the marsh's hydrology in the midst of such development presents a challenging set of questions, complicated by the fact that these few acres of marsh have also become habitat for the endangered salt marsh sparrow. Because the marsh has been so damaged by tidal restrictions, it hasn't accreted material in step with sea level rise. There's concern that letting the tides return all at once would drown the nests. But Slade hopes that humans can, by using satellite data, historical photos, increasingly accurate modeling programs, and on-the-ground observation and research, create dynamic management plans, even for specific sites like this that have a highly specific confluence of factors affecting them.

Many federal and state organizations like the refuge are working on a long overdue effort to build relationships with Indigenous communities to gain a better understanding of what a healthy marsh looked like in the past, which they hope would provide a more robust sense of how to keep marshes healthy in the future. Along the Atlantic coast of the United States, salt marshes were sites of Indigenous foraging, harvesting, and land management through the use of fire to help maintain grass populations. Restoring Native access and traditional ecological knowledge to these sites, Sue tells me, will be a key factor in mapping a future course for salt marshes.

Sue directs my attention across the marsh platform where a unique confluence of these macro- and micro-changes are present. This marsh is experiencing an intersection of conditions that is different from the marsh across the Webhannet river, which is different from the marsh upriver, and different from what is happening elsewhere in New England, elsewhere in the United States, elsewhere in the world.

The implementation of management plans and the research to prove the need is often slow, happening over many years. Even then, the results can be inconclusive. But there are people out there who are reading the landscape, adapting their own knowledge via their on-the-ground learning, in order to help salt marshes adapt.

Our stories, too, can seek to be adaptive, even as they will be flawed and perhaps short-sighted as we strive with an inevitably limited perception to decipher more-than-human landscapes. And we can't all become salt marsh biologists. Perhaps we can't even fully undo the conditioning that tends to place us at the center of our stories. But I think what we *can* do might be as simple as arriving in a landscape with openness and a desire to learn. This, itself, is a decentering practice.

Striving to be adaptive, working to listen beyond our conditioned minds, reaching for a language that is read in shades of green rather than letters on a screen: this is the work of bringing the land back from the margins, into the center. And time is short. The sea is coming.

WILD TRANSGRESSION

Myths are the foram fossils of our narrative histories—the small relics of the long ago, narratives specific to their time but with meaning to convey to us now. Myths are large enough to hold the vastness of what is beyond us, even within the constraining form of language. As we witness what is happening to our landscapes, myths can whisper a way of moving, a way of being, a way of understanding what is and what is to come.

There is a myth that made a home in me while I was pregnant and has been at work on me since. I did not understand why until I went to the salt marshes.

In the Book of Exodus, Jochebed becomes pregnant with Moses during Pharaoh's decree that all male children born to the Hebrew slaves must be thrown into the Nile River. As it appears in the Torah, this part of the story is recounted in just two sentences: "The woman conceived and bore a son; and when she saw that he was a fine baby, she hid him three months. When she could hide him no longer, she got a papyrus basket for him, and plastered it with bitumen and pitch; she put the child in it and placed it among the reeds on the bank of the river."

The midrash—rabbinic interpretation and commentary—offers more detail: Jochebed weaves the basket of bulrushes, a grasslike plant that grows in wetlands and would have been found along the banks of the Nile. "Paper reed" was known as a valuable material for its flexibility and ability to withstand "the pressure of both soft and hard things." She coats the outside of the basket with pitch and the inside with bitumen. In some versions, she weaves a canopy over the basket.

A woman whose son has been condemned to death does the only thing she can do to give him a chance at life: weaves a basket, places him inside, and abandons him. Can you feel Jochebed's grief? Her fear? Her faith? Can you imagine the moment when she must walk away from Moses, the water lapping at the woven reeds?

Exodus continues. Baby Moses is promptly discovered in his basket and taken in by Pharaoh's daughter, who seeks out a midwife to care for the child. The midrash tells us that this is Jochebed herself—a known and respected midwife among the Hebrews—who comes to nurse Moses, never revealing she is the mother. And so, in secrecy, the two are reunited.

The practice of midwifery, therefore, becomes an act of transgression, a subversion of the will of the powers that be and an assertion of the feminine as an agent of change to bring about a different future. In Exodus, Shiphrah and Puah are named as the Hebrew midwives who blatantly disobey the king of Egypt in their decision to "let the boys live." Some rabbinic traditions identify Shiphrah and Puah as none other than Jochebed and her daughter, Miriam. Jochebed's transgression in saving the lives of these infants, including her own son, ultimately liberates her people. The metaphor of Exodus itself is a birth story, in this sense of liberation and the birth of a nation.

* * *

As long as women have been bearing children, midwives have been enabling the transition of birth. They assist in the transformative, bloody work of bringing someone—both mother and child—across a threshold. From womb to world. From saltwater to air. From woman to mother.

Labor is a wilder way of being in the world than any other I have experienced as an adult. To give birth is to be repeatedly plunged into a crashing sea. My mind lost control of my body—in itself terrifying. Being in our bodies through the process of birth—however one does it, whether in a hospital or at home, vaginally or via C-section, with or without pain management—decenters a story we are so often told: that our rational minds are, and ought to be, in control. In labor we are worked upon by ancient biological processes. We are viscerally, unrelentingly reminded that we are animal. We experience the transgression of the wild. That bewildering encroachment.

Labor was a timeless time. Contractions warped seconds into hours. *Ride out each contraction like a wave*, a wistful book had advised me a few weeks prior, and I'd tucked this comforting image into my pocket for when I'd need it.

Fuck the waves! I thought as another eruption of body-splitting pain bloomed within me, snaked into my lower back, pushed bile out of my throat. The world was rent apart and stitched together again, and dawn and dusk and dawn stretched and snapped, and Aspen was crying on my chest. We had crossed the portal. The two of us became, in that process of birth, so utterly porous, so wild, that one living, breathing, body emerged from another. She had been born, a child. I had been reborn, a mother.

This universal act by which each of us has found our way into the world carries a transgression of what is wild upon what is civilized. The transgression of the will of the body upon the will of the mind.

❊ ❊ ❊

Jochebed and the other Hebrew midwives who quietly worked against Pharaoh's decree by helping the birthing mothers deliver, conceal, and care for their children were also playing a symbolic role in the wider story of the Israelites. Their midwifery became existential, writes scholar of Hebrew literature Inbar Raveh, as "their insistence on the perpetuation of life is a revolutionary act in the context of slavery. It demonstrates hope for the future of the newborn and the power to imagine a different future, without slavery and oppression." And so, just as a midwife delivers a child, the Israelites are delivered from slavery to freedom.

I am sometimes troubled by stories, biblical and otherwise, that bring us through trial and transformation and then provide us with an ending, an answer. Or perhaps I am not so much troubled by the existence of resolution as I am by our tendency to dwell on it. What happens if we dwell instead within beginnings and middles? In, for example, the forty years of wandering in the wilderness?

In our moment here on our Earth, we are not at an ending. We are not at the point in the story where God offers us a covenant or opens the door to the promised land. Nor are we at the point of the abrupt end of apocalypse. Biblical narratives can bestow upon us a certain passivity—ironically, both in their guarantee of redemption and new beginnings and in their normalizing of the world ending. But neither of those outcomes does much to turn our attention to the present. And, in actuality, there will be no *ending*—in any human way of thinking about it. For there is no such thing.

I don't believe that we, in our lifetimes, will achieve a merciful resolution to the planet-wide ecological crisis. But this is not to say that we wash our hands of outcomes; rather, with all the more rigor and witness, we must strive to attune our minds, bodies, and spirits to the now, this moment in which the work can be done. The hard work. The present-tense work we have to do, despite not knowing what is after. The work of seeing and caring for the living world, even in all the pain, even in the face of a death decree. The work of measuring salt marsh erosion, reading the forams in the peat, telling the stories, testifying, defending, loving, cultivating.

Here we find ourselves yet again at the edge: working in the uncertainty, working in the mystery, and rooted, grounded, with our feet in the eroding muck.

When mythologist Martin Shaw tells a story—or crawls into a story and becomes it for a while—he first invites his listeners not to focus on the "ending" to the myth but to notice, rather, where in the story they find themselves. Myths, he says, can work on us like this. They can provide us with an image or a scrap of meaning that will settle into us at the same time that it *unsettles* something within us.

A goose's egg, rolled away from the nest.

A basket by the river.

I ask: Where do I find myself in Exodus?

I answer: In the moment when Jochebed places her child into a basket and walks away.

What does this moment have to tell me? Who is Jochebed today?

She is, I think, the mother who must do the impossible. The mother who can neither know nor guarantee her child's future but acts in service to it anyway, standing upon the foundation of her present love. For that is all she can do. She is the mother who, awash with despair and fear, chooses to believe that her boy will live. She is the mother who gathers bulrushes by the water. She is the mother who knows how to weave a basket.

Just as Jochebed intimately knows the process of childbirth as a midwife, her parting with Moses strikes me as yet another act of midwifery. Leaving her child at the lapping cusp of land and water is an act of creating a threshold, an opening. Within a rending of worlds comes the creation of a new path.

I read reports of what is coming. A prediction that critical features of the ocean's circulatory system could collapse this century; a report of consecutive heat waves that should have been once-in-millennium events; data that warn of record low levels of

Arctic sea ice. *Transgression*, I learn, is also the word for when the ocean encroaches where it should not on land.

I wonder if, in becoming a parent, I've committed to leaving my daughter by the banks of a river, if among the things she will inherit from me is a shifting edge. She will grow into an Earth in the grips of change and transformation. I cannot see what this will look like. I wonder about the extent of the shelter I can provide to her. I wonder how to become a weaver of baskets. What, today, are my bitumen and pitch? What is my bulrush? What are the tools of weaving?

Cosmic forces are ever at work on the sea. The unknown lurks in the swirling waters beyond the snails and the fiddler crabs, in the deep dark. And that swirling water sometimes rises up and spills beyond its usual constraints. The tide line can be a place of gentle, predictable ebb and flow. It can also be a place of crashing waves, spraying foam, unstoppable flood. Just as the salt marsh cordgrass welcomes the sea, our own porous edges are the places from which we can welcome wildness.

Welcoming the transgression of the wild upon our bodies calls us to a place that is often uncomfortable or painful. We have to rest in questions, not answers. The unknown, not certainty.

Just as tides and marshes can teach us about navigating our wild edges, so too can myth pull us into relationships of ebb and flow. We have to be willing for parts of ourselves to erode away, little by little.

It is because of Jochebed's act of great trust and faith in God that she is able to do the unimaginable. God rewards Jochebed with a long life. She follows her son through the parted sea into the promised land and freedom. The midrash says that she is granted such a long life that she survives each of her three children, and that, at the end of Moses's life, his two siblings already gone, he begs God to spare him and thereby spare his mother this further loss, the death of his siblings having already "blunted" her teeth.

"Will more of her teeth be blunted by my death?" he implores.

Judaism is matrilineal, passed down through the mother. It is the tradition of my mother and hers and hers, back to ancient Egypt and before. Jochebed is, in a way, midwife to all of us who descended from her acts of faith. And Jochebed, it seems, was destined to be a woman defined by thresholds and liminal spaces. The midrash says, too, that she herself was conceived en route from one home to another, and then born between the walls at the entrance to Egypt.

Part of our inheritance from her is instruction on how to exist *between*, to become creatures who welcome the transgression of wildness because we are, after all—in the coursing of our blood and the beating of our hearts and in the snaking networks of our veins and nerves—wild. And it is our wild selves who best navigate edges.

We, mothers of blunted teeth, must do the work, must walk the path, despite the pain.

And so, again and again, though my rational mind resists and tempts me always to turn back, I find that my feet are walking with Jochebed, down to the Nile. Aspen is with me.

We descend together to that uncertain edge.

FLOOD

In southern Louisiana, the mouth of the Mississippi River utters its thick, ground-swelling command of a voice like God speaking to Moses atop a quaking Mount Sinai. It is a relentlessly creative force, a builder of worlds.

Earth's fourth longest river, spanning a valley that is twice as large as the Nile, gave repeated birth to this landscape, coming into its modern form over the last nine thousand years as its tributaries pulled at their own banks and spilled into the Mississippi, who swallowed the tons of suspended sediment from the interior rivers of the continent. The Mississippi's watershed stretches from the Rockies to the Appalachians and drains 1.2 million square miles over thirty-one states and two Canadian provinces. Over many thousands of years it has unloaded its water and sediments into the Gulf of Mexico, building a shifting mosaic of vast, highly productive coastal wetlands. When the river reached the Gulf, the waters slowed, the river's load of millions of metric tons of annual sediments settled (it's estimated that, historically, the Mississippi carried 400–460 million metric tons of sediment during the Holocene), and delta complexes formed: salt marshes, bays, lakes, swamps, and barrier islands. Smaller rivers and bayous formed in the coastal plain.

In this way, Louisiana's marshes have historically had a ceaseless, foundational flow of Earth in the form of waterborne sediment. Even as the tides eroded wetlands or sea levels climbed, the river periodically overflowed its banks, building the land up again. Every so often, this sediment would plug the route of the river and the course of the river, and the shape and location of the delta would shift. This delta would come to span more than twelve thousand square kilometers on land and more than thirty thousand square kilometers underwater.

Indigenous peoples lived here in respectful and cautious relationship to the water, understanding its tendency to flood and break patterns. Jeffery Darensbourg, a doctor of cognitive science who specializes in Indigenous languages and linguistics, is an enrolled member of the Atakapa Ishak Nation of southwest Louisiana and southeast Texas. Ishak means "the human beings," and his people have called this area home for millennia. It is a place they have contributed to shaping and naming, and a place they have been shaped and named by. "Wilderness is a completely foreign concept to Indigenous thinking," he tells me. "We never lived in 'wilderness.' Not one space where native people lived was it 'wilderness.' The environment was constantly being shaped."

Where the Vermilion River empties into the Gulf of Mexico, there is an artificial channel called Four Mile Cutoff, built so ships could carry oil field workers out to the Gulf. "Right where Four Mile Cutoff enters the Gulf, there is a shell midden," says Jeffery. Shell middens—mounds consisting primarily of shells—are sites of cultural importance, often built over the course of centuries, and often in places where Indigenous people would gather annually or seasonally. Jeffery continues:

> [It] was built by my tribe over the course of thousands of years. As I recall, it was shaped sort of like an alligator at one point. It's a place where we would break our pots every year, so it's covered in thousands of pieces of pottery. I was walking along it, and I found a piece of flint that had been struck on one side and used as a grinder on

the other. I know from my research that that flint came
from Arkansas. It was a commonly traded item. So I think
about things traded all the way down there from Arkansas, and about how the shell midden would keep erosion
from happening. Building mounds had an advantage for
survival. Some mounds were for burial, but most of them
were not. They were mostly ceremonial places, but also
places of retreat.

Ceremony, trade, and planned retreat were among the defining uses of this landscape before colonization. This way of being
with the landscape, Jeffery explains to me from his home in New
Orleans, is held within the original name of this city: *Bulbancha*.
He adds:

> Thinking of the Mississippi River as one thing is not a
> Native conception. There are different names, different
> parts of the river. The river around [New Orleans] is called
> *Bulbancha*—"place of foreign tongues" or "place of other
> languages"—which means you're likely to find a bunch of
> people speaking different languages. Which should tell
> you that it's a trade zone between nations.

Bulbancha was a hub of commerce that included the seasonal arrival and departure of many distinct Indigenous nations,
including the Chitimacha, Choctaw, Natchez, Houma, Chawasha,
Washa, Acolapissa, Tunica-Biloxi, Bayogoula, Taensa, and Atakapa
Ishak. It was not permanently settled for reasons clear to these
peoples: because it was a network of wetlands that frequently
flooded.

The French city of New Orleans was founded in 1718, and
many of the threads that held the live transmission of Native language and culture in this place were severed. Settlers extinguished

place names and erased histories. Many of the Indigenous peoples died from disease. As elsewhere, these violent legacies trace into today. For Jeffery's people, who spoke Ishakkoy ("human being talk"), "there are no more speakers of Ishakkoy from any sort of continuous transmission," he wrote in an essay for *Southern Cultures*. "That, in itself, is an environmental loss."

* * *

By 1858, more than one thousand miles of levees on either side of the Mississippi had been constructed to control the river's flooding, disrupting the sediment flow from the Mississippi into the coastal plain. In 1901, oil and gas reserves were discovered beneath southern Louisiana's marshes and swamps, and the fossil fuel industry set to work on the delta, digging wells and dredging canals throughout the marshes. Canals ran as much as sixteen feet deep and 150 feet wide in order to transport rigs and crews. They also disrupted the hydrology of the wetlands, bringing saltwater into freshwater marshes and killing the freshwater plants whose roots held soil in place and who supplied annual cycles of detritus to the marsh platform. Dredged materials from the canals were piled onto adjacent marshes, causing them to sink under the weight. With far less organic plant material and fresh sediment inputs, the edges of the marshes began to crumble into the sea. Open ponds gained area within the meadows, and the wind gained speed over the water, eroding the edges further.

Then came the flood of 1927. Following months of outbreaks of extreme weather across the Mississippi's tributaries, the river swelled and burst its levees in dozens of places in the Lower Mississippi Valley. More than 600,000 people were left homeless. Between 250 and 1,000 people were killed. The response from the federal government was not to retreat from the powerful water but to build better. The Flood Control Act of 1928 made the US

Army Corps of Engineers responsible for preventing another disaster of this magnitude. The levees swarmed the riverbanks.

In the late 1930s, the oil and gas industry moved offshore, and thousands of wells, underwater pipelines, and yet more canals followed. Decades later, under all of these pressures, as many as fifty square miles of wetlands were vanishing annually, and approximately a quarter of the country's oil and gas resources were moving through Louisiana's coast. More than fifty thousand wells have been excavated, accessed by upward of ten thousand miles of canals. From the 1930s to today, Louisiana has lost a quarter of its wetlands, more than the rest of the continental United States combined. Rising seas have only compounded the problem. Depending on how well we respond to coming changes in climate, between one thousand and three thousand square miles are predicted to vanish in the next fifty years.

* * *

Driving along LA-23 South from New Orleans and into Plaquemines Parish, Louisiana, I don't see the Mississippi, though it flows just to the east of the highway, rarely more than 1,000 feet away. It has been bound behind the levee.

It's surreal that this flowing body of water—so expansive and far-reaching that it is carrying waters and sediments from the Niobrara and Platte rivers in Nebraska, the place of my birth and earliest years—is invisible to my eye, even though the mighty river is *right there*. Just there, on the other side of the oil and gas infrastructure.

The road is a narrow ribbon of raised land, the river on one side, the wetlands on the other. Many of the houses we pass initially remind me of daddy longlegs, except they appear so eerily unnatural that I revise my thoughts: they are more like machines in alien invasion movies. Some of the structures must be twenty feet off the ground, standing atop dozens of thin legs of cement blocks, so that when the water inevitably rises up, it will flow beneath, not through. The houses are getting higher and higher, my companions tell me. There are many homes, too, that remain flush on the ground, homes of those who cannot afford to rise.

I'm the outsider of the group, but my fellow travelers, who were either born in or are long-term residents of New Orleans— two artists, Heather and Hannah, and a photojournalist, Bryan— seem frequently stunned into silence as well. Most disconcerting are the dozens of cranes, like skeletons of insect-devoured leaves, that stand behind a twenty-eight-and-a-half-foot tall steel flood wall. Within this wall is Venture Global Plaquemines LNG, a brand-new liquefied natural gas export facility. At 630 acres, it's significantly larger than New Orleans's French Quarter. At $13.2 billion, the project's financing then constituted the largest transaction in the history of our planet (and it secured another $7.8 billion for the second phase of the project). A colorful sign, hung on the flood wall and nearly as tall, reads *Building a Future for Plaquemines Parish.*

If the structure survives several decades here before being permanently inundated, a local resident speculates, it will have made its investors their money back. Recent US census data ranked Plaquemines Parish the fourth highest county in the nation in terms of percentage of population decrease (three other counties in Louisiana also made the top ten). But the parking lots alongside LNG hold hundreds of cars. There are fewer and fewer local opportunities for employment.

Today, the state of Louisiana owns 20 percent of the coast; the rest is private and corporate. The largest holder is the Louisiana Land and Exploration Company, a subsidiary of ConocoPhillips, which owns 636,000 acres, stretching 120 miles east to west and 85 miles north to south, across eight parishes.

The four of us are on our way to meet captain Richie Blink of Delta Discovery Tours. He is going to take us out on his converted shrimp boat into the Plaquemines Delta Complex and show us the salt marshes. Richie is in his midthirties with a youthful round face, an initial shyness, and a widely sought-after expertise about this landscape. He grew up in Plaquemines, in a family that lived "hand to mouth," he says, off of the marsh ecosystem. He once attempted what he calls the "suburban hell lifestyle" of Baton Rouge, but he ultimately returned here to his home. Now he works with his partner to make their home and the land surrounding it as flood resilient as possible, planting water-tolerant trees and wetland grasses. "It's our wish to live here as long as we can, until there is a permanent inundation, because we feel strongly that people need to be living on the bleeding edge of climate change to help pioneer more resilient ways of living and building," says Richie. For his professional work, he gives educational delta tours on the shrimp boat he refurbished. Several people I reached out to for interviews ahead of my trip here asked, independently of each other, if I'd be "going out on the boat with Richie." I take him to be somewhat of a household name for anyone interested in what's happening here, at one of the world's fastest-eroding edges.

Before the tour, Richie gives us a PowerPoint presentation on the history of the Mississippi Delta. We sit away from the bugs and the humidity in his newly acquired, fixer-upper building on Ice House Road. An older fellow walks in partway through with a question for Richie. He looks around blinking, a bit perplexed, and finally says with a smile, "This sure wasn't a church last time I was here." He's referring, I learn, both to the upcycled church pews we're sitting in and to the fact that this building was, before Richie moved in, a local bar.

Out on the water, past the floodgates, the sandwich terns are squeaking overhead. Richie points out double-crested cormorant, snowy egret, willet, and tricolored heron. The marsh grasses sway. *Spartina alterniflora* grows here, too. I take deep breaths, try to push the image of the LNG terminal out of my mind, and, for a brief moment, I have the mistaken impression that all is well out here with the birds.

But then we come to the Lemon Trees, the local name for what I mistake for a barrier island. It is, in fact, an ancient Indigenous mound, and it is at the confluence of the forces at work on the delta today.

This mound is locally called "Lemon Trees" because, knowing the site's significance, older white locals generally kept a respectful distance when out on their boats, apart from the occasional leaving of what they called "offerings." The legend goes that someone once left several lemons on the bank, which grew into fruit-bearing trees. A landmark atop a landmark. Today the lemon trees are bleached skeletons that are fully submerged underwater. Richie remembers vibrant live oak growing here when he was young, after the lemon trees had died. The oaks are now skeletons, too.

The layered history and ecology of this site is a complex one. In the years since the mound was abandoned, it has become an eroding salt marsh, as well as a site of restoration efforts. Several years ago, Hurricane Ida permanently inundated several hundred yards of its remaining land. There are experiments underway to plant mangroves in the hopes of offering the marsh deeper roots.

Richie keeps the boat on the water, close enough for us to see the biodegradable bags of oyster shells that line the banks. The Coalition to Restore Coastal Louisiana partnered with the Grand Bayou Indian Village community to do the installation, which is an ancient marsh management technique. Already, the oysters have created a productive reef and are armoring the bank, slowing the erosion.

The long list of other types of restoration efforts across southern Louisiana speaks to the extent of the problem: ridge restoration, marsh creation, land bridges, diversions of the Mississippi, hydrologic restoration, barrier island maintenance,

shoreline protection, bank stabilization, programmatic restoration, structural improvements (new levees, for example), and
nonstructural improvements (elevating homes, floodproofing,
and voluntary acquisitions of buildings that are likely to be inundated). Louisiana's Coastal Restoration Plan calls for $50 billion
over fifty years to mitigate land loss. Much of the coastal restoration funding comes from the oil and gas industry itself.

Time grows thin. NOAA recently took the names of thirty-
one places in this area off the nautical charts because they no longer exist.

"Everyone is for coastal restoration, but not many want to
do the bold work to make the delta as sustainable as it can be,"
Richie says. "Maybe this place shouldn't have been permanently
settled in the first place. Even the Indigenous mounds that are
outside here are seasonal camps. We could all leave south Louisiana, and the river would take care of it all. It would bust the
levee, water would flow, there would be a very sustainable delta
somewhere. But we've created more or less the largest port complex on the planet here. Everything we've done is for economic
certainty. These natural systems will work themselves out; it's the
humans that want to make it messy. Want to bend physics to make
it work."

The truth is, though I don't have eyes trained to see it, the
water out here in the delta is the most surreal and eerie thing of
all. We come to an old family camp that once stood on land, a
stilted structure that was built, like many fish camps, at the edge
of what was once a healthy salt marsh, legs firmly in the peat. Now
it's a quarter mile into open water. It serves as a landing place now
only for seabirds who flit between the empty rooms, flying to and
fro through the windowless walls.

HURRICANE

Hurricane Ida made landfall in southern Louisiana on August 29, on the sixteenth anniversary of Hurricane Katrina. It was a Category 4 storm. The sea surged between three and nine feet in places like Grand Isle and Port Fourchon. Winds sustained at 150 miles per hour.

Like those in New Orleans who lived inside the levees, Heather Bird Harris—one of the artists who accompanied me on Richie's boat, and who goes by Bird—and her family were under voluntary evacuation orders. She and her husband and their two children—two and four at the time—flew to her parents' home on the coast of Rhode Island. Bird and her husband had been in New Orleans for a decade at that point. When she tells me that's the place "where they fell in love," I can't tell if she means with each other or with a place, though I believe she means both. Bird is white; her husband, son, and daughter are Black; and they were excited to start a family within New Orleans's rich and thriving Black culture.

I met Bird as I was beginning to write this book, and we connected as mothers who were struggling to express the interconnected strands of love, land, grief, fear, and how to provide for our children's well-being. She was the one who invited me to come to New Orleans, to see the rising water firsthand.

It was while Bird's family was safely evacuated in Rhode Island, as Ida bore down in Louisiana, that her son Jade looked out over the calm, sun-dazzled sea in New England and spoke the words that would set in motion their family's decision to permanently leave their beloved, flood-prone city.

"You know what an ocean is?" Jade said, as if simply stating a well-understood fact. "It's water so high, over all the cities, that you can't even see the bottom."

Bird remembers looking at her son, thinking: "Oh my goodness, you're four, and you're looking at a beautiful ocean, and you see a flood."

Back at home, Jade's school had frequently closed for flooding. There were sunny days when the family simply couldn't go outside because their street had turned into a toxic river. Bird realized that morning in Rhode Island that "the boundaries between water and land and his recent memory had already been blurred." Several days later, Ida hit New England. The downtown of her parents' town flooded. "It was like," Bird says, "there's really no escaping this."

Bird is a visual artist and abstract painter whose work explores land loss, layered histories, and mothering in ecological crisis. She lists the births of both of her children on her CV. She makes her own paints and inks from Earth pigments that she collects from salt marsh peat, backyard soil, river mud, stones, and bricks. These she mixes with water and synthetic color. Her paintings are a dance between control and un-control, letting the water and pigment move each other organically. Through them, she explores the beauty of water and also the fear that water now evokes in her. She observes in her work "the way that water will settle earth into edges that look like the coastline of Louisiana. Or the edges of a flower petal. Or lots of little inlets. It [might] look like rivers." Witnessing these processes on a small scale helps her make sense of the massive scale of what is happening on the southern coastline. "The way that water is moving the Earth currently is part of a greater system, and it's OK," she says. "The infrastructure that we have built: that's the issue."

I ask if she thinks that the work of mothering right now is learning to live at the edge. She hesitates. After Ida, her family moved to Atlanta, away from the coast, and so this is a line of inquiry that stings. For her, it is less a theoretical question, about a way of being in the world, and more a literal question, about inhabiting a vulnerable coastline. "It's possible [to live] at the edge if you can learn responsiveness and how to be in a reciprocal relationship with the water and with the land," she says. "I think that's the hard part, and that's where all that stress comes from, because we weren't taught that . . . And the cities weren't built to support that, and therefore the places that we love so much can't sustain themselves."

Her latest work has a new edge to it, this one imposed: it's a series of large canvases that are split evenly down the middle, with paints made from soil and pigment from her former backyard in New Orleans on one side, and paints made from soil pigments from her new backyard in Atlanta on the other. Two landscapes, side by side but never meeting. In making these works, she observes the way the sediment moves differently on both sides, just as she observes how the stress and anxiety have dropped away from her children's shoulders in Atlanta, just as she lives, daily, within the profound heartache of having left a beloved place.

A precise definition of home is hard for her to pin down. "It's just anything that ebbs and flows through your life, based on what you need. It's very fluid for me right now."

I think this is true to an extent for many of us who are witnessing changes to the places we call home. There is an unsettling fluidity to the boundaries of where we live, whether in the shifting patterns of the seasons or the threat of wildfire. But this is especially true in places like New Orleans. Everyone I meet here is acutely aware of the presence of water. The people I speak to are either planning to leave, actively wrestling with whether to stay or go, or they are determined to stay, in full view of coming floods.

If you put a willow tree into a foot of water, Jeffery Darensbourg tells me, the next day it will sprout a new branch several inches above the surface. Meaning that, when floods happen, you can look to see where the willows have grown new branches to know how high the flood waters came, and therefore how high to build a place of safety and retreat. "That indicates a way of living with water and not against it," he says.

For his part, Jeffery plans to leave New Orleans in the next several years. "It's a place that has constantly flooded and will flood—for all time periods. That part can never be changed." He does not yet know where he'll go.

* * *

The morning of our boat ride with Richie, I had coffee with Alex Kolker, professor of earth and environmental sciences at the Louisiana Universities Marine Consortium. He sees this question of home and edges on a much longer timescale:

> A lot of deltaic wetlands are about five to seven thousand years old, which is about the age of human civilization. Some of our earliest civilizations were coastal river deltas. You had the Tigris-Euphrates, which the Bible says is the garden of Eden. You have the Nile River in Egypt, the Indus River delta in India. Maybe that's not an accident. But over that time of seven thousand years, we've seen cultures rise and flourish and also fall apart. And the environment sometimes plays a part in that.

How, he wonders aloud, does this present moment of land erosion and sea level rise fit into the rise and fall of cultures and civilizations? "What does that mean," he asks, "for those of us who go through periods of rapid transformation and change?"

It's a rhetorical question, not directed at me specifically, and it sits there, unanswered between us while we eat our pastries in the sunshine. A question that billows and buffets like a storm cloud.

* * *

Meanwhile, the Mississippi River still works its own will.

On the east bank of Plaquemines Parish, the river has opened a new cut, turning a previously narrow cut channel into an 850-foot-wide distributary called Neptune Pass.

For years, coastal advocates have been working toward human-made, large-scale diversions of the river that would resupply sediment to disappearing wetlands and build new land. Such projects often have a billion-dollar price tag. But this one the river accomplished on its own. Satellite imagery of this new pass shows the beginning of a new delta formation. Thin arms of vegetated sediment are appearing. New marshes are growing.

The Army Corps of Engineers is considering closing the pass because it's diverting 16 percent of the river's flow at its mouth, slowing ship navigation. Many are urging them to wait and give the river a chance, to leave it unbound, so that it can create the worlds it has always known how to create.

TIDE-WORK

"The shore is an ancient world," writes Rachel Carson, "for as long as there has been an earth and sea there has been this place of the meeting of land and water. Yet it is a world that keeps alive the sense of continuing creation and of the relentless drive of life."

The mystery of the border between land and sea is that it is ever in flux. It does not hold still. It is a boundary mediated by hydrodynamic, geologic, and cosmic forces.

Let's return, briefly, to Silverledges.

As the moon pulls water over the face of the Earth twice daily, the Sheepscot climbs and descends its banks. At high tide, the water rises to meet the feet of the slanted stone that leads down to the shore and that has been exposed only for twelve thousand years, a negligible amount of time in Earth's 4.5-billion-year history. Six hours later, the water has retreated, the top layer of sand has dried. This tiny world has shifted. The seaweed lies a bit differently over the rocks. Shells and pebbles have been rolled to new locations. I cannot say whether, day to day and tide to tide, these aggregated differences mean very much. Though I imagine they mean something to the creatures who live in this liminal space of water and land, where the alternating, fleeting presences of flood and drought, water and sun, shape how and when each life moves through their worlds, heightens or lessens one's chance of being predated, another's chance at a meal.

Where the sweep of water erases the path taken and reveals the next way.

For a long time, I thought that the way to deal with the climate crisis was to make a pathway into the light. But that's a linear way of thinking. For we, too, exist within inundation, within the clarifying shape of darkness. The tightening grip of grief. The threshold is crossed again and again.

Human beings are not delineated points that make clean cuts. We are messes of relationship. We are blurred boundaries. We are porous. We are made up of trillions of individual bacteria, of recycled air. We are powered and sustained by the foods we consume. We harbor DDE and PFAS. We carry stories and myths.

"A mother and daughter are an edge," writes Terry Tempest Williams in *When Women Were Birds*. "Edges are ecotones, transitional zones, places of danger or opportunity. House-dwelling tension. When I stand on the edge of the land and sea, I feel this tension, this fluid line of transition. High tide. Low tide. It is the sea's reach and retreat that reminds me we have been human for only a very short time."

I am a mother in a time of rising seas.
We are all mothers in a time of rising seas.

My job is to teach my daughter fluidity. Responsiveness. I am not talking about passivity or apathy; rather, to exist at the blurred boundary between joy and grief, agency and letting go, unraveling and becoming, life and loss. This, perhaps, has always been the case, since we have been human beings. But we have to come, again, to see it. Smell it. Taste it. Breathe it.

Can we be as fluid as the tide? Can we wax and wane, remake the patterns? Can we be like the periwinkle? The foraminifera?

Inhabiting the edge together, inclusively, is where the edge becomes a place of interconnection, possibility, and relationship.

Edge work is tide work. Ebb and flow. Repeated movements. Subtly shifting patterns. Repeat. Repeat. It is living within the change, not outside of it.

For there is no longer any outside of the change.

The work of mothering is to walk down to the edge. It is, I think, the only place where the walls come down.

PART VI

HOMEMAKING
Tending the Seasons

What folly to separate the urgent life will of the hollyhock
outside my door from the other lives, the family, I hold dear.
My life demands a radically domestic ecological thought.

—Camille Dungy, *Soil*

INHABITING

Among the books on my shelf is a 1975 edition of *Webster's New Collegiate Dictionary*. I've kept it, in part, because I can't remember if it was my mother's when she was in school or if I purchased it at a used bookstore. The former possibility has given it a sentimental value (albeit quite possibly a made-up one). In it, *homemaker* is defined as "(n) one who manages a household esp. as a wife and mother." Today, the *Cambridge Dictionary* defines the word as "a person who manages a home and often raises children instead of earning money from a job." In the *Oxford English Dictionary*: "a person who runs his or her own household; one skilled at domestic tasks; a housewife or househusband."

That the gendered language has largely been removed over the last four decades is progress. But let's continue to implode this definition. Let's honor as valuable, necessary, and deeply worthy those who put their minds, bodies, and spirits to creating dwellings and spaces in which others are cared for, tended to, and made to feel welcome. Let's pull it outside of its assumed contrast to "earning money," thus wrenching it free of capitalism. Let's think more inclusively about what "home" and "housework" mean. Let's make the walls of our homes porous and inclusive to the more-than-human world beyond.

In doing so, let's turn once more to Robin Wall Kimmerer, the home-creator who inspired this book: "a good mother . . . creates a home where all of life's beings can flourish," Kimmerer writes. That is the kind of homemaker I long to be. And that's the kind of "good mother"—the one who is engaged in the work of radical inclusiveness, who is in relationship to more-than-human kin, who dwells within a home that is not a silo but a village—that I want to be as well. A physical space, yes, but also a way of being, a way of inhabiting that we can carry with us and practice, no matter where we are.

On the shifting ground of the edge, how do we make such a home, a way of holding steady, though the waters may roil around us?

❊ ❊ ❊

There is a row of trees growing along the west fence of our backyard. They are spindly with thin canopies. They are missing patches of bark, with some branches free of leaves year-round. The leaves that do emerge in the spring get chewed by some insect we never see. The trees are not as majestic as the large white pine that grows tall and wide in the center of the yard, nor are they as iconic as the red maples that line the eastern fence and turn bright red and orange come fall. Friends have asked what kinds of trees the west-fence trees are. Either Andrew or I always answer, "I don't know," at which point I briefly think, "Maybe we *should* know." And then I forget about the trees again.

I'm writing these words as we pass the one-year anniversary of moving to this house. As we approached this milestone over the last few months, having been next to those trees day in and out, I still hadn't given them much thought. My attention was caught up in the other acts of making a home. The physical acts of moving, arranging, rearranging, putting in a garden and tending to it, walking and biking and driving the new streets. And the emotional acts: saying farewell to one place and then making a different sort of internal and external space for another one, navigating the new. Moving still takes a far greater emotional toll than I expect it will. I get attached to places. I mourn them when I leave.

The scraggly trees have served as backdrop to it all, making only brief appearances in my consciousness. Over the winter, I worried about whether or not they'd fall in a storm, if they could withstand the weight of wet snow. In late summer, I offered them a bit of gratitude for the sparse shade they provided on the hottest days.

As that first summer in this house turned into a bright fall, and fall into a warm winter, and winter into a wet spring, and a wet spring into an even wetter summer—I turned over and over in my mind what this new home means. I fretted about it. I conjured other homes in daydreams, places I've lived before but no longer have in my life. The house on Comanche Street in Norman, Oklahoma, with the rose rocks built into the flagstone exterior and the pear tree that dropped rock-hard fruit onto our car; or Lost Farm on Nantucket, where my brother and I did much of our growing up, now inhabited by the person who took my father's job when he retired and moved back to Nebraska. I've wondered if it was the right choice to leave our caretaking opportunity in Washington. I've worried that, as an adult and as a mother, I haven't gotten home right.

I carried this worry even as we returned to the deeply welcome, familiar sensory surroundings of the Northeast. As we put plants in the yard of this new house, and as Aspen delighted in the round-bellied robins that bounced through the yard. Even as this became the place where the three of us snuggle on the couch to watch old episodes of *Reading Rainbow* and *Mister Rogers*, Aspen only begrudgingly sharing the popcorn, and where family frequently drops by, and the neighbors brought us all of the irises they'd dug up from their front lawn to plant in our own. Even then I kept finding myself caught between missing homes I'd never get back and wondering if our *true* home was still out there, somewhere, undiscovered.

One day last week, for some reason or for no reason at all, I thought: *it's time to find out what kind of trees those are.* I went outside and plucked a leaf, then pulled a small green book, *Tree Finder,* off the shelf and started flipping through. With only so many northeastern deciduous trees with ridged leaves, I ruled out birch and beech and came to the elms. Hackberry, a member of the elm family, looked like the closest fit. I then consulted the more in-depth *Trees of North America,* which confirmed it.

"They're hackberries!" I announced. Then there didn't seem much else to say about it, so we sat down to dinner and didn't mention the trees again.

I didn't realize how closely Aspen had been paying attention. The next day, I was doing odds and ends in the kitchen when Aspen piped up from the living room: "I need to get a leaf, Mom."

"A leaf?" And then, looking over, I saw she was sitting cross-legged on the floor, flipping through *Tree Finder.* I went outside and pulled a leaf from one of the trees and brought it in to her.

"Hmm . . ." she said, holding the leaf against random pages. She made a show of flipping back and forth through the book. "Hummmm. . . ." And then, "Maybe it's a . . . *hackberry!*"

Since then, no matter how many times that little green book goes back on the shelf, it disappears again. She's kept it close. I've found it in her canvas tote, in the corner of her bed, in her red wagon.

And I realized that, of course, this is it. *This* is getting it right. Knowing the name of the trees is part of it. But really, it's this little girl who is not worried one iota about whether we're in the right place, because she spends her time and energy simply being here: fully present, unendingly curious, silly, rooted and rooting further.

We are in our fifth season living in this house. We are still learning.

Here, in five seasons, are five practices of homemaking.

45

WONDER (SUMMER)

The U-Haul was waiting for us when we pulled into our new driveway for the first time. My mom was so eager to have us back in New England that she volunteered to drive it across the country from Seattle to the coast of Maine. She and her friend Jim made the trip in three epic days. Grandma adrenaline. A good friend volunteered to drive our car for us, via a slightly different route. She did it in just under two weeks, taking her time to enjoy the sights along the way. We were grateful to avoid the fifty-plus hours of driving, and so we flew back with almost-two-year-old Aspen and three backpacks. We made that journey in just under six hours.

We'd been gone for a year. It had been, in many ways, a hard one.

Our little gray house in Portland's Libbytown neighborhood was baking in the July sun that first afternoon. My brother and his partner showed up with a bag of ice and cold beer. My cousin and her husband came with a frosted three-layer cake, rimmed with ripe berries. (They also confessed to being the ones who had mowed our lawn the week before we arrived.) The U-Haul was unloaded within an hour. Our bed was assembled, our bookshelves built, our rugs rolled out. Some friends came with two bags of potting soil and vegetable seedlings they had started, which they put into our raised beds for us. So began our garden. In the weeks to follow, we dug out two large beds in the front yard, planted them with perennial flowers. Bees came to pollinate them. Squirrels ate all our squash. Andrew planted two apple trees and a pear tree in the back. We met the neighbors.

All to say: those first months were nothing extraordinary. There was no great revelation to be transcribed here. I even considered deleting the above words. But I've kept them, in the end, precisely because they are small and ordinary. They are the daily, mundane, joyful, wonderful, tedious acts that make a place into a home.

Joy and wonder do not need to be great and grand. They are often in the direct experience of the everyday. I remember, for instance, childhood walks in Oklahoma. We would lift a piece of moist, decaying bark and find a garter snake twined beneath, a lightning strike of yellow down his back. That same flash of light might later run down the center of the storming sky. That sky, which held a stubbornly untamable wild, right there above our heads, no matter how tamed the land below.

These perfunctory sorts of joy and wonder are critical practices of homemaking. While they may sound frivolous or indulgent, they are necessary. Joy is not an escape but an anchor. Wonder is not a distraction but a portal. It is often in the daily. Joy is in direct experience. It is at our feet or whispering in our ears, and still it does not narrow our gaze. It makes us expansive. It fortifies, grounds, sustains, feeds. It surpasses the ego. If we are to do the work ahead, in all of our anger and grief and fear, we must make our home, our harbor, in joy. A place of safe return. We must make a practice of living from and through our wonder. Without them, despair threatens to overwhelm. And despair does not serve us or others.

Joy and wonder constitute a type of learning and sharing of experience that Heather Bird Harris defined to me as "rhizomatic." Not hierarchical or prescribed, but dynamic and spreading into numerous pathways and possibilities. Aspen has taught me more about joy in the last three years than I have learned in the last thirty-six. She crawls slowly behind ants just to see where they'll go. She throws up her hands and says, "*What* in the *world!?*" in reference to herself, when she knows she is being silly. She cries out in the middle of the night because she can't find the squishy blue truck she went to sleep holding. Beyond meeting her basic needs, I think nurturing and cultivating her joy and wonder is one of the best things I can do for her. Though it is often she who shows me how to do this.

In mothering, and in homemaking, there is always opportunity to notice those flashes of lightning, along the snake's back and along the wide arc of the sky. There is always the potential of being struck.

MUSIC (FALL)

Beatrice Harrison, renowned cellist of the early twentieth century, enjoyed practicing outdoors in her English garden. Once, when playing Rimsky-Korsakov's "Chant Hindu," she heard her notes echoed back to her. A nightingale, drawn by her playing, had come to sing with her cello. She played ascending and descending notes. "The voice of the bird followed me," she recalled. "It seemed a miracle."

In early October, I visited the Audubon nature trail at Scarborough Marsh. A thick wall of cloud was retreating, and the maple branches were arms raised in devotion, draped in fiery cloaks that spat sparks of the emerging sun. The cordgrass was gold and green and red-brown. Cattails tufted out their bronze seed. I collected a handful, and it was unbearably delicate and soft, lighter than air. The breeze nearly tugged it from my open palm. The proud, stout bayberry held its sheen of emerald green. The purple-crowned heads of New England aster bowed over the trail, alongside them the dwindling bloom of the goldenrod, a dozen setting suns. The sumac was blood red. Birds chipped and chirped in the trees, darting and bobbing in blurs of wings across the trail ahead of me. I didn't know who they were. But their notes played a familiar tune somewhere in the recesses of my mind.

It was my first time in this place, but home bounded in my chest. My body knew it before I did: a sensory knowledge; an embodied, encoded memory. I *knew* this place. I had been here before.

But no, I've never been here, my thoughts insisted.

Oh yes you have, said my body.

I felt what the intuited recognition was in my limbs and in my ears before the clear image came into my mind. The palette of colors and shapes and sounds into which I had been folded conjured the image of Lost Farm, hundreds of miles away and out to sea. My physical body was here, but my memory had been transported. It was as if the marsh and that family home were overlaid, a double exposure. It was my sensory being that spoke the overlapping layers of place to me in a language I could never hope to translate here. It spoke, too, the depth and range of emotion that followed. Joy. Grief. Love. Longing. All of this, before my mind connected the dots.

"Not surprising," I then thought to myself, my left-hemisphere logic kicking in. Scarborough Marsh and Lost Farm share many of the same ecological features. They are both in New England, they are both tempered by proximity to the coast, they both have woods and brackish water and meadows. Probably even the same species of birds, heading southward on their winter migration.

Logic briefly satisfied, I returned to my astonishment. Because it was not my intellect that first made this connection. It was the bayberry and the aster and the cattail and the birds whose names I did not know but whose voices had been tucked away in my mind like forgotten lullabies.

At the time of this walk, Lost Farm had come to live up to its name. It was a lost place. My family no longer lived there after my dad retired and returned to his childhood home of Nebraska. Our twenty-year span of time on that land was over, and my heart ached for a home that was home no more. But in that familiar wave of grief that arose in memory, in the conjuring of Lost Farm through sensory recognition, I was comforted by a new knowledge: that Lost Farm lived not only in my neural memory, in the way that I usually thought of brain-kept memory, but in my *bodily memory* as well. It had been written into some internal, sensory map. I carried the imprint of that landscape with me.

But why? Logic again interrupted. *And how?*

It was, I realized, the memory-stimulating effect of the *soundscape* that truly surprised, and therefore most interested me. Somehow, the sounds of Scarborough Marsh had brought Lost Farm to my mind's eye, as clear as a developing photograph. Was I making that up? Could that be true?

✳ ✳ ✳

A few days after my walk at the marsh, I planted garlic cloves. I had read they were supposed to remain dormant until spring, when they would then grow into zesty scapes. But they grew several inches by late October and then stopped abruptly, as if realizing the world above the soil was not as it should be. Temperatures in southern Maine reached seventy degrees on November 12. But the garlic couldn't retreat back into the ground, and so it stayed there, exposed, slowly losing its green over the next several months as temperatures sporadically dove below freezing. Then, approaching Thanksgiving, the rhododendron sent out buds, like a cuckoo clock someone forgot to wind, keeping a time that no longer matched that of the external world. I noticed all of this and didn't have any idea what to do about it. What was there to do about a world losing track of its time?

Around then, I received an email from my uncle Kevin in Seattle. He CC'ed most of our extended family, suggesting we all bring our copies of *Rise Up Singing*—a songbook with the words and chords to more than 1,000 folksongs, gospels, and ballads—to

Thanksgiving. The plan was to meet at my aunt and uncle's house in Concord, New Hampshire. More of us were gathering than had been able to in a long time.

Uncle Kevin was always singing. He'd call one of his daughters just to sing them a song. He sang in the car, while skiing, in his local folk song circle. When we visited their family last Thanksgiving in Seattle, he sang to Aspen, even though, at fourteen months old, she was a little put off by his loud voice and his face a foot from hers. He chose an especially long song with many verses and sang it all the way through, insistent, trying to make eye contact with her the whole time. *That's so Kevin*, I remember thinking.

He suggested in his email that, over Thanksgiving, we sing some rounds. Rounds are musical compositions with no fixed ending. In a simple round, one line of melody is sung by all of the voices, who join the melody at different times, so that one melodic thread layers and folds over itself, different bars coinciding at different moments, creating harmonies. It's a beautiful and simple way of singing, inclusive and accessible. There is room for all of the voices.

My mom and her five siblings shared a childhood in a large, haunted farmhouse on 72nd street in Omaha, Nebraska. (Everyone who grew up in that house has at least one convincing ghost story.) It was a colorful and chaotic dwelling. The kitchen wallpaper featured stylized drawings of French Revolution soldiers. As a teenager, my mom painted an eight-foot-tall giraffe on the wall of the downstairs bedroom. That was my favorite room in the house as a child. Oil paintings of fruit and rural landscapes hung on the walls in the living room. Musical instruments were tucked in corners. It was the only house I'd ever been in where it felt like there was life in the walls as much as there was life in the people who lived between them. That it was haunted never surprised or scared me.

But as an adult, I came to know that the house—long since sold to another family, all the walls painted over in neutral tones—had held something dark, too. Alongside the disembodied footsteps on the stairs and the voices in the empty hall there had been a truer haunting. Alongside the genuine love the siblings feel for each other are deep family wounds that have, for each of them, been slow to heal.

Folk music runs thick in our blood on the Scudder side of my family. Music is, I think, one of the few unblemished forms of inheritance. It seems able to hold my mother's side of the family together in the moments when little else can. My grandmother was an opera singer. She and my grandfather helped found the Omaha Folk Song Society. They were big fans of Pete Seeger. For my mom and her siblings, passing music onto my generation has been, I think, to pass along something that feels graciously unfraught, one of the unpolluted ways of loving that existed in that house. The music has been handed down, with care and respect, like a family jewel, its form intact.

Thanksgiving Day arrived, boisterous. There were eighteen of us, ages one to sixty-nine, aunts, uncles, cousins, cousins' children, and, for much of the day, no one sat still for more than a handful of moments. Conversations were started, unfinished, returned to, forgotten. Things bubbled on the stove. Dustings of flour were repeatedly swept from the floor.

Several hours before we ate, the bulk of the cooking done and the table set, we gathered close in the living room. Children on laps. Some adults seated on the floor. Extra chairs brought in. Though there were a number of adept guitar, fiddle, and piano players among us, we opted for no instruments apart from our voices. We pulled out our copies of *Rise Up Singing*. There was a moment of hesitation. Then we started to sing.

We sang "Ah, Poor Bird" and "Rose, Rose" and "One Bottle of Pop" and "Kookaburra" and "Why Shouldn't My Goose." There might have been a short pause between songs. Then one of us would remember a round we learned long ago. We took turns choosing and suggesting and teaching each other. Laughter ran through us as often as the melody did.

The tune and the harmonies moved around and around our circle. When our voices were singing, there was nothing in me but the notes and the next notes moving toward, and in, and through, and the sounds of those notes traveling through the vessels of each of the members of my family, each voice its own timbre and shape, each voice making space for the others, sharing the song. Tunes I had not heard or sung in decades, but now remembered my grandfather or my mom singing to me, returned easily, having never been forgotten. Aspen sat on my lap, quiet and listening, patting her knees with her hands.

This hour of singing together created a subtle shift in our family. Where there was often tension in these gatherings—people ready to raise the walls by about this time—there was none after our song circle. For the rest of the evening, we kept returning to the shape of that circle. We told stories. We listened to each other. People moved in and out, tended to children, did the dishes, got some more pie. But the circle held its shape.

And there it was again: the conjuring of home through sound and song. A certainty of belonging woven into a series of notes. This time not Lost Farm, but a sense of being at home within the music itself and within the love of singing that had lived for generations in my family.

✳ ✳ ✳

It took me some time to connect the experiences, to realize that two of my most acute, most deeply embodied experiences of home in recent memory had been prompted by song. The singing of birds and then the singing of my family. In two different places, with a different set of voices (really, a different set of *species*), and with different memories stimulated—but still, the feeling itself had been the same. A deep sense of belonging, existential and physical, emotional and spiritual.

Could those two experiences be connected? What did song have to do with such feeling? Could the same sensation be triggered by both birds and humans?

I retraced my steps and started back where I had begun: at the marsh.

First, I confirmed that the same species of birds were likely to have been present in both of these particular landscapes at this time of year. Yes. Among them: Eastern towhee. Pine warbler. Black-capped chickadee. Tufted titmouse. Dark-eyed junco. I listened to recordings of their songs. I did know them! Eastern towhee, I remember my dad teaching me, sings *drink your tea*. And black-capped chickadee sings *chickadee-dee-dee-dee*.

There is a difference between bird calls and bird songs. Birds call or sing for a variety of reasons: as warnings, to establish territory, to compete for and attract mates. Whether there is further meaning or intention behind their compositions is a question Western science at least has yet to answer. But I will leave the intentions of the birds aside for the moment. What I was curious about: Do our human minds hear these bird sounds as music? And, if so, what is the effect?

It turns out that the songs of birds often have both rhythmic variation and combinations of notes that would be easily recognizable as music to the ears of human beings. The authors of a paper published by the *American Association for the Advancement of Science* write that "some bird songs resemble musical compositions; for example, the canyon wren's trill cascades down the musical scale like the opening of Chopin's 'Revolutionary' Etude."

This wren, they found, sings in a chromatic scale, whereas others, like the hermit thrush, sing in the pentatonic.

A study published in *Current Biology* compared the rhythms of wild thrush nightingales and domestic zebra finches to rhythms from human musical traditions around the world. They found that the nightingale's complex repertoire features "universal rhythm categories, with patterns that were surprisingly similar to those of music," while the zebra finch sings a simpler song, a repeated motif with a metronomic rhythm. Such similarities in rhythm across species, the authors hope, will contribute to our understanding that, "like music and language, the song of many bird species is culturally transmitted through learning, and it forms dialects reminiscent of local musical traditions or different languages." Some songbird species, like the American goldfinch, sing in melodies and rhythms that are so rapid and complex it can be difficult for our brains to follow them. But it nonetheless seems clear that the human mind is *capable* of hearing birdsong not just as a series of sounds or notes but as music.

Next, I wanted to know: how and why did recognizable music move me so deeply in both of those experiences? How did it stir such memory and emotion?

We know part of the answer but not all of it. Here is what happens when the human brain hears a sound. Say you hear a single, isolated note: an open G plucked on a cello. Sound waves travel through the ear canal to the eardrum, which vibrates. The vibrations then reach three bones in the middle ear where they are amplified and sent to the spiral-shaped cochlea. Here, hair cells sort the vibration into elementary frequencies. The auditory nerve then transmits this information, now an electrical signal, to the brain stem and then to the brain's auditory cortex, where the sound is represented in a spatial arrangement, a frequency map. Our brain's fine-tuned ability to process sound would deliver us valuable information: direction of the sound's source, perhaps a new focus of our attention to that sound; an understanding that the sound came from a musical instrument, and perhaps recognition of the instrument itself or even an ability to name the note.

But *music* has a far more complex relationship to the human brain than sound does. Look at what happens when our brain hears not just a single, plucked note but a melody. Say that same G is bowed on a cello, and this time it is the G that begins the Prelude to Bach's Cello Suite No. 1; an arpeggio follows, and the notes continue, combining to create perhaps the most beloved and recognizable cello piece of all time. The same neural process repeats itself—eardrum to cochlea to auditory cortex—but it simultaneously radiates beyond, spilling far past the brain's sound processing systems.

Music stimulates the visual and motor cortices; the cerebellum, which is related to rhythm, timing, and fine-tuning movement; the amygdala, which has a prominent role in emotion processes and emotional learning; the hippocampus, a crucial part of the brain for storing memory; and the mesolimbic system, which serves as the primary reward center of our brain. And just as the relationship between a series of individual tones transforms them into music, all of these parts of our brain work together to integrate layers of sound across time and space so that it becomes possible for us to decipher a series of sounds as song.

Even the *type* of music we're listening to has been traced to different patterns of neural stimulation. Our brains, for example, have a special category for music that is sung, versus instrumental music. Different parts of our brain light up depending on whether we were listening to music or playing it, and again whether we were improvising music or reading a musical score. The subtleties of music prompt neurological responses even on the cellular level: neural cells will react differently to the exact same tone when it is part of an ascending series of notes or when it is part of a descending one.

Music also has demonstrable effects on the physical body. A study at Cornell University had participants listen to different musical compositions that were expected to evoke strong emotions: happiness, fear, or sadness. While they were listening, their physiological responses via heart rate, blood pressure, and respiration were measured. The study found that the types of music resulted in specific physiological changes that were consistent across the subjects. Music has also been found to influence clinical health recoveries, and music therapy is often used in medical settings to reduce anxiety and fear in patients.

We still don't have a clear idea why any of this is the case. Nor can we pinpoint music's origins. Archaeological evidence of sophisticated fifty-thousand-year-old bone flutes suggests the possibility that music-making has been a human tradition for several hundred thousand years. There are theories that song, dance, and rhythm were central factors in the emergence of human consciousness itself. It is wonderful, is it not, to think that music comes as naturally and as wildly to us as it does to the nightingale?

Even today, music in the human experience is believed to be culturally universal. Reacting to music precedes language acquisition in infants. In utero, a near-term fetus will respond to a song if it has been exposed to that song for numerous weeks. Infants can recognize familiar melodies, as well as changes in tempo and rhythm.

Why sound in the form of music affects us so profoundly is perhaps a question we will not find the answer to, at least in my lifetime.

So—where had I gotten in my inquiry? The species of songbirds at Lost Farm and Scarborough Marsh were much the same. Birdsong has been demonstrated to be structured in ways similar to human music and recognizable to us as such. Music has been shown to activate memory and promote a physical and emotional sense of well-being.

I still had a question: beyond well-being, comfort, and safety, there seemed to be a distinctly place-based element to hearing music that was not only familiar but associated with home. Because, especially at the marsh, the familiarity of the birdsong not only caused me to remember a beloved place but, in turn, made the marsh itself—an unfamiliar landscape—feel like a home-place where I was safe and comfortable. In that way, it seems that a soundscape can offer us a place-based orientation or grounding. An internal centering that can outwardly center us as well.

What, then, is the role of music in homemaking? For these two encounters with music had enacted within me some deeply ingrained sense of home. Homemaking, then, is not just something we do but something that can be done *to* us. The world around us can give us this gift. Our bodies can receive sensory input as an experience of true well-being.

* * *

Young zebra finches learn to sing from adult males in their community, songs they are able to remember and repeat, just as human infants learn to speak from an adult tutor. Songbirds even share with us a "transitional babbling phase" before they're able to clearly articulate.

Local populations of white-crowned sparrows sing in a "geographic mosaic of dialects," sharing certain features in their songs that are specific to their place of birth. In competing for territory and mates, these birds grow into adults who have learned a set of songs that are locally unique, within a community that is adapted to the environmental conditions immediately around them. Thus, this species of sparrow receives not only songs from their families and communities but *place*-specific songs that could help maintain the population's geographic location.

Our human minds, too, evolved to know and respond to what we hear in the world around us. The soundscape continues to feed us necessary information, even if many of us are no longer taught how to tune our awareness to it. In 2009, an Indigenous musician in the Yoreme community of northwestern Mexico told a puzzled ethnologist that, in the Yoreme language, one can sing in both sound and color. Yoreme ceremonial music was first received from the mouse and the bird, sounds from which the Yoreme created the drum and the flute. In playing these instruments, one is not simply making music but recreating a specific ecological soundscape, and, therefore, participating in and reaffirming the Yoreme relationship with place. Sacred music for the Yoreme is landscape-specific, multisensory, and a means of maintaining and carrying forward this relationship.

Just as my conscious mind was struggling to keep up with and trust the innate knowledge of my body at the marsh, Western science has been slow to catch up with the idea that music, landscape, and culture are not separate functions of the human experience but are intertwined. And especially when they are *intentionally* or ceremonially intertwined, we come into a deeper experience of being not only within a place but participants in it.

The cultural transmissions of song in my upbringing were not only shared in a setting of safety and comfort (tucked in bed, for example) but also often sung before or after a story from my mom's childhood. Perhaps this is part of why that sense of home-through-song has stayed so strongly with me. Not only is music an unbroken inheritance in my family, but it endures as a universal inheritance of humanity more broadly. I have yet to meet a human who does not enjoy music. Could this universal inclination for melody and rhythm constitute one of the paths we might walk toward healing our relationship with the living world?

In *Sounds Wild and Broken*, biologist David George Haskell confirms the way in which culture extends beyond language and words, and deep into the realm of the senses. "Like many singing birds, human culture is transmitted by sound, as well as by sight and touch," he writes. "Aural memory, then, allows us to understand and navigate both the human and beyond-human worlds."

Aural memory. This was the phrase I had been searching for. Both the marsh and my family's song circle triggered such memory and, in doing so, reoriented me to some of my earliest lessons of navigating the world. My father teaching me the song of the eastern towhee, my mother singing "Kookaburra" to me before bed. Each experience of song was nested in an early experience of being at home.

For that is what home is, isn't it? Not walls and a roof but a place, and the songs we learn in order to be in it. Home is the unique way that each of us becomes attuned to the world. And it is an ongoing becoming. Within landscape, and soundscape, is the entwining of human culture and ecology in ways that are both healing and harmful. We learn and then begin to hum and to sing the sounds of our places, like the melody of a round, so that that line of song plays over itself again and again, layered and layering. The circle extends. Our mind maps what our senses experience. We map places into ourselves. We remember. We sing.

❊ ❊ ❊

And so, with "Ah, Poor Bird" and *drink your tea* running through my mind, I think of the orientation to home that I want to pass on to Aspen:

> *Singing simple songs in a circle.*
> *A practice of no fixed endings.*
> *Trust in the body.*
> *The ever-present possibility of healing.*
> *The imperative to listen.*
> *Creating and tending to an inclusive circle of care.*

A circle of care. A place for every voice. A way for the notes to travel through us and on to others.

❊ ❊ ❊

After Thanksgiving, we keep singing in our family of three. On through our celebrations of the Solstice and Hanukkah and Christmas. Through the winter, into spring. Aspen requests songs and variations of songs. The Kookaburra sits in the old gum tree, then in a yogurt tree, a pizza tree, a bunny tree. Aspen keeps patting her knees. My cousin Emma and I start a monthly song circle in our community.

The songs are like lit candles that kept burning. When I fell in love with the right whales and then dove into grief, when I came to the edge of what I know and walked into the fear that was on the other side, I returned to that circle.

The circle continues to hold space for songs and for more than songs. After Thanksgiving, a family text chain forms. The six siblings share jokes and wish each other happy birthdays. There is a lightness to it all that I've never noticed between them. I wonder whether it was because we sang together, but I can't be sure. Obviously, there's more to it, but whether the singing wove its own bit of healing, or the singing became possible because healing had been done, it seems the songs marked a change.

The circle keeps showing up, inviting us in. We are practicing what it means to extend it and to welcome others. To keep the circle of care with us and within us, to make space in it for others. This is done mostly in small ways around our home. We decide not to mow as much of our lawn as we did last year. We mow the center to keep the ticks out and give Aspen easy space to run but leave a wide swath to do what it will. Tiny, delicate wildflowers and orange mushrooms like frisbees and sweet-smelling grass grows. We try to be better listeners. To honor the wisdom of our ears. We learn the voices of the northern cardinal, robin, and nuthatch. I accept that the garlic will not recover from its early entry. I remember that there will be another opportunity to plant. The Earth will turn through its days and nights and seasons. I remember that this circling is the one that makes all of the other circles possible.

✳ ✳ ✳

Seven months after we form that Thanksgiving circle, my uncle Kevin will die suddenly. It will be unfair and far too soon, as death often is. The news will arrive from Seattle like a glacier calving from a distance, a hushed and violent crash into the sea.

The circle, then, will seem to break. We will bear the unbearable weight of an abrupt ending, a voice cut short.

But that inheritance, that multigenerational circle of song, will prove resilient once again. It will withstand what feels ready to crumble. Ahead of our gathering to celebrate his life, his wife of forty years and their two daughters, smiling through tears, will ask if we would, please, come together to sing.

We'll bring copies of *Rise Up Singing*. And rise our voices will.

A PARTICULAR LOVE (WINTER)

Long, long ago, Saint Kevin retreated to the wilderness for his observance of Lent, as was his custom. There he remained forty days secluded in a small, simple hut with naught but a roof over his head and a window to let in light and fresh air. He spent his time reading and praying, occasionally lifting one hand out of the window, where he held it steady, in all his devotion, heavenward.

One day, his hand thus extended, a blackbird landed on his palm, took it for a nest, and laid an egg.

Kevin, feeling the bird and the egg in his hand, did not withdraw his arm back into the hut but left it there raised to heaven, day and night, night and day, turn after turn of the Earth, until the egg hatched, and the young bird fledged. The mother bird and the baby bird departed on their own time, of their own will.

* * *

It's early March, the beginning of Lent, several weeks before Easter and the onset of spring, when we drive to Strafford, Vermont, to spend a weekend with Mark and Lisa Kutolowski and their children. In their observance of Lent, Mark and Lisa are eating only foods that are grown or produced in the New England region, a respectable challenge in the northeastern winter. (Anna and Luke, two years old and eight months old respectively, are exempted from participating.) Lisa kindly warned me ahead of time that this means no coffee or black tea, and while I briefly consider joining them in their abstention during our visit, I choose the coffee instead. Aspen rarely sleeps past 5:00 a.m., more often rising closer to 4:30. We pack an ample stash of caffeine.

The last several miles of our drive are over an icy dirt road, and Andrew rightly wonders if we'll be able to leave again on Sunday, given the eighteen inches of snow expected during our stay. There's already a fresh foot on the ground, and it gives the illusion of arriving amid endless winter, but, in truth, the last several months have been far warmer than usual. Winter is not a New England resident this year but a fickle houseguest, coming and going. In Portland, it was fifty-five degrees on January 1.

As we pull up, Lisa, in leggings and an embroidered skirt, brown hair knotted at the back of her neck, steps onto the porch, waving. Luke is strapped to her back in a onesie snowsuit, peering around her shoulder. He's one of those babies whose face is so well defined and expressive you feel you know exactly what he'll look like twenty years from now and, because of this, are tempted to strike up a conversation with him about this evening's expected blizzard.

We step into the house, recently constructed, the unessential details left undone for now—the tile backsplash behind the kitchen sink and stove, the backboards on the stairs, half of the porch. The bones of one of last year's flock of chickens are stewing in a crockpot, and the briny scent of broth makes the kitchen seem even cozier. This year's chicks and guinea keets are staying warm under a large bulb, several rooms away, in the space that will eventually be Lisa's commercial bread kitchen. Anna is shyly hugging Mark's leg at first but is soon singing songs, jumping on the couch, and telling us about her favorite books. This is their communal space and guest house, where we'll be staying the next several nights. Mark, Lisa, Anna, and Luke live a hundred yards up and over a hill, in a yurt.

At 5:30, late winter sun sinking, we follow the family, with Anna leading the way, across the road and down a forested trail well-packed by snowshoes. We come alongside Abbott Brook trickling below thick bridges of snow and arrive at the chapel, another yurt (yes, they are so very Vermont).

It is time for Vespers, evening prayer.

We've come to see Mark and Lisa, Roman Catholics living a quasi-monastic life on a homestead, because they are braiding together a relationship to the land with their faith. Pairing homesteading with ritual, syncing together church liturgy and the liturgy of the land.

Mark is a trained wilderness guide, a wild foods expert, and a devout Catholic with short silver hair and beard to match. He eats butter by the tablespoon, has a strong academic streak, and has a goofy sense of humor. I met him nearly a decade ago, working under the guidance and mentorship of Steve Blackmer at Kairos Earth. One of my strongest memories of Mark is from that time, during a winter staff retreat in northern New Hampshire. Temperatures had plummeted—negative thirty degrees Fahrenheit at night and failing to climb anywhere near zero during the day. It was the kind of cold where, if you threw a cup of boiling water into the air, it never hit the ground, instead instantly turning to ice crystals. Such was the forecast for our three-day stay in an off-grid cabin in the middle of the woods with no electricity or running water. Five of us were there, drinking tea made of boiled snow and huddling close to the woodstove. I was dreading going to sleep that first night—imagining how quickly the stove would cool, and how temperatures outside were expected to fall well into the range that the tag on the inside of my sleeping bag labeled as "risk"—when Mark announced he was going to build and sleep in a snow cave. I occasionally awoke that night to rub warmth back into my nose, wondering if we'd find him frozen to death in the morning. But he trudged in after dawn, eyebrows and eyelashes encrusted in ice, hungry for breakfast. Someone got out the butter. Since then, I still think to myself that if the world goes to shit, we'd better go find Mark.

As a young man, Mark committed to life as an Oblate of Saint Benedict at Mount Saviour Monastery. An oblate is a lay follower, in this case one committed to follow a way of life laid out by Saint Benedict, the father of Western monasticism, who established the Benedictine Rule in the sixth century. As an oblate, Mark is not obliged to observe the Rule in full as a vowed monk would—practicing celibacy or living within the walls of a monastery—but he is expected to pray the liturgical hours and to seek holiness within his life, manifesting Christ's presence in the world and society.

When I first knew Mark, he was longing for a family and religious community, but the desire for wildness and wilderness that defined his faith left him apart from much of mainstream Catholicism. Then he met Lisa, a professional bread baker and an accomplished singer with a smile like the sun parting clouds.

We've come to see them because I'm curious about faith-based practices of living with the land that draw upon my Judeo-Christian roots (paired with my mother's Jewish heritage, my father's side of the family is Catholic, all the way back to distant ancestors in Switzerland). Mark and Lisa are trying to rebuild a way of life that has largely been lost within Western culture. Living an explicitly spiritual life in partnership with the land, with an eye toward generations: not only Anna and Luke but those who come after them, and inclusive, too, of the generations of trees, the coyotes, and the barred owls.

Lisa was down at the chapel earlier, stoking the wood stove. Inside the yurt, branches radiate down the ceiling from the skylight at the top and crisscross the circular walls, making up the internal bones of the structure. Snow and ice skitter audibly down the canvas roof. On the far wall is a simple altar: a table draped in white and purple cloth, with an icon of Christ, a vase of bare branches, and several dozen candles, a handful of which Mark and Lisa light. Anna has her own altar with a bird's nest, a candle, a collection of polished stones, and a tangle of green moss. She and Aspen run around throughout the service. Luke stays strapped to his mom.

Cast in flickers of firelight, we arrange ourselves in a semi-circle. Lisa and I kneel on sheepskins on the floor, made from lambs they raised over the summer and culled in the fall. Mark and Andrew sit on folding chairs. Lisa passes around small, black binders containing liturgies, readings, hymns, and prayers. Some are typed, some are handwritten and photocopied. Mark and Lisa take turns with the psalms and gospel readings. We all sing together, *Look down on us, O Kindly Lord, and see how with repentant tears / We have begun the sacred fast which is to last for forty days.* Lisa's voice is sweet and clear, Mark's earnest and slightly off-key.

The Liturgy of the Hours is a canonical means of timekeeping, marking both the day's hours and the year's seasons through practices of Christian devotion, structuring time around prayer at regular intervals: Vigils, Lauds, Terce, Sext, None, Vespers, Compline. It began with the Jewish practice of praying the Psalms and continues within Christianity as a means of drawing one's attention back, again and again, to God. Each involves spoken prayer, Gospel readings, psalms, and hymns, the specifics of which change depending on the hour of the day, the season of the year, and the preference of the community or individual. It is a ritual that finds strength in its ancient structure and its ability to bend. It's like what Augustine said, Mark tells me: "the beauty ever ancient, ever new."

Back at the guesthouse, we have dinner, say goodnight.

By bedtime, a heavy curtain of snow is falling.

✳ ✳ ✳

Morning: still snowing. The land is one undulating mound of white, a pale sky hanging behind a forest enveloped in this sudden winter. We pray Lauds upstairs in the guesthouse. (Were the weather warmer, we would be outdoors.)

> *O God, come to our assistance*
> *O Lord, make haste to help us.*
> *Praise be to the Father, the Son and Holy Spirit*
> *Both now and forever. Amen.*

I am neither Catholic nor Christian, but this prayer is not so different from the entreaties that frequently run through my mind. I say secular or vaguely religious versions of such things when I am overwhelmed, ready to throw up my hands. But Mark and Lisa say this prayer as part of their daily work, to orient them back to their calling to live well on this land.

"I think love is particular in its fullest flourishing," Mark says. "To actually have a specific place we're in loving relationship with. It's *these* plants, it's *this* topsoil, it's *these* trees. It becomes very particular and very personal. And very vulnerable, too. In a beautiful way, the fate of this land and our sense of well-being are interwoven. There's a real sense of our bodies belonging in a place. This is who we are, where we're of."

They are, Lisa tells me, relearning how to live on a human scale. With both restraint and constraint. There is a natural spiritual desire for the infinite, they tell me, but we live in a time when many have confused it, seeking limitlessness in our physical (and, increasingly, virtual) presence on a finite Earth. But "if we can be *finite* in our human realm," says Mark, "then we have a chance of actually living well with all the other creatures."

Where they are able, they are drawing upon what is immediately around them for sustenance. Their hope is that, ultimately, between 80 and 90 percent of their caloric intake will come from this land. Next year, they'll implement a management regime that will begin the process of restoring the struggling meadow of native grasses that runs down the hillside.

Their yurt has no electricity or running water, and very little barrier between the sounds and light of the world outside. After the sun sets in the evening, they do only what they can do by candlelight. They hear the owls and coyotes at night and awake to sunrise and birds in the morning. Their home space mediates their relationship to time and space, tying them more closely to the seasons and rhythms of the living world.

Meanwhile, the liturgical calendar of the church mirrors the seasons of the land. Advent is the darkest and quietest time of the year. It's not unusual for the first daffodil to bloom on Easter.

In ways literal and symbolic, they are working to keep the boundaries between themselves and the land, and between themselves and God, thin. They break from what they are doing, whether weeding the vegetable garden or chopping wood, to pray the hours. It is not always easy, or convenient, they both tell me. They continue to learn hard lessons.

This is *axis mundi*: an ever revolving around that divine center, not only when it is easy but also when it is challenging. They make the conscious, repeated choice to hold themselves close.

Mark and Lisa bought this land with the intention to share it, with both the other creatures who reside here and with other people. They hope that eventually a community of fifteen to twenty will come here to join them, share in the bounty, pray the hours, raise the children, and leave the land healthier for the next generation. They currently have one long-term resident who lives full time in the guest house. Around fifty people come annually for shorter periods of spiritual retreat.

"I think when we're not rooted in a place, it's almost impossible to think generationally," says Lisa. Mark and Lisa are working within their faith tradition to reimagine land ownership as both communal and accessible, not individual and fenced in.

"It's the loss of cultural wisdom," says Lisa. "We hope and pray that we're able to make a turn and that what we're doing is a gift to future generations. But we can't go back. And there's a lot of things that we're doing very imperfectly because so much wisdom was lost."

That wisdom and knowledge was lost generations ago for many of European descent in the United States. And systemic racism continues to sever generational knowledge, the passing down of cultural tradition, and the possibility of a place-based knowledge that can be passed down in the form of home and skills on the land, for Indigenous people, Black people, and people of color.

In his article for *The Atlantic*, "The Case for Reparations," Ta-Nehisi Coates writes that the wealth of white households is, on average, twenty times greater than that of Black households, adding that "the concentration of poverty has been paired with a concentration of melanin. The resulting conflagration has been devastating." This includes access to and participation in the food system. In her book *Farming While Black*, Leah Penniman of Soul Fire Farm writes: "In 1910, at the height of Black landownership [in America], 16 million acres of farmland—14 percent of the total—was owned and cultivated by Black families. Now less than 1 percent of farms are Black-owned." Mainstream American ideals that gatekeep generational wealth, access to land, and, significantly, maternal care continue to have calamitous consequences. Black women in the United States are three to four times more likely to die from complications surrounding pregnancy and childbirth than white women.

Thinking generationally as a mother is a privilege in our country. Sharing what we have—in Mark and Lisa's case, in the form of access to fertile land—is one way to begin to heal, to both return and help to safekeep that cultural wisdom.

After our lunch of foraged fiddleheads, local beef, and roasted potatoes and carrots, Aspen falls asleep for a long nap. Lisa and I strap on snowshoes, and I follow her to Table Rock. It's a well-known local landmark. Though it's covered in several feet of snow, I can see its magnificence. It is a single oblong stone, perhaps twenty feet long and fifteen feet wide, that sits several feet off the ground, on a narrow base that is also part of this continuous piece of rock. The ground below has been sheltered from snow and is bare, apart from autumn's leaves, turned deep purple-brown. Moss trails and drips from the underside of the stone.

Lisa likes to imagine how anyone who would have come across Table Rock, even thousands of years ago, would have remarked upon it, found it to be meaningful. She and Mark want to reopen public access to it, and Lisa wonders aloud if they should clear space around it and add benches or just let it be as it is.

There are different ways, she says, of marking and honoring sacred spaces.

* * *

I think back to the barn owls. That sense of belonging that is at once tuned to the infinite and grounded in place. That does not separate spirit from land but finds ways of weaving us together with both.

I want to share in full the answers Mark and Lisa gave when I asked each of them how becoming a parent in a time of climate crisis has changed their relationship to the land and their relationship to God. I asked them how it informs their practices of homemaking in this place, and here's what they said.

Mark: "It deepens and intensifies the beauty and the vulnerability of belonging. Even more so, it's not just about waiting it out through our lifetimes. The choices that we make, ecological and cultural and spiritual, will be passed forward to these beings who we love more than anything we can imagine. And it intensifies the sobriety of seeing the situation we're facing and also the desire to do everything we can to bring about healing. It also intensifies the egocentric desire to grasp and control and obscure the balance of doing what I can, and then letting go and trusting. There's a greater intensity of feeling, especially when I really allow myself to think: 'what's it going to be like for them fifty years from now?' Spiritually, too, I think one of the greatest gifts in this time—when we can try, but we can't make [guarantees] for our children—is that the hope that I have isn't about things going well. Hope rests in the fact that there's this infinite Love, and I know that even in the worst ever possible human circumstances, people have drawn strength and hope and light from connecting with the presence of God. I want Anna and Luke to know that, no matter what is going on in the wider world or what may be collapsing, there's unlimited spiritual power and love that they can access. That's also part of what we're trying to cultivate: an environment where they may be able to feel that."

Lisa: "With so much uncertainty, one of the things we've talked about in terms of parenting is this desire to be building something real here, with food systems, and also this awareness all the time that, with so much uncertainty, we really don't know what's going to happen. It's good and prudent and beautiful to steward this piece of land, but we don't know the fate of this land. What cannot be taken from our children is a deep sense of their belonging in the world and knowing that they are beloved children of God, and that they have that spirit and they're connected. So even if things wildly change, they'll know how to listen and know and observe and be in relationship with land and also have land-based skills. I think they're likely going to live through difficult times. And that just seems like what we can give them: the opportunity to serve and live beautiful lives. Beautiful, in the sense of real."

❊ ❊ ❊

In the evening, the skies cleared of snow and tomorrow's road home already well-plowed in the way of rural Vermont roads, we head back to the chapel for evening prayer. This time we observe children's Vespers, which includes interactive songs and short stories of saints. Mark tells the story of Saint Kevin and the blackbird. And then the story of Saint Cuthbert, who prayed in the North Sea.

With the waters climbing up to his neck, Cuthbert would sing the psalms from dusk until daybreak. One night, a curious novice crept to the shore to observe this master in prayer. When Cuthbert emerged from the frigid waters at dawn, his feet numbed with cold, the novice was astonished to witness two otters crawl from the sea and wrap themselves around Cuthbert's feet, restoring his warmth.

48

REBIRTH (SPRING)

After a year on Nantucket, Nathan and I moved back to Oklahoma to live with our mom. On one particular day, I was doing what I often did after high school at fifteen years old: hiding out in my room, eating Hostess cupcakes, and watching sitcom reruns on my very tiny television. This was deliciously luxurious: we didn't have cable TV until well into our teenage years, and we didn't grow up with junk food. As my brother and I were given more freedom, I enjoyed squandering it with unhealthy habits. Between the end of the school day and the beginning of homework, I immersed myself in pop culture and processed sugar, making up for lost time: *Friends, Frasier, The Drew Carey Show.* Nutter Butters. The box of assorted candy bars I was supposed to sell to neighbors as part of a fundraiser for orchestra but kept eating instead.

A knock at the door. Mom was still working; Nathan was out with friends. Three eager smiles took up the space on our small concrete porch. Two girls and a boy, all about my age.

"Are you Chelsea?"

"Yes?"

"We're from—Baptist Church. Can we talk to you for a minute?"

In their eyes, a foreboding shine of expectation. A memory surfaced: scribbling down my name and address on a note card. A friend had brought me to what I will always remember as the "hellfire service" at her Baptist church. That one about how even babies will burn in hell if they haven't been baptized. Afterward, an adult in nice clothes had thrust a form and pen into my hand and then waited, too close by, for me to fill it out.

From inside the door, I again said, "Yes?"

We climbed the stairs to my small room, crowded with four of us, but the three didn't seem to mind.

"Chelsea, do you know about the salvation of Jesus Christ?"

"No . . ." I said, half expecting tinny sitcom laughter to fill the space of silence that followed.

They all smiled and nodded, not quite pity, but a pained sort of understanding.

"Jesus died for our sins," said the blonde girl. "And if you accept Jesus into your heart, your sins will be forgiven." I struggled to remember what counted as a sin and whether I'd committed any.

They told me what it meant to be capital-S *Saved*. They told me it was never too late. They told me I could still be reborn. Born again. This time, a child of God. I was having a hard time telling their voices apart. One of them, or all of them, directed a question at me: "Chelsea, if you died today, what would you say to Jesus to be allowed into heaven?"

I think I audibly gulped, then gave what I could already tell was the wrong answer. "I guess I'd say that I try to be a good person. I try to be kind. I don't hurt people." I mumbled something about being Jewish.

"Chelsea,"—why did they keep saying my name like that?—"unless you accept Jesus Christ into your heart, you will burn in hell for all eternity," said the boy.

They let that sink in for a moment.

Another memory surfaced. My friend who took me to church explaining how long eternity is, as if she'd known this conversation was coming for me. *The time it would take for a single dove to move the biggest mountain you can imagine,* she had said, *if it had to carry it away grain of sand by grain of sand, and fly each grain to the other side of the earth.* "Yeah . . . that's a long time," I'd replied noncommittally.

"So . . . are you prepared to accept Him now?" asked one of the girls. They leaned in.

I am, I thought in all my teenage angst, *a lone dove moving a mountain.*

Their disappointment was palpable as they left, the fate of my soul hanging in the balance.

I was angry and hurt. But something else, too. There was a welling sense of loss pooling in me. This I didn't expect. The only part of it I could articulate was: "fuck them, but I'm tempted." Not tempted because I was afraid of hell—of "Jesus . . . *or else!*"—but because no one else had yet recognized—nor had I explicitly recognized in myself—the part of me that was, indeed, religious. That deep part of me that was so hungry for God. Even in that moment, I didn't really know that about myself. I knew only that I was, for the first time, aware of feeling spiritually empty.

If you grew up in Oklahoma in the 1990s and early 2000s and were religious, you were almost certainly Christian. If you were Christian, you were very likely evangelical. That I did not fit into this paradigm had been made clear. But I didn't have another one.

When my mom got home, and I told her what happened, she called the church and did my shouting for me. They didn't knock again.

But it would take me more than a decade to unravel God from my sense of betrayal and mistrust. For those years, I pursued and repeatedly rejected faith. Five years of undergraduate work in religious studies, two years of a master's degree in comparative theological studies. It would take moving to Amman, Jordan, and back. It would take denial. Gnashing of teeth. It would take books read and essays written and countless interfaith events, through all of which I remained intent, always, on how *other* people think about faith. I kept learning about paradigms I didn't fit into. I kept trying to feed that hunger from a distance, but I remained hungry.

Then, I found mysticism. I found the definition of divinity that is beyond all definition. I was told, gently, by Steve Blackmer, that another word for the sacred is mystery, is Earth. Then, finally, I heard the word differently.

God.

I heard it among the maple trees and the vernal pools and the ticks and the black bear tracks at Church of the Woods.

Something in me was, indeed, reborn.

✻ ✻ ✻

It's our first spring in our new house, and everything is waking up. Rising again. The first spring after planting a garden is all anticipation. What will come back? How well will it grow? In the garden's unfurling is that ineffable sense of connection, of what Seamus Heaney writes of Saint Kevin, after the blackbird lands in his palm: that he finds himself "linked into the network of eternal life."

Just like our bodies, our home spaces are thin places. Whether our walls are canvas or brick. The sacred and the mundane run through and interrupt each other. The sacred might erupt unexpectedly in the rain that softly falls on the roof. In a child's laugh. In our noticing the robin's nest in the tree. In the touch of one body to another. In the lobelia that takes months to bloom but then unfolds the most glorious purple. We might encounter the sacred as we kneel in the garden or put seeds in the window box, anticipating the sight of green rising through soil. And between it all is the tedium, the often-mindless routine, the day-to-day acts of living as *Homo sapiens.*

We might forget the robin's nest is there at all until we see what remains of it: the blue eggshell, empty and broken on the ground. And we'll feel the flutter of hope that the chick fledged and flew, found its way into the air.

My journey to understand the sacred continues. Always, in mystery. Always, with the failure of words and language. I see it in the lightning. I hear it in the notes that rain down from the trees and in the songs of the chickadees. I'm showing up to the journey now. I stumble. I'm learning. I sometimes feel the sacred in my chest, bounding. That first meeting with a righteous God in my teenage bedroom is the cracked robin's egg on the sidewalk: empty, able to be left behind. Something else has grown wings and taken to the sky.

49

RITUAL (SUMMER)

Our favorite hike near Earthsea is a short leg of Vermont's Long Trail, beginning a little over a mile from our property as the crow flies. We've done this hike several times a year since we lived in nearby Jeffersonville—eight years ago now—a repetition Andrew and I enjoy and know well. We've hiked in heavy snow, in rain, in the thaw of mud, amid autumn's leaves, in the black fly–ridden days of early summer. First we climb a steep, beech-and-birch-tunneled logging road, the owner having granted right-of-way to hikers; then we cross a bridge deeper into the forest, which transitions to hemlock and maple trees and brings us onto what in the winter will be used as snowmobile trails. Eventually, we come to what is, depending on the season, either a narrow and trickling or wide and babbling brook, out onto a trail that winds up farther into the woods around several massive boulders, and we arrive at one of the Long Trail's sweet little three-sided shelters. There are four bunks inside, a table between them. It's always swept clean, the broom left leaning on the same place along the wall, dutifully used and replaced by whomever last stayed the night. We eat our lunch at the picnic table outside, then do it all in reverse.

We don't make it anywhere near the shelter this time. Not because Aspen can't make it this far (we have a carrier pack for when her legs tire), but because of the eastern newt.

These amphibians begin their lives in the water, then emerge onto dry land as juveniles, at which point they are called red efts.

I like this about amphibians—that they change and transform so utterly that they earn themselves new names along the way.

The eft stage, which lasts two to seven years, is the only state of being in which I've seen them, because it's the only time our worlds naturally intersect. They climb into the realm of rock, dirt, and dry air as bright orange newts, an inch or two long, soft and shiny, with yellow and black eyes. I've always resisted the temptation to pick one up, but I imagine they are squishy and a bit sticky. When they reach adulthood, their final form, when they may properly be called eastern newts, they'll return to the water—ponds, lakes, and marshes—where the females will lay their eggs. The process will begin again.

This, too, is a sort of ritual.

Today on our hike it is red eft season. Here on the trail are so, so many. When we spot the first one, Aspen slowly approaches and crouches down next to it, a little unsure at the start, and then fully absorbed. She doesn't try to grab or touch it, taking seriously Andrew's gentle caution that they are sensitive and don't like to be handled. But she wants to get close. She stays crouched, and the eft holds still, also presumably a bit unsure of the intentions of this giant creature looming overhead. A couple minutes later, Andrew and I try to urge her onward, both of us swatting the mosquitos who have found an easy feast in our lack of movement, and both of us eager to work our legs up the mountain, reach our usual destination, repeat this particular ritual in our own predictable way.

But the game is up. The only way Aspen is willing to leave the company of this new friend is in the search for more. Over the next ninety minutes, we'll make it about a quarter mile into what we'd hoped would be at least a six-mile hike. We will spend our time looking for efts.

"There's one!" one of us will say.

Aspen will run over, carefully crouch next to it, and set about playing Red Light, Green Light, a new favorite game.

"Green light, little buddy!" she'll say. The eft will freeze. *"Green light,* little friend." Nothing. And then: "GREEN LIGHT!!" The little buddy will give a start and take off for the shelter of the greenery along the trail. "Red light," we find, has a higher rate of success.

Aspen will do this perhaps two dozen times as we walk, not our usual start-to-finish on the trail but eft-to-eft. We make our meandering, zigzagging, mosquito-ridden, slow way.

By the time we get back to the car, the feeling is unanimous: every little friend was an utterly worthy destination.

✻ ✻ ✻

Later, I look up that word, *ritual,* in my *Oxford Dictionary of World Religions,* wondering if an eft's life is, in fact, something like a ritual.

But from the first sentence of the long *ritual* entry, I can sense that whatever poor soul was assigned to write it must have been overwhelmed. It reads: "Actions repeated in regular and predictable ways, both in religious and secular contexts, serving so many purposes that summary is impossible."

This, happily, would seem to give me license to explore the word broadly. Let's consider, then, the life of the red eft as a ritual, across many generations. Amphibious lives that repeat in regular and predictable ways. Each begins in water, finds land, returns to water, mates, dies.

But this is rather detached, and it leaves open the deeper question of whether there is intent or meaning behind the eft's repeated, predictable actions. Many would say "no"—at least, not beyond biological programming and the urge for survival.

But there's something else in that vague definition of ritual that I like. What if we apply this same phrase to both an individual red eft and to the eastern newt as a species: "serving so many purposes that summary is impossible"?

For isn't it true that we could never possibly summarize the many purposes, the many ways of being worthy, of any one creature?

An atheist can no more disprove God's existence than a believer can prove it. A scientist could not claim the lack of an eft's personhood or intent any more than I could claim meaning in his rites of passage from water to land to water, from salamander to eft to salamander.

"Impossible to summarize" could be taken as a cop-out, a convenient avoidance. But it also leaves the little fellows with some agency and some mystery. Worthy destinations, indeed.

CREATING POSSIBLE FUTURES

When I began writing this book, if you had asked me if I have hope for the future, I would have answered an unequivocal, underlined, and italicized "_Yes_." I probably would have put at least one exclamation point there as well.

"My daughter being in this world means that I don't have a choice about whether or not to hope," was my common refrain. "I have to believe in the future." This was a comforting statement.

Lately, I have been more honest with myself. The truth is my hope is fickle. I doubt just as often. Headlines from this summer read: "July 4 Was Earth's Hottest Day in over 100,000 Years—Breaking Record for 2nd Day in a Row"; "Heat Records Are Broken around the Globe as Earth Warms, Fast"; "A Desperate Push to Save Florida's Coral: Get It Out of the Sea"; "Sentinel of Southwest: Saguaro Cacti Are Collapsing, Dying in Arizona Heat." Climate refugees are set adrift and left to drown. Florida's oceans reach one hundred degrees Fahrenheit. Earth experiences its hottest summer on record. "Global boiling," I read in one article, and I need to go outside to take gulps of fresh air.

I want to keep hope's fire burning on this burning Earth. But especially in the quiet, in the dark, my hope flickers like a candle when someone has opened a door and let the gale in. Sometimes the flame goes out.

* * *

The Lamoille River, along which our Earthsea land sits, flooded just before I wrote this chapter, as did several of Vermont's other rivers, including the Winooski in Montpelier, which turned the downtown streets of the state's small capital city into a wide river. "Historic and catastrophic" were the governor's words. The Lamoille, normally gauged at between three and five feet, crested at twenty-one feet after torrential rains. In downtown Johnson, the river climbed halfway to the ceiling of the only local grocery store. It broke into the new health clinic, built recently to aid in the opioid crisis that has gripped this town.

The three of us drove to Johnson several days later, as the waters were receding. On the way, we passed a one-story barn with a white horizontal line drawn across it a foot below the roof. Beneath the line, the words: "High water line 2023. In God We Trust." Everywhere we went, the river had left its shadow across the landscape, a layer of gray silt coating everything the waters had risen to touch. Silt on the trunks of trees, silt on the hedges and bushes, silt on people's gardens and the walls of their homes.

In town, a few buildings upriver from the store, which was being gutted into dumpsters, a sheet was nailed to the outside of a house, "WE NEED FEMA" spray painted on it in red letters. The town website said, "DO NOT DRINK THE WATER." Sludge from the inundated wastewater treatment plant was still flowing into the river and into the town's supply of drinking water. Two more inches of rain fell in the three days we stayed. People in yellow vests carrying clipboards went door to door, business to business. Air quality was poor because of wildfire smoke from Canada. Our rickety cabin, fifty feet up the hillside, was spared. Across the road, the Lamoille had changed shape, eroded the sandy banks and cut a new channel. Its waters ran thick and brown, full of debris.

Another veil of denial—"New England is still okay for now"—was removed.

Poof. The candle goes out.

What is always on hope's heels, waiting to walk through that open door, is despair. Despair eats up all the space in the darkness. When that happens, I cannot relight the wick. I lose the thread. I lose the words.

* * *

The oldest living tree in the world is a quaking aspen, *Populus tremuloides*, in Utah's Fishlake National Forest. Named *Pando*—Latin for "I spread"—this aspen is also the world's largest organism, weighing in at thirteen million pounds. What began as a single seed has grown a root system that spans more than one hundred acres. Above ground grows an aspen grove with 47,000 individual silver-white trunks, slender and elegant, whispering to each other via heart-shaped leaves. These individual trees are, really, genetically identical sprouts of the same being—a beingness held within and maintained by the vast root system beneath.

The aboveground shoots are relatively short-lived on the timescale of trees. They endure for a little longer than the average human life, between eighty-five and 135 years. The roots, however, are ancient. At least twelve thousand years old by most estimates, though an unconfirmed eighty thousand years is frequently cited as well.

We often associate a tree's longevity with its trunk, an outward expansion of rings, a wrinkling and thickening bark. But where aspen trees grow in such clonal colonies—though no other approaches Pando's extraordinary size—the roots are the tree's means of survival and endurance. In particular, they protect the tree from wildfire. Though the aboveground trunks might be consumed, left as smoke and ash, the roots will remain largely unscathed. Thus, when its world burns, an aspen colony finds its patient resurrection. After a fire, the tree is reborn.

Here in Maine, the primary role of quaking aspen is as a pioneer species. They arrive in a landscape after fire or intensive logging has claimed a long-standing forest. Alongside paper birch, they take root and begin to heal the soil, forming an early successional forest. Thus, aspens are pioneers not in the sense of crowding out or uprooting what had long grown; they are pioneers in the sense of paving the way for new life, in the sense of healing wounds, creating habitat that will be suitable for others, making new opportunities for establishment and belonging. An aspen tree in this context accepts the natural length of its life. Its purpose is, in part, to cultivate fertile ground, with an eye toward what and who comes next.

The quaking leaves of aspen trees have inspired in diverse cultures the belief that their rustling in the wind speaks to a connection to the spirit world. The Greeks made shields from aspen wood, and their heroes journeyed into the underworld wearing crowns of aspen leaves to facilitate their passage and safe return. The Celts, too, harvested wood from this "shield tree," the whispering tree, to protect themselves, physically and spiritually. Their protective qualities led to aspens being planted near dwellings.

In both Scotland and Ireland, the trees were once thought to communicate via the wind: carrying messages to the ancestors in the spirit realm and bestowing upon listeners in this realm the gift of inspiration and poetry. In the Scottish Highlands, it was said that an aspen leaf placed under one's tongue would bestow the gift of more eloquent speech.

And so the aspen tree exists within that realm of deep belonging: arising from ancient roots, attuned to the whispers of the sacred.

All of these are among the reasons we gave our daughter this name. It's not that we wish to weigh her down with any burden of expectation that she embody some idealized version of an enlightened being; rather, we gave her this name because she deserves a world where her truest belonging is possible. We gave her this name because the responsibility of that belonging is ours. She is the tree we planted. Now we must tend to the world around her.

Her name holds within it our embodied vision for this world. Not our hope for it, nor even our certain belief that such a world will come about, but the vision through which we do the work, now, to bring that world into being.

* * *

When I try to imagine different versions of the future, from the opposing vantage points of both hope and despair, the images are always blurry. I feel disembodied. And in an age when so much is disembodied, so much becoming virtual, so much of our attention oriented to the screen, I feel less and less interested in casting my mind ahead, away from what is here, around me.

And so—just as I've long known despair to be—hope has become an unreliable narrator. Too shaky a foundation on which to repair the world.

And so I choose instead that which holds me steady, that which clears the fog from my eyes, that which does not flicker but only burns brighter no matter my grief, my anger.

I choose love.

It is upon love that I will do what I can to heal; it is upon love that I will kneel to pray, it is upon love that I will guide our daughter's feet. This is the practice of inscendence that I am called to.

> May Aspen grow into a world where she can flourish.
> May she find courage, resiliency, and ancient knowledge
> in deep roots.

May she hear the whispers of the divine in the wind.
May she learn to endure the fires when they come, in
whatever form they come.
May she know generosity and an open heart.
May she make fertile ground for others.

May she have that chance.
May all of our children have that chance.

This is my prayer.

And this is my work: it is upon love that I will walk in and with this world.

I don't know what that future will look like. I cannot know that. But I know how to listen for love's call. I am learning how to answer it.

✻ ✻ ✻

And now, as I recently heard Gregory Alan Isakov sing, let's put all the words away.

Outside my window, and outside yours, is a wide and wild, wounded and sacred world.

Let's venture out together.

Let's begin, and continue, and begin again the work of being good mothers.

Let's remember to love and nurture this Earth as she deserves.

So that our children and our more-than-human kin might find themselves at home,

    generation

        after generation

            after generation.

ACKNOWLEDGMENTS

Among the many humbling lessons that I learned while writing this book is that a book is one part of a vast ecosystem, a network of life-giving, world-shaping, critical support.

Enormous thanks to my editor at Broadleaf, Valerie Weaver-Zercher, for believing in this book from the very beginning and for having the clarity, insight, and keen eye to help transform it from a scrappy proposal into a finished manuscript. Thank you to the team at Broadleaf for supporting this work and bringing it into the world.

My unending gratitude to the kind, knowledgeable, and generous people who took the time to speak to me and share their expertise: Melanie White of the Clearwater Marine Aquarium, who spends many of her days in a tiny airplane looking for North Atlantic right whales; Bri Benvenuti of Ducks Unlimited, who taught me about the incredible nesting practices of saltmarsh sparrows; Bob Morrill, who patiently answered my early questions about whales; Joe Kelley of the University of Maine, who has spent his life among marshes in Maine and Louisiana, and who introduced me to the mysterious world of foraminifera; Philip Hamilton, for your open heart and fervent commitment to the protection of right whales; Scott Kraus, for your pioneering work in right whale research and for making both the beauty and the plight of this species widely known; Tom Murison, for sharing with me the brave and noble work of his sister, Laurie, who dedicated her life to the well-being of marine mammals; Roger Christie and Wendy Sisson—Roger for graciously speaking to me about your childhood and your great-aunt and adopted mother, Rachel Carson, and Wendy for helping to arrange our stay at the Southport cottage; Jennifer S. Walker at

Rowan University and Catherine Davis at North Carolina State University, for your expert eyes on my foraminifera chapters; Hannah Chalew, for joining us on the boat with Richie and for sharing your experience as a mother and an artist in a flood-prone city; Bryan Tarnowski, for being on the boat and helping to document all that is occurring in southern Louisiana; Harry and Debi Hartford of Thurston and Peters Sugarhouse, for always welcoming me among your trees and always sending me home with maple ice cream; Corrine Michaud-LeBlanc of the Maine Department of Inland Fisheries and Wildlife's "Beginning with Habitat" program; and Shelley Megquier of Maine Farmland Trust.

Special thanks to: Clay George, for inviting me to coastal Georgia and taking me out to see the whale mothers and calves—that was a life-changing experience; thanks to Trip and Ashley, for making space for me in the boat and for sharing your wisdom and some good laughs. Thanks to Rachel Stearns and Susan Adamowicz for bringing me out in the field at the Rachel Carson National Wildlife Refuge. Thanks to Rachel for letting me test the shear strength of the peat and call out the kilopascal readings! Thanks to Susan for helping me see a salt marsh in all its shades of green. Thanks to Richie Blink for the salt marsh tour and for your generous way of sharing knowledge and the integrity with which you are a witness at the front lines of rising seas. To Alex Kolker of the Louisiana Universities Marine Consortium, for meeting with me in Louisiana and helping me understand the deep time scale of planetary forces at work on marshes. To Jeffery Darensbourg, for bringing me into a deeper understanding of the Indigenous history of, and continued presence in, Bulbancha and southern Louisiana. To Slade Moore, for taking me on a tour of salt marshes in southern Maine, for patiently and thoroughly answering my many questions, and for your work in ensuring a future for marshes in Maine. To Mark and Lisa, dear friends, for hosting my family at your homestead, for reminding me of ways of living at a human scale, and for your necessary work braiding together the land and the sacred. To Bird Harris, who became a dear friend throughout the writing of this book: thank you for reaching out to me, for making my trip to Louisiana not only possible but incredibly rich and vibrant, for sharing your experience as a mother, and for creating work that so beautifully renders shifting edges.

Thank you to the many people in my writing community who read parts of this book and offered their feedback, encouragement, and helpful edits. I'm looking at you, Jenny and Laura! You were with me, and this book, from the first drafts through the last, and I am so grateful. You have been anchors. Thanks to Kate, Jenna, and Kirsten, brilliant women of the EON writing group, for having conversations about motherhood that stretched and challenged my understanding and assumptions. Thank you to my trusty Wednesday night memoir group: Pat, Ken, Will, Mike, and, of course, Uncle Steve. I'm grateful to have you as long-term fellow writers and trusted readers. Special thanks to Rebecca Dawson Webb, who runs our memoir group, and who served as a writing coach for me in the first months of writing this book. You asked the hard questions, offered strong encouragement, and kept me grounded and focused. Thank you to Scott Russell Sanders, who has been a mentor, teacher, and friend to me and my family: you were the first writer to call me a writer. Thanks also to Ruth; I strive to write stories as marvelously crafted as your quilts. Thank you to Steve Blackmer, most trusted friend.

Thank you to the team at *Emergence Magazine*, who did me the great honor of offering me my first job as a writer. Thanks to Hannah, Devin, Michelle, Noah, and the Studio Airport crew. Thanks to Seana, for your ever steady and kind presence and unbelievable work ethic. Special thanks to executive editor Emmanuel Vaughan-Lee: I would not be the writer I am today without the stories you entrusted me to write. Thank you, too, to the Kalliopeia Foundation.

Thank you to Bethany Ritz, my first editor, who could always see straight through to the heart of my writing even when I could not and who, with grace and care, made me a stronger writer.

Gratitude and love to my community of friends and family who helped me not only through writing this book but who have taught me to be a better mother, sister, daughter, friend, ally, and ecological citizen.

Of course, this book ecosystem would not exist without the living ecosystems that inspired it. Thank you to the many creatures and beings whose voices appear in these chapters and who permitted me a glimpse into their worlds. You taught me, surprised me, mystified me, challenged me. You opened my heart and expanded my understanding of community. You taught me new ways of mothering, new ways of being mothered.

Thank you to my father-in-law, Ellsworth, who has read (and emailed me about!) everything I've ever written and has unfailingly supported my family. Thank you to my father, Ernie, for teaching me to see the living world—especially plants—as valuable, interesting, and utterly worthy of our attention. Thank you to my stepmom, Kathleen, for your ceaseless encouragement and confidence. Thank you to my mother, Asia. I would not be the mother I am without your example as a mom to me, and as Aspen's beloved Bubba. You taught me to be creative and to follow my heart. Thank you to my brother, Nathan. I don't know where or who I would be without you. You are my best friend. I love you.

And how to possibly thank you, Andrew and Aspen? Lights of my life, dearest companions. To Andrew, my first and most trusted reader, my husband, my love: you made writing this book possible, but more than that, you are here, by my side, creating the life that makes me want to write. And to Aspen, our most beloved, our sweet little tree. You renew my world every day. Without you, none of these words would be.

NOTES

INTRODUCTION

xiv   ***"brains of men who are regularly engaged in caring for their children change":*** Chelsea Conaboy, *Mother Brain: How Neuroscience Is Rewriting the Story of Motherhood* (New York: Henry Holt, 2022), 17.

xv   ***"I live my life in widening circles":*** Rainer Maria Rilke, "Widening Circles," in *Rilke's Book of Hours: Love Poems to God*, trans. Joanna Macy and Anita Barrows (New York: Riverhead Books, 2005), 45.

xv   ***physiological, psychological, and sociological processes and metamorphoses of motherhood:*** Lucy Jones, *Matrescence: On the Metamorphosis of Pregnancy, Childbirth and Motherhood* (London: Allen Lane, 2023), 17.

xvi   ***"making kin and making kind":*** Donna J. Haraway, *Staying with the Trouble: Making Kin in the Chthulucene* (Raleigh, NC: Duke University Press, 2016), 102–3.

xvii   ***"no one cares for children entirely on their own":*** Angela Garbes, *Essential Labor: Mothering as Social Change* (New York: Harper Wave, 2022), 9.

xvii   ***supporting and nurturing life:*** Garbes, *Essential Labor*, 9.

xvii   ***"the earth whose skin you are":*** Joy Harjo, "Remember," *Emergence Magazine*, accessed September 17, 2021, https://emergencemagazine.org/poem/remember/.

xvii   ***"human perception that makes the world a gift":*** Robin Wall Kimmerer, *Braiding Sweetgrass: Indigenous Wisdom, Scientific Knowledge, and the Teachings of Plants* (Minneapolis, MN: Milkweed Editions, 2013), 30.

xxi   ***in the heaven of the contented:*** Rupert Gethin, *The Foundations of Buddhism* (Oxford: Oxford University Press, 1998), 17–18.

xxii   ***"companion species":*** Haraway, *Staying with the Trouble*, 11.

CHAPTER 1: HEARTBEAT

5   A version of this chapter first appeared as the essay "New Life in Spring": Chelsea Steinauer-Scudder, "New Life in Spring: Pregnancy and the Coronavirus," *Emergence Magazine*, March 19, 2020, https://emergencemagazine.org/op_ed/new-life-in-spring/.

CHAPTER 2: AXIS MUNDI

7   ***holiest places are often mountains:*** Mircea Eliade, *The Sacred and the Profane, The Nature of Religion: The Significance of Religious Myth, Symbolism, and Ritual within Life and Culture,* 1st ed. (New York: Harper Torchbook, 1961).

10   ***"influence of the entire universe converges on every spot":*** Scott Russell Sanders, *Staying Put: Making a Home in a Restless World* (Boston: Beacon Press, 1993), 115–16.

10   A version of the following four chapters first appeared as the essay "Coming into Being: Reflections on Mothering in the Apocalypse": Chelsea Steinauer-Scudder, "Coming into Being: Reflections on Mothering in the Apocalypse," *Emergence Magazine,* October 26, 2022, https://emergencemagazine.org/essay/coming-into-being/.

CHAPTER 3: COMING INTO BEING

13   ***"creaking architecture of my own mind":*** Charles Foster, "Against Nature Writing," *Emergence Magazine,* July 21, 2021, https://emergencemagazine.org/essay/against-nature-writing/.

CHAPTER 4: THE GOOD MOTHER

15   ***people displaced by climate-related disasters:*** Sources for the data in this paragraph come from: "Endangered and Threatened Wildlife and Plants; Removal of 23 Extinct Species From the Lists of Endangered and Threatened Wildlife and Plants," Federal Register, September 30, 2021, https://www.federalregister.gov/documents/2021/09/30/2021-21219/endangered-and-threatened-wildlife-and-plants-removal-of-23-extinct-species-from-the-

lists-of; Susan Cosier, "The World Needs Topsoil to Grow 95% of Its Food—but It's Rapidly Disappearing," *The Guardian*, May 30, 2019, https://www.theguardian.com/us-news/2019/may/30/topsoil-farming-agriculture-food-toxic-america; and "Climate Refugees—the World's Forgotten Victims," World Economic Forum, June 18, 2021, https://www.weforum.org/agenda/2021/06/climate-refugees-the-world-s-forgotten-victims/.

16   ***to pose with it for photographs:*** Linda Hogan, *Dwellings: A Spiritual History of the Living World* (New York: W. W. Norton & Company, 1995), 72.

16   ***"a remedy that will heal the wound":*** Hogan, *Dwellings*, 76.

17   ***"all of life's beings can flourish":*** Robin Wall Kimmerer, *Braiding Sweetgrass: Indigenous Wisdom, Scientific Knowledge, and the Teachings of Plants* (Minneapolis, MN: Milkweed Editions, 2013), 97.

CHAPTER 5: A MOTHERING LANGUAGE

18   ***"promoting the diversity of the community":*** Suzanne Simard, *Finding the Mother Tree: Discovering the Wisdom of the Forest* (New York: Alfred A. Knopf, 2021), 286.

18   ***"helping them to prepare for changes ahead":*** Simard, *Finding the Mother Tree*, 287.

18   ***An article in the New Yorker:*** Rivka Galchen, "Green Dream," *The New Yorker*, October 11, 2021.

22   ***"most secret, motivating depths":*** Joseph Campbell, *Myths to Live By: How We Re-Create Ancient Legends in Our Daily Lives to Release Human Potential*, 11th ed. (Toronto: Bantam Books, 1988), 24.

CHAPTER 6: ASCENDANCE

28   ***massive storm system barreled through:*** Sarah Yang, "Sensing Distant Tornadoes, Birds Flew the Coop. What Tipped Them Off?" *Berkeley News*, December 8, 2014, https://news.berkeley.edu/2014/12/18/infrasound-as-early-storm-warning-for-birds.

28   ***returned home when it was safe:*** Henry M. Streby et al., "Tornadic Storm Avoidance Behavior in Breeding Songbirds," *Current Biology* 25, no. 1 (January 5, 2015): 98–102, doi:10.1016/j.cub.2014.10.079.

29   *"bird's-eye view closer to God's":* Anna Badkhen, *Bright Unbearable Reality* (New York: New York Review of Books, 2022), 58.

29   *"they fly robed in the waters":* "*Rig-Veda* Book 1: HYMN CLXIV. Viśvedevas," *Rig-Veda*, trans. Ralph T. H. Griffith [1896], accessed July 2023, https://sacred-texts.com/hin/rigveda/rv01164.htm.

29   *god of magic and wisdom:* Antoaneta Roussi, "Ancient Egyptians Mummified Millions of Birds. Where Did They Get Them?" *National Geographic*, November 13, 2019, https://www.nationalgeographic.com/history/article/egyptians-mummified-millions-ibis-birds-how.

30   *"also our own sacred nature":* Llewellyn Vaughan-Lee, ed., *Spiritual Ecology: The Cry of the Earth*, 2nd ed. (Point Reyes, California: The Golden Sufi Center, 2016), v.

31   *"but in the spirit of relatedness":* Martin Shaw, *Scatterlings: Getting Claimed in the Age of Amnesia* (Ashland, Oregon: White Cloud Press, 2016), 11.

CHAPTER 7: SETTING BEARINGS

35   *a prayer for the health of her child:* Helen Curry, *The Way of the Labyrinth: A Powerful Meditation for Everyday Life* (New York: Penguin Compass, 2000), 29.

36   *"everyday anguish that shapes the habits of being":* bell hooks, *Belonging: A Culture of Place* (New York: Routledge, 2009), 1.

36   *"very fabric of North America's ecosystem is unraveling":* John W. Fitzpatrick and Peter P. Marra, "Opinion | The Crisis for Birds Is a Crisis for Us All," *New York Times*, September 19, 2019, https://www.nytimes.com/2019/09/19/opinion/crisis-birds-north-america.html.

36   *twenty million people were being internally displaced:* Oxfam International, "Forced from Home: Climate-Fuelled Displacement," May 25, 2022, https://www.oxfam.org/en/research/forced-home-climate-fuelled-displacement.

CHAPTER 8: HOOPOE, I

38   *"when they pondered on the journey's length":* Farid ud-Din Attar, *The Conference of the Birds*, trans. Afkham Darbandi and Dick Davis (London: Penguin Books, 1984), 35.

CHAPTER 9: SENSORY ORIENTATION

41 **the means of their practiced actions of making a home:** D. S. Bunn, A. B. Warburton, and R. D. S. Wilson, *The Barn Owl* (London: T & AD Poyser Ltd, 1982), 107.

43 **a dense, curved wall that amplifies sound:** Masakazu Konishi, "How the Owl Tracks Its Prey: Experiments with Trained Barn Owls Reveal How Their Acute Sense of Hearing Enables Them to Catch Prey in the Dark," *American Scientist* 61, no. 4 (1973): 414–24.

44 **will be louder in her left ear:** Eric I. Knudsen, "The Hearing of the Barn Owl," *Scientific American* 245, no. 6 (1981): 113–25.

44 **opening is directed at a slight upward angle:** S. F. Volman, "Directional Hearing in Owls: Neurobiology, Behaviour and Evolution," in *Perception and Motor Control in Birds: An Ecological Approach*, ed. Mark N. O. Davies and Patrick R. Green (Berlin, Heidelberg: Springer, 1994), 292–314, doi:10.1007/978-3-642-75869-0_17.

44 **processed into information about the sound's location:** Knudsen, "The Hearing of the Barn Owl," 113–25.

44 **the auditory center of her midbrain:** The auditory center of the avian midbrain is called the MLd (nucleus mesencephalicus lateralis pars dorsalis). It corresponds to the mammalian auditory structure, the inferior colliculus. [Knudsen, "The Hearing of the Barn Owl," 113–25.]

44 **a two-dimensional map of the owl's world:** Volman, "Directional Hearing in Owls," 292–314.

45 **the position of the vole is accurately displayed:** Volman, "Directional Hearing in Owls," 292–314.

45 **performed poorly in subsequent flight tests:** Konishi, "How the Owl Tracks Its Prey," 414–24.

47 **decision-making and planning in relation to the landscape:** This paragraph sourced from: David A. Raichlen and Gene E. Alexander, "Why Your Brain Needs Exercise," *Scientific American*, April 1, 2021, https://www.scientificamerican.com/video/why-your-brain-needs-exercise1/.

47 **ability to remember specific, personal events within the context of their occurrence:** Timothy A. Allen and Norbert J. Fortin, "The Evolution of Episodic Memory," *Proceedings of the National Academy of Sciences of the United States of America* 110 (2013): 10379–86.

47   *"process and encode environmental and geographical data":* Eran
      Ben-Elia, "An Exploratory Real-World Wayfinding Experiment: A
      Comparison of Drivers' Spatial Learning with a Paper Map vs. Turn-
      by-Turn Audiovisual Route Guidance," *Transportation Research
      Interdisciplinary Perspectives* 9 (March 2021): 100280, doi:10.1016/j.
      trip.2020.100280.

47   *"storing relationships between linguistic entities in the form of
      narratives":* Neil Burgess, Eleanor A. Maguire, and John O'Keefe,
      "The Human Hippocampus and Spatial and Episodic Mem-
      ory," *Neuron* 35, no. 4 (August 15, 2002): 625–41, doi:10.1016/
      S0896-6273(02)00830-9.

48   *theoretical possibility of a common neural ancestry:* This paragraph
      sourced from: Allen and Fortin, "The Evolution of Episodic Mem-
      ory," 10379–86.

48   *"negatively impact the integrity of the hippocampus":* Louisa
      Dahmani and Véronique D. Bohbot, "Habitual Use of GPS Nega-
      tively Impacts Spatial Memory during Self-Guided Navigation,"
      Scientific Reports 10, no. 1 (April 14, 2020): 6310, doi:10.1038/
      s41598-020-62877-0.

49   *fewer chicks fledging from the nest:* Wouter Halfwerk et al.,
      "Negative Impact of Traffic Noise on Avian Reproductive Suc-
      cess," *Journal of Applied Ecology* 48, no. 1 (February 2011): 210–19,
      doi:10.1111/j.1365-2664.2010.01914.x.

CHAPTER 11: DISRUPTED NAVIGATION

51   *as many as half a million birds:* "Azraq Wetland Reserve
      Rehabilitation Helped Attract Variety of Birds—RSCN," *Jor-
      dan Times,* July 5, 2018, https://jordantimes.com/news/local/
      azraq-wetland-reserve-rehabilitation-helped-attract-variety-
      birds-%E2%80%94-rscn.

52   *the birds started coming back:* "Waterbird Population in 'Remark-
      able Decline'—Census," *Jordan Times,* April 18, 2018, https://
      jordantimes.com/news/local/waterbird-population-remarkable-
      decline%E2%80%99-%E2%80%94-census.

52   *now sits many meters below ground:* Elizabeth Whitman, "A Land
      without Water: The Scramble to Stop Jordan from Running Dry,"

Nature 573, no. 7772 (September 4, 2019): 20–23, doi:10.1038/d41586-019-02600-w.

52   *a marked decline in the numbers of northern shovelers:* T. Qaneer et al., "Waterbird Census in Jordan over the Period of 2000–2013," *Bulletin of the Mediterranean Waterbirds Network,* no. 1 (January 2013): 1–8, https://www.researchgate.net/publication/321062265_Waterbird_census_in_Jordan_over_the_period_2001_to_2013.

53   *half a million Syrians, mostly women and children:* Rana F. Sweis, "Jordan's Schools Buckle Under Weight of Syrian Refugees," *New York Times,* October 6, 2013, https://www.nytimes.com/2013/10/07/world/middleeast/jordans-schools-buckle-under-weight-of-syrian-refugees.html.

53   *the ruthless violence of a dictator in response to pro-democracy protests:* Peter H. Gleick, "Water, Drought, Climate Change, and Conflict in Syria," *Weather, Climate, and Society* 6, no. 3 (July 2014): 331–40, doi:10.1175/WCAS-D-13-00059.1.

55   *faucets often run dry, sometimes for days at a time:* Karen Zraick, "Jordan Is Running Out of Water, a Grim Glimpse of the Future," *New York Times,* November 9, 2022, https://www.nytimes.com/2022/11/09/world/middleeast/jordan-water-cop-27.html.

CHAPTER 13: QUICKENING

59   *"a strange shape for the soul":* James L. Allen Jr., "Yeats's Bird-Soul Symbolism," *Twentieth Century Literature* 6, no. 3 (1960): 117–22, doi:10.2307/441010.

60   *"rubs the wrong way against logic":* Linda Hogan, *Dwellings: A Spiritual History of the Living World* (New York: W. W. Norton & Company, 1995), 16–17.

CHAPTER 14: UNRAVELING

61   *the word death and the phrase realm of death:* Sara El-Sayed Kitat, "The Veneration of the Owl in Græco-Roman Egypt," *International Journal of History and Cultural Studies* 5, no. 2 (2019): 1–20.

62   *"its auditory system becomes calibrated to its head and ears":* Volman, "Directional Hearing in Owls," 292–314.

CHAPTER 15: HOOPOE, IV

67   *"It is yourselves you see and what you are":* Attar, *The Conference of the Birds,* 219.

CHAPTER 16: BODIES IN ORBIT

73   *do not seem to maintain long-term bonds:* Scott D. Kraus and Rosalind M. Rolland, eds., *The Urban Whale: North Atlantic Right Whales at the Crossroads* (Cambridge, Massachusetts: Harvard University Press, 2007), 19.

74   *reproductive health well into her old age:* Philip K. Hamilton et al., "Age Structure and Longevity in North Atlantic Right Whales *Eubalaena Glacialis* and Their Relation to Reproduction," *Marine Ecology Progress Series* 171 (October 1, 1998): 285–92, doi:10.3354/meps171285.

CHAPTER 17: BLOODLINES, MILKLINES

81   *The list goes on:* "North Atlantic Right Whale Catalog," New England Aquarium, https://rwcatalog.neaq.org/#/whales.

82   *which is atop a gigantic whale:* Jean-Loïc Le Quellec, "The Long Tail of a Whale," in Whale on the Rock, dir. Sang-mog Lee (Ulsan: Ulsan Petroglyph Museum, 2017), 9–43, https://www.researchgate.net/publication/322077902_2017_-_The_Long_Tail_of_a_Whale_In_Sang-mog_Lee_dir_Whale_on_the_Rock_Ulsan_Ulsan_Petroglyph_Museum_pp_9-43?_tp=eyJjb25oZXhoIjp7ImZpcnNoUGFnZSI6InBiYmxpY2F0aW9uIiwicGFnZSI6Il9kaXJlY3QifX0.

82   *as Kerri ní Dochartaigh so beautifully writes:* Kerri ní Dochartaigh, "When You Could Hear the Trees," *Emergence Magazine* 4 (November 9, 2023), https://emergencemagazine.org/essay/when-you-could-hear-the-trees/.

CHAPTER 18: SCRIMSHAW

84   *much of the Western world was lit by whale oil:* Peter Applebome, "They Used to Say Whale Oil Was Indispensable, Too," *New York*

Times, August 3, 2008, https://www.nytimes.com/2008/08/03/nyregion/03towns.html.

84   *a frenzy of slaughter for centuries:* Ana S. L. Rodrigues et al., "Forgotten Mediterranean Calving Grounds of Grey and North Atlantic Right Whales: Evidence from Roman Archaeological Records," *Proceedings: Biological Sciences* 285, no. 1882 (2018): 1–9.

84   *"where our children's grandchildren will go for bread":* Jessica Boyall, "The Art of Whaling: Illustrations from the Logbooks of Nantucket Whaleships," *The Public Domain Review,* January 13, 2021, https://publicdomainreview.org/essay/the-art-of-whaling/.

85   *Many of the 2,500 members of the Wampanoag:* Boyall, "The Art of Whaling."

85   *then hauling them to shore for processing:* Boyall, "The Art of Whaling."

85   *gone for as many as three years at a time:* Nathaniel Philbrick, "How Nantucket Came to Be the Whaling Capital of the World," *Smithsonian Magazine,* December 2015, https://www.smithsonianmag.com/history/nantucket-came-to-be-whaling-capital-of-world-180957198/.

85   *forty to fifty whales' worth of oil:* Philbrick, "How Nantucket Came to Be."

85   *"there were 472 fatherless children on Nantucket":* Philbrick, "How Nantucket Came to Be."

86   *spiraling Nantucket into economic depression:* Michelle Cartwright Soverino, "From the Egan Art Collection, Rodney Charman's 'The Great Fire of 1846,'" Egan Maritime Institute, July 12, 2019, accessed September 4, 2023, https://eganmaritime.org/news/the-great-fire-of-1846.

86   *depleted the world's populations of whales by as much as 90 percent:* Joe Roman et al., "Whales as Marine Ecosystem Engineers," *Frontiers in Ecology and the Environment* 12, no. 7 (September 2014): 377–85, doi:10.1890/130220.

86   *Nantucket had dominated this industry:* Boyall, "The Art of Whaling."

86   *granted right whales international protection:* The above information in this paragraph sourced from: Kraus and Rolland, *The Urban Whale,* 5.

CHAPTER 19: FLUKEPRINT

88   *a breakwater that dampens the waves inside the print:* R. Levy et al., "A Theory for the Hydrodynamic Origin of Whale Flukeprints," *International Journal of Non-Linear Mechanics* 46, no. 4 (May 2011): 616–26, doi:10.1016/j.ijnonlinmec.2010.12.009.

88   *the entire body of a whale meant a whale was slaughtered:* Boyall, "The Art of Whaling."

CHAPTER 21: URBAN WHALE

90   *is a primary cause of death for large whales:* This paragraph sourced from: Erica Gies, "Sharing the Seas," *Corporate Knights* 17, no. 4 (2018): 18–21.

91   *"elegant dewatering mechanism":* David W. Laist, *North Atlantic Right Whales: From Hunted Leviathan to Conservation Icon* (Washington, DC: Johns Hopkins University Press, 2017), 34–45.

91   *slow starvation from the inability to feed or from infection:* Amy R. Knowlton et al., "Effects of Fishing Rope Strength on the Severity of Large Whale Entanglements," *Conservation Biology* 30, no. 2 (April 2016): 318–28, doi:10.1111/cobi.12590.

91   *like a tree around a fence:* Michael J. Moore, *We Are All Whalers: The Plight of Whales and Our Responsibility* (Chicago: The University of Chicago Press, 2021), 120.

91   *Moore, who has performed dozens of North Atlantic right whale necropsies:* Moore, *We Are All Whalers,* 35.

92   *establishing speed restrictions, and modifying shipping routes:* Gregory K. Silber et al., "The Role of the International Maritime Organization in Reducing Vessel Threat to Whales: Process, Options, Action and Effectiveness," *Marine Policy* 36, no. 6 (November 1, 2012): 1221–33, doi:10.1016/j.marpol.2012.03.008.

92   *speed restrictions within defined marine mammal management areas:* Vanessa Pirotta et al., "Consequences of Global Shipping Traffic for Marine Giants," *Frontiers in Ecology and the Environment* 17, no. 1 (February 2019): 39–47, https://www.jstor.org/stable/26623725.

92   *success is contingent on widespread compliance:* David W. Laist, Amy R. Knowlton, and Daniel Pendleton, "Effectiveness of Mandatory

Vessel Speed Limits for Protecting North Atlantic Right Whales," *Endangered Species Research* 23, no. 2 (February 28, 2014): 133–147, https://www.int-res.com/abstracts/esr/v23/n2/p133–147/.

93   *from the Gulf of Maine to the Gulf of St. Lawrence in Canada:* This paragraph sourced from: Erin L. Meyer-Gutbrod et al., "Ocean Regime Shift Is Driving Collapse of the North Atlantic Right Whale Population," *Oceanography* 34, no. 3 (September 2021): 22–31, https://www.jstor.org/stable/27051387; Andrew J. Pershing and Daniel E. Pendleton, "Can Right Whales Outswim Climate Change? Can We?," *Oceanography* 34, no. 3 (September 2021): 19–21, https://www.jstor.org/stable/27051386.

93   *a direct correlation to the number of right whale calves being born:* Pershing and Pendleton, "Can Right Whales Outswim?," 19–21.

93   *susceptible to being impacted by a limited availability of prey:* Rosalind M. Rolland et al., "Health of North Atlantic Right Whales *Eubalaena Glacialis* over Three Decades: From Individual Health to Demographic and Population Health Trends," *Marine Ecology Progress Series* 542 (January 19, 2016): 265–282, https://www.int-res.com/abstracts/meps/v542/p265–282/.

93   *a significant decline in the calving rate:* Meyer-Gutbrod et al., "Ocean Regime Shift Is Driving," 22–31.

94   *having found where their food had gone:* Meyer-Gutbrod et al., "Ocean Regime Shift Is Driving," 22–31.

94   *twelve in the Gulf of St. Lawrence and five in the United States:* Meyer-Gutbrod et al., "Ocean Regime Shift Is Driving," 22–31.

94   *it is more likely that there were closer to 150 deaths:* Philip Hamilton, interview conducted by Chelsea Steinauer-Scudder, January 21, 2024.

94   *less food availability and to human-caused injury and mortality:* Pershing and Pendleton, "Can Right Whales Outswim?," 19–21.

94   *species could be functionally extinct within three decades:* Nicholas R. Record et al., "Rapid Climate-Driven Circulation Changes Threaten Conservation of Endangered North Atlantic Right Whales," *Oceanography* 32, no. 2 (June 2019): 162–69.

95   *enough to threaten the recovery of the entire population:* Nicholas R. Record, "The Intertwined Futures of Whales and Humans," *Oceanography* 34, no. 3 (August 2021): 16–18.

95   *swimming alone near a pier in Beaufort, North Carolina:* Hina Alam, "Endangered North Atlantic Right Whale Baby Found Dead near North Carolina," *Global News*, January 12, 2023, https://globalnews. ca/news/9405526/north-atlantic-right-whale-baby-dead/.

95   *they cannot survive without their mothers:* Almost exactly a year later, as I am editing this chapter, a newly born right whale calf is struck by a ship's propellor. This is the child of a right whale mother named Juno. The calf is expected to die. [John Yoon, "Rare North Atlantic Right Whale Calf IS Expected to Die from Injuries," *New York Times*, January 11, 2024, https://www.nytimes. com/2024/01/11/science/north-atlantic-right-whale-calf-boat. html.]

96   *an estimated 920,500 vertical fishing lines:* Moore, *We Are All Whalers*, 169.

96   *an estimated $1.5 billion a year to the state's economy:* Kevin Miller, "Maine Lobster Industry Wins Reprieve but Environmentalists Say Whales Will Die," *NPR*, January 4, 2023, https://www.npr. org/2023/01/04/1146637583/maine-lobster-industry-wins-reprieve-but-environmentalists-say-whales-will-die.

97   *"this rider will doom the right whale to extinction":* Maxine Joselow, "To Protect Lobstermen, Spending Bill Might Speed Whales' Extinction, Advocates Say," *Washington Post*, December 20, 2022, https:// www.washingtonpost.com/climate-environment/2022/12/20/ right-whales-maine-spending-bill/.

97   *"the problem of whale trauma has continued to get worse":* Moore, *We Are All Whalers*, 176.

CHAPTER 22: DEVOUR

99   *the man understands the language of birds:* Jean-Loïc Le Quellec, "The Long Tail of a Whale," in Whale on the Rock, dir. Sang-mog Lee (Ulsan: Ulsan Petroglyph Museum, 2017), 9–43, https://www. researchgate.net/publication/322077902_2017_-_The_Long_ Tail_of_a_Whale_In_Sang-mog_Lee_dir_Whale_on_the_Rock_ Ulsan_Ulsan_Petroglyph_Museum_pp_9-43?_tp=eyJjb250ZXh 0Ijp7lmZpcnN0UGFnZSI6InBiYmxpY2F0aW9uIiwicGFnZSI6Il 9kaXJlY3QifX0.

99 *Similar stories are told by the Inupiaq and the Nunivak:* Le Quellec, "The Long Tail of a Whale," 9–43.

99 *until the beast spat him back out in irritation:* Le Quellec, "The Long Tail of a Whale," 9–43.

100 *"having endured a second wonderful imprisonment in the womb":* Le Quellec, "The Long Tail of a Whale," 9–43.

100 *"where Jonah saw the 'mysteries' in the whale's belly":* Le Quellec, "The Long Tail of a Whale," 9–43.

100 *fled the father (God) by reentering the womb of the mother (whale):* Le Quellec, "The Long Tail of a Whale," 9–43.

CHAPTER 24: WHALEFALL

110 *blue whales have been reduced by an estimated 99 percent:* Christopher E. Doughty et al., "Global Nutrient Transport in a World of Giants," *Proceedings of the National Academy of Sciences* 113, no. 4 (October 26, 2015): 868–73, doi:10.1073/pnas.1502549112.

110 *comparatively little is known about them:* Roman et al., "Whales as Marine Ecosystem Engineers," 377–385.

110 *from saltwater to freshwater, and from sea to land:* Roman et al., "Whales as Marine Ecosystem Engineers," 377–385.

111 *"the death of a whale can prove not a tragedy but a turning point":* Rebecca Giggs, *Fathoms: The World in the Whale* (New York: Simon & Schuster, 2020), 21.

CHAPTER 25: CHIMERA

112 *"distinct organisms living with one another":* Elena E. Giorgi, "I Am My Mother's Chimera. Chances Are, So Are You," *HuffPost,* March 18, 2016, https://www.huffpost.com/entry/i-am-my-mothers-chimera-b_9464250.

113 *transferred postnatally through nursing:* Viviane Callier, "Baby's Cells Can Manipulate Mom's Body for Decades," *Smithsonian Magazine,* September 2, 2015, https://www.smithsonianmag.com/science-nature/babys-cells-can-manipulate-moms-body-decades-180956493/.

113   ***they became heart cells and helped her heal:*** Robert Mar-
tone, "Scientists Discover Children's Cells Living in Mothers'
Brains," *Scientific American*, December 4, 2012, https://www.
scientificamerican.com/article/scientists-discover-childrens-
cells-living-in-mothers-brain/.

113   ***contributing to the health of the mother's heart:*** Abigail Tucker,
"The New Science of Motherhood," *Smithsonian Magazine*, May 2021,
https://www.smithsonianmag.com/science-nature/new-science-
motherhood-180977456/.

CHAPTER 29: CULTIVATING ROOTS

133   ***"cannot possibly flourish alone":*** Wendell Berry, *The Unsettling of
America: Culture and Agriculture* (Berkeley, California: Counter-
point, 2015), 24.

CHAPTER 30: CUTTING DOWN THE WORLD

138   ***increasingly circumscribed as the wizard grows wiser:*** In Le Guin's
Earthsea universe, only men can be mages.

138   ***"To light a candle is to cast a shadow":*** Ursula K. Le Guin, *A Wizard
of Earthsea* (New York: Houghton Mifflin, 2012), 51.

139   ***covered with hides or waterproof birch bark:*** Frederick Matthew
Wiseman, *The Voice of the Dawn: An Autohistory of the Abenaki
Nation* (Hanover: University Press of New England, 2001),
24–29.

139   ***Spruce and hemlock roots were used for cords and lacing:*** Wiseman,
The Voice of the Dawn, 29.

139   ***"strapped to a joyously carved wooden cradleboard":*** Wiseman, *The
Voice of the Dawn*, 37.

140   ***"a source of our living and health":*** Wiseman, *The Voice of the Dawn*,
42.

140   ***corn, beans, squash, and artichokes:*** Wiseman, *The Voice of the
Dawn*, 58.

140   ***"an interdiction I will follow":*** Wiseman, *The Voice of the Dawn*,
69–70.

140   *"New England consumed more than 260 million cords of firewood":* This paragraph sourced from: William Cronon, *Changes in the Land: Indians, Colonists, and the Ecology of New England* (New York: Hill & Wang, 2003), 109–110, 120, quote from 121.

141   *"a property system that taught them to treat land as capital":* Cronon, *Changes in the Land*, 77.

141   *"the motion of body and hand":* Le Guin, *A Wizard of Earthsea*, 60.

142   *"supremacy of the Caucasian race in our land":* Garland E. Allen, "'Culling the Herd': Eugenics and the Conservation Movement in the United States, 1900–1940," *Journal of the History of Biology* 46, no. 1 (Spring 2013): 31–72, https://www.jstor.org/stable/42628761.

143   *performed on women identified as being poor:* Mark Bushnell, "Vermont Eugenics," Accessed September 4, 2023, https://www.uvm.edu/~lkaelber/eugenics/VT/VT.html.

144   *were deemed to represent a persistent threat to the projects of colonialism:* Bushnell, "Vermont Eugenics"; and Hope Greenberg and Nancy Gallagher, "What Is Eugenics?: Eugenics Project: A Documentary History, UVM," Accessed January 28, 2024, https://www.uvm.edu/%7Eeugenics/famstudies.html#who.

144   *"sterilizing at least 25 percent of Native American women":* Jane Lawrence, "The Indian Health Service and the Sterilization of Native American Women," *American Indian Quarterly* 24, no. 3 (Summer 2000): 400–419.

144   *estimated seventy thousand people in America endured forced sterilization in the twentieth century:* Adam Cohen, "The Supreme Court Ruling That Led to 70,000 Forced Sterilizations," *Fresh Air* (podcast), March 7, 2016, https://www.npr.org/sections/health-shots/2016/03/07/469478098/the-supreme-court-ruling-that-led-to-70-000-forced-sterilizations.

144   *"in this other forest from which they came":* Ursula K. Le Guin, *The Word for World Is Forest* (New York: Tom Doherty Associates, 1972), 56.

CHAPTER 31: RESTRAINED GROWTH

146   *difficult for harmful intruders like fungi to spread internally:* Peter Wohlleben, *The Hidden Life of Trees: What They Feel, How They*

Communicate, trans. Jane Billinghurst (Vancouver: Greystone Books, 2015), 33.

147 **"the center of forest communication, protection, and sentience":** Simard, *Finding the Mother Tree*, 5.

147 **"ensuring the community in which they were raising their kin was healthy":** Simard, *Finding the Mother Tree*, 270.

148 **"well-being depends on their community":** Wohlleben, *The Hidden Life of Trees*, 17.

151 **"the flight of birds, the great slow gestures of trees":** Le Guin, *A Wizard of Earthsea*, 98.

151 **"It's what all parents do":** Simard, *Finding the Mother Tree*, 5.

CHAPTER 32: CREATION STORY

152 **"freedom to imagine who might live there":** Julie Phillips, "Ursula K. Le Guin Was a Creator of Worlds," *Humanities* 40, no. 1 (winter 2019), cover story, https://www.neh.gov/article/ursula-k-le-guin-was-creator-worlds.

155 **"whose roots are deeper than the forest":** Ursula K. Le Guin, *The Word for World Is Forest* (New York: Tor, 2010), 60.

CHAPTER 33: TREE SEED

157 **considering the adoption of a tree ordinance:** The South Portland city council successfully passed a citywide tree ordinance in 2023.

160 A version of this chapter first appeared as the essay "Firebreak" in Emergence Magazine: Chelsea Steinauer-Scudder, "Firebreak," *Emergence Magazine*, July 9, 2021, https://emergencemagazine.org/op_ed/firebreak/.

CHAPTER 34: VULNERABLE NEST

169 A version of this chapter first appeared as the essays "Above Water" and "The Way of the Goldfinch" in Emergence Magazine: Chelsea Steinauer-Scudder, "Above Water," *Emergence Magazine*, April 20, 2020, https://emergencemagazine.org/op_ed/above-water/; and Chelsea Steinauer-Scudder, "The Way of the Goldfinch," *Emergence*

Magazine, July 13, 2020, https://emergencemagazine.org/op_ed/
the-way-of-the-goldfinch/.

CHAPTER 35: POROUS BOUNDARIES

170 *"in a miniature ocean within his mother's womb":* Rachel Carson,
The Sea Around Us (New York: Oxford University Press, 2018), 14.

171 *"the spectacle of living creatures faced by the cosmic realities of their
world":* Rachel Carson, *The Edge of the Sea* (Boston: Houghton Mifflin Company, 1998), 7.

CHAPTER 36: BETWEEN THE TIDES

173 *smiling bays, and pooling coves between them:* Carson, *The Edge of
the Sea*, 42–43.

175 *present in a majority of blood samples collected:* Christopher R.
Kirman et al., "Biomonitoring Equivalents for DDT/DDE," *Regula-
tory Toxicology and Pharmacology*, 60, no 2 (2011): 172–180, https://
www.sciencedirect.com/science/article/pii/S0273230011000651.

176 *"before I go back to my barnacles":* Rachel Carson, *Always, Rachel:
The Letters of Rachel Carson and Dorothy Freeman, 1952–1964*, ed.
Dorothy Freeman and Martha E. Freeman (Boston: Beacon Press,
1994), 92.

177 *"grazing on the intertidal rocks":* Carson, *The Edge of the Sea*, 50.

177 *writes about ways of being outdoors with children:* Rachel Carson,
The Sense of Wonder, 2nd ed. (Berkeley, California: The Nature
Company, 1956).

177 *not come here again until Dorothy scattered her ashes:* Linda Lear,
Rachel Carson: Witness for Nature (Boston: Mariner Books, 2009),
466, 474, 483.

180 *"We live in an age of rising seas":* Rachel Carson, *The Sea Trilogy*, ed.
Sandra Steingraber (Library of America: 2021), 285.

CHAPTER 37: EDGE EROSION

184 *Grasses and forbs took to the soil:* Kimberly Sebold, *From Marsh to
Farm: The Landscape Transformation of Coastal New Jersey* (Washington, DC: National Park Service, n.d), 13.

185   *three to four times higher in the northeastern United States than the global average:* J. C. Carey et al., "The Declining Role of Organic Matter in New England Salt Marshes," *Estuaries and Coasts* 40, no. 3 (2017): 626–39.

185   *"as it has over the last 100 years":* "2022 Sea Level Rise Technical Report," National Oceanic and Atmospheric Administration, Accessed September 4, 2023, https://oceanservice.noaa.gov/hazards/sealevelrise/sealevelrise-tech-report-sections.html.

188   *which would drown today's healthy, intact salt marshes:* Keryn B. Gedan, Andrew H. Altieri, and Mark D. Bertness, "Uncertain Future of New England Salt Marshes," *Marine Ecology Progress Series* 434 (2011): 229–38.

188   *armoring it against marsh migration as well:* Gedan, Altieri, and Bertness, "Uncertain Future of New England Salt Marshes," 229–38.

188   *marshes may be lagging behind rising oceans:* Carey et al., "The Declining Role," 626–39.

CHAPTER 38: PASSAGEWAYS

189   *"extreme marginal environment":* H. Saffert and E. Thomas, "Living Foraminifera and Total Populations in Salt Marsh Peat Cores: Kelsey Marsh (Clinton, CT) and the Great Marshes (Barnstable, MA)," *Marine Micropaleontology* 33, no. 3–4 (April 1998): 175–202, doi:10.1016/S0377-8398(97)00035-2.

190   *shells and skeletons were relatively new evolutionary inventions:* This paragraph sourced from: Ewen Callaway, "Oldest *Homo Sapiens* Fossil Claim Rewrites Our Species' History," *Nature*, June 7, 2017, doi:10.1038/nature.2017.22114; and "Foraminifera," British Geological Survey, Accessed August 29, 2023, https://www.bgs.ac.uk/discovering-geology/fossils-and-geological-time/foraminifera/.

190   *that exist between the chambers of their shells:* Marcelle K. Boudagher-Fadel, "Biology and Evolutionary History of Larger Benthic Foraminifera," in *Evolution and Geological Significance of Larger Benthic Foraminifera*, 2nd ed. (London: UCL Press, 2018), 1–44.

190   *which are photosynthesizing algae:* University College London, "Foraminifera," Postgraduate Unit of Micropalaeontology, Department

of Earth Sciences, 2002, https://www.ucl.ac.uk/GeolSci/micropal/
foram.html.

191   *Forams also evolve rapidly across generations:* Boudagher-Fadel,
      "Biology and Evolutionary History of Larger Benthic Foraminifera,"
      1–44.

191   *geological reconstructions of deep time marine conditions:* Pratul
      Kumar Saraswati, *Foraminiferal Micropaleontology for Understand-
      ing Earth's History,* ed. Pratul Kumar Saraswati (Amsterdam: Else-
      vier, 2021), 1–24, doi:10.1016/B978-0-12-823957-5.00010-X.

191   *glacial freezing and melting during the Quarternary:* "Foramin-
      ifera," British Geological Survey.

191   *"the evolution of life and the environment on Earth":* Saraswati, *Fora-
      miniferal Micropaleontology for Understanding Earth's History,* 1–24.

192   *intertidal waters of coastal salt marshes:* Boudagher-Fadel, "Biology
      and Evolutionary History," 1–44.

192   *anoxic environment where other organisms are not well-preserved:*
      Neil E. Tibert and David B. Scott, "Ostracodes and Agglutinated
      Foraminifera as Indicators of Paleoenvironmental Change in an
      Early Carboniferous Brackish Bay, Atlantic Canada," *PALAIOS* 14,
      no. 3 (June 1999): 246–60, doi:10.2307/3515437.

192   *changes in sea levels in coastal marshes over time:* Saffert and
      Thomas, "Living Foraminifera and Total Populations," 175–202.

192   *to eight centimeters above mean high water:* W. Roland Gehrels,
      "Determining Relative Sea-Level Change from Salt-Marsh Fora-
      minifera and Plant Zones on the Coast of Maine, U.S.A.," *Journal of
      Coastal Research* 10, no. 4 (Autumn 1994): 990–1009, https://www.
      jstor.org/stable/4298291.

194   *"open and greedy for surprising new and old connections":* Donna J.
      Haraway, *Staying with the Trouble: Making Kin in the Chthulucene*
      (Durham and London: Duke University Press, 2016), 101.

CHAPTER 39: RECLAIM

196   *expansion of farming into marshland and protected the land from
      floods:* Sebold, *From Marsh to Farm,* 2.

197   *so that they could grow freshwater crops:* Keryn D. Bromberg and
      Mark D. Bertness, "Reconstructing New England Salt Marsh Losses

Using Historical Maps," *Estuaries* 28, no. 6 (December 2005): 823–832, https://www.jstor.org/stable/3526949.

197   *"and its methods will be American":* Sebold, *From Marsh to Farm*, 5.

197   *somewhere between 37 and 80 percent:* Bromberg and Bertness, "Reconstructing New England Salt Marsh Losses," 823–832; and Mark D. Bertness, Patrick J. Ewanchuk, and Brian Reed Silliman, "Anthropogenic Modification of New England Salt Marsh Landscapes," *Proceedings of the National Academy of Sciences of the United States of America* 99, no. 3 (February 2002): 1395–1398, https://www.jstor.org/stable/3057772.

198   *"severing our language from that which supports and sustains it":* David Abram, *The Spell of the Sensuous: Perception and Language in a More-Than-Human World*, 2nd ed. (New York: Vintage Books, 2017), 263.

CHAPTER 40: WILD TRANSGRESSION

202   *"among the reeds on the bank of the river":* Michael D. Coogan, ed., "Exodus 2:2–3," in *The New Oxford Annotated Bible: New Revised Standard Edition with the Apocrypha*, 3rd ed. (Oxford: Oxford University Press, 2001).

203   *"the pressure of both soft and hard things":* "Rashi on Exodus 2:11:1," Sefaria, https://www.sefaria.org/Rashi_on_Exodus.2.11.1?ven=Pentateuch_with_Rashi%27s_commentary_by_M._Rosenbaum_and_A.M._Silbermann,_1929-1934&lang=bi.

203   *liberation and the birth of a nation:* Inbar Raveh, "'They Let the Children Live': The Midwives at a Political Crossroads," *Nashim: A Journal of Jewish Women's Studies & Gender Issues*, no. 24 (Spring 2013): 11–26.

205   *"without slavery and oppression":* Raveh, "'They Let the Children Live,'" 12.

207   *record low levels of Arctic sea ice:* David Wallace-Wells, "The Ocean Is Looking More Menacing," *New York Times*, June 1, 2023, https://www.nytimes.com/2023/06/01/opinion/the-ocean-is-looking-more-menacing.html.

208 *"Will more of her teeth be blunted":* Tamar Kadari, "Jochebed: Midrash and Aggadah," Jewish Women's Archive, Accessed January 30, 2024, https://jwa.org/encyclopedia/article/jochebed-midrash-and-aggadah.

CHAPTER 41: FLOOD

209 *valley that is twice as large as the Nile:* John M. Barry, *Rising Tide: The Great Mississippi Flood of 1927 and How It Changed America* (New York: Simon & Schuster, 1998).

209 *over thirty-one states and two Canadian provinces:* Betsy Mason, "Map Shows Every River That Flows to the Mighty Mississippi," *National Geographic*, September 23, 2016, https://www.nationalgeographic.com/culture/article/mississippi-river-watershed-map.

209 *400–460 million metric tons of sediment during the Holocene:* Catherine Russell et al., "Geological Evolution of the Mississippi River into the Anthropocene," *The Anthropocene Review* 8, no. 2 (August 2021): 115–40, doi:10.1177/20530196211045527.

210 *more than thirty thousand square kilometers underwater:* Russell et al., "Geological Evolution of the Mississippi," 115–40.

211 *Acolapissa, Tunica-Biloxi, Bayogoula, Taensa, and Atakapa Ishak:* Rain Prud'homme-Cranford, Darryl Barthé, and Andrew J. Jolivétte, *Louisiana Creole Peoplehood: Afro-Indigeneity and Community* (Seattle: University of Washington Press, 2022).

212 *"in itself, is an environmental loss":* Jeffrey U. Darensbourg, "Hunting Memories of the Grass Things," *Southern Cultures* 27, no. 1, Accessed August 29, 2023, https://www.southerncultures.org/article/hunting-memories-of-the-grass-things/.

212 *sediment flow from the Mississippi into the coastal plain:* Barry, *Rising Tide.*

212 *eroding the edges further:* Bob Marshall, The Lens, and ProPublica, "Losing Ground: Southeast Louisiana Is Disappearing, Quickly," *Scientific American*, August 28, 2014, https://www.scientificamerican.com/article/losing-ground-southeast-louisiana-is-disappearing-quickly/.

213   ***were moving through Louisiana's coast:*** Jason P. Theriot, *American Energy, Imperiled Coast: Oil and Gas Development in Louisiana's Wetlands* (Baton Rouge: LSU Press, 2014).

213   ***predicted to vanish in the next fifty years:*** "Louisiana's Comprehensive Master Plan for a Sustainable Coast, 2023, 4th ed.," Coastal Protection and Restoration Authority of Louisiana, May 25, 2023, 39, 230531_CPRA_MP_Final-for-web_spreads.pdf (la.gov).

214   ***the largest transaction in the history of our planet:*** "Venture Global Announces Final Investment Decision and Financial Close for Plaquemines LNG," Venture Global LNG, May 25, 2022, https://venturegloballng.com/press/venture-global-announces-final-investment-decision-and-financial-close-for-plaquemines-lng/.

214   ***in terms of percentage of population decrease in 2022:*** Faimon A. Roberts III, "Four Louisiana Parishes Rank in Top 10 in US for Population Loss in 2022," NOLA.com, March 30, 2023, https://www.nola.com/news/politics/four-louisiana-parishes-are-top-10-in-us-in-population-loss/article_31761734-cf12-11ed-aa0e-ef5a86a9828b.html.

CHAPTER 43: TIDE-WORK

223   ***"sense of continuing creation and of the relentless drive of life":*** Carson, *The Edge of the Sea*, 2.

224   ***"we have been human for only a very short time":*** Terry Tempest Williams, *When Women Were Birds: Fifty-Four Variations on Voice* (New York: Picador, 2012), 18–19.

CHAPTER 46: MUSIC (FALL)

235   ***"It seemed a miracle:"*** Dalya Alberge, "The Cello and the Nightingale: 1924 Duet Was Faked, BBC Admits," *The Guardian*, April 8, 2022, https://www.theguardian.com/media/2022/apr/08/the-cello-and-the-nightingale-1924-duet-was-faked-bbc-admits.

243   ***decipher a series of sounds as song:*** Samata R Sharma and David Silbersweig, "Setting the Stage: Neurobiological Effects of Music on

the Brain," *Crossroads of Music and Medicine*, no. 6 (2018), https://remix.berklee.edu/mh-exchange-music-medicine/6.

243 **special category for music that is sung:** Sam V. Norman-Haignere et al., "A Neural Population Selective for Song in Human Auditory Cortex," *Current Biology* 32, no. 7 (April 11, 2022): 1470–1484.e12, doi:10.1016/j.cub.2022.01.069.

243 **when it is part of a descending one:** Norman M. Weinberger, "Music and the Brain," *Scientific American* 291, no. 5 (2004): 88–95.

244 **physiological changes that were consistent across the subjects:** Carol L. Krumhansl, "An Exploratory Study of Musical Emotions and Psychophysiology," *Canadian Journal of Experimental Psychology* 51, no. 4 (December 1997): 336–353, doi:10.1037/1196-1961.51.4.336.

244 **a human tradition for several hundred thousand years:** Patricia M. Gray et al., "The Music of Nature and the Nature of Music," *Science* 291, no. 5501 (January 2001): 52–54, https://www.jstor.org/stable/3082167

244 **as well as changes in tempo and rhythm:** Weinberger, "Music and the Brain," 88–95.

245 **before they're able to clearly articulate:** Sanne Moorman et al., "Human-like Brain Hemispheric Dominance in Birdsong Learning," *Proceedings of the National Academy of Sciences* 109, no. 31 (July 2012): 12782–12787, doi:10.1073/pnas.1207207109.

245 **that could help maintain the population's geographic location:** This paragraph sourced from: Michael A. Cunningham and Myron Charles Baker, "Vocal Learning in White-Crowned Sparrows: Sensitive Phase and Song Dialects," *Behavioral Ecology and Sociobiology* 13, no. 4 (1983): 259–269, https://www.jstor.org/stable/4599635.

246 **a means of maintaining and carrying forward this relationship:** Helena Simonett, "Envisioned, Ensounded, Enacted: Sacred Ecology and Indigenous Musical Experience in Yoreme Ceremonies of Northwest Mexico," *Ethnomusicology* 58, no. 1 (2014): 110 –132, doi:10.5406/ethnomusicology.58.1.0110.

247 **"allows us to understand and navigate both the human and beyond-human worlds":** David George Haskell, *Sounds Wild and Broken: Sonic Marvels, Evolution's Creativity, and the Crisis of Sensory Extinction* (New York: Viking, 2022), 323.

CHAPTER 47: A PARTICULAR LOVE (WINTER)

257 *"resulting conflagration has been devastating":* Ta-Nehisi Coates, "The Case for Reparations," *The Atlantic*, June 2014, https://www.theatlantic.com/magazine/archive/2014/06/the-case-for-reparations/361631/.

257 *"less than 1 percent of farms are Black-owned":* Leah Penniman, *Farming While Black: Soul Fire Farm's Practical Guide to Liberation on the Land* (White River Junction: Chelsea Green Publishing, 2018), 7.

CHAPTER 50: CREATING POSSIBLE FUTURES

270 *"Collapsing, Dying in Arizona Heat":* Mary Whitfill Roeloffs, "July 4 Was Earth's Hottest Day in over 100,000 Years—Breaking Record for 2nd Day in a Row," *Forbes*, July 5, 2023, https://www.forbes.com/sites/maryroeloffs/2023/07/05/july-4-was-earths-hottest-day-in-over-100000-years-breaking-record-for-2nd-day-in-a-row/?sh=5a5d502267dd.

Catrin Einhorn and Jason Gulley, "A Desperate Push to Save Florida's Coral: Get It Out of the Sea," *New York Times*, July 31, 2023, https://www.nytimes.com/2023/07/31/climate/coral-reefs-heat-florida-ocean-temperatures.html.

Brad Plumer and Elena Shao, "Heat Records Are Broken around the Globe as Earth Warms, Fast," *New York Times*, July 6, 2023, https://www.nytimes.com/2023/07/06/climate/climate-change-record-heat.html.

Saman Shafiq, "'Sentinel of Southwest': Saguaro Cacti Are Collapsing, Dying in Arizona Heat," *USA TODAY*, July 26, 2023, https://www.usatoday.com/story/news/nation/2023/07/26/saguaro-cactus-dying-arizona-heat-reuters/70470713007/.